Vincent L Milner, Joseph F. Berg

Paganism, Popery and Christianity

The Blessing of an Open Bible, as Shown in the History of Christianity, from the Time of our Saviour to the present day

Vincent L Milner, Joseph F. Berg

Paganism, Popery and Christianity
The Blessing of an Open Bible, as Shown in the History of Christianity, from the Time of our Saviour to the present day

ISBN/EAN: 9783337104122

Printed in Europe, USA, Canada, Australia, Japan

Cover: Foto ©Lupo / pixelio.de

More available books at **www.hansebooks.com**

Paganism, Popery, and Christianity;

OR, THE BLESSING OF AN

OPEN BIBLE,

AS SHOWN IN THE HISTORY OF CHRISTIANITY, FROM THE TIME
OF OUR SAVIOUR TO THE PRESENT DAY.

By VINCENT W. MILNER.

WITH A VIEW OF THE

Latest Developments of Rome's Hostility to the Bible,

AS EXHIBITED IN THE SANDWICH ISLANDS, IN TUSCANY, MADEIRA,
IN IRELAND, FRANCE, ETC.

AND AN

EXPOSE OF THE ABSURDITIES OF THE IMMACULATE CONCEPTION,
AND THE IDOLATROUS VENERATION OF THE VIRGIN MARY.

BY

REV. JOSEPH F. BERG, D.D.

AUTHOR OF "THE JESUITS," "CHURCH AND STATE," ETC. ETC.

PHILADELPHIA:
J. W. BRADLEY, 48 N. FOURTH ST.
AUBURN, N. Y.: H. A. YATES, No. 57 GENESEE STREET.
NEW HAVEN: M. BRADLEY, 24 HIGH ST.
1855.

Entered according to Act of Congress, in the year 1855, by

J. W. BRADLEY,

In the Clerk's Office of the District Court of the United States, in and for the Eastern District of Pennsylvania.

PHILADELPHIA:
STEREOTYPED BY GEORGE CHARLES,
PRINTED BY KING & BAIRD.

INTRODUCTION.

The design of the following pages is to trace the progressive power of Christianity from the beginning of the Christian era to the present day. The influence of the Bible is best appreciated in the light of history; and the argument which is most obvious to every candid mind, and which defies all the sophistry of infidelity, is that which every unprejudiced reader deduces from the facts inscribed, not merely in books, but in the character of nations, which have been brought under the law of divine revelation. The world's history is a running commentary upon the truth that the highest developments of art and science are utterly impotent as reformatory agencies. The periods in ancient, as well as in modern history, most distinguished for the perfection of the fine arts, have uniformly been the most profligate and corrupt. The age of Pericles and Alcibiades in Greece, and the Augustan age of Rome, are illustrations in point. The most rational systems of philosophy were equally powerless in producing the moral reformation in the masses, without which no nation can be permanently prosperous and happy. On the other hand, we find the Bible and the most refined civilization uniformly associated with the purest morality and the highest exaltation of national character. The surest means of securing the blessings of enlightened, liberal, and equitable legislation and government, is found in obedience to the code of laws presented in the Bible. The art of printing and all the brightest inventions of science are no safeguard, unless they are consecrated by the pure morality of divine revelation. A more interesting theme cannot easily be selected than the history of the struggle between moral light and darkness, presented in the contest between Paganism, Popery, and Christianity. Throughout the world's annals the truth is seen running like a thread of gold, that the happiness of the race is identified with an open Bible. This fact is alone suggestive of its divine origin; and the more recent events of the present century, the current history of our own time, abundantly establish the power of the Scriptures in promoting the dearest interests of humanity.

CONTENTS.

THE COMING AND MINISTRY OF OUR SAVIOUR	9
SCENES IN THE SIEGE OF JERUSALEM BY THE ROMANS, A. D., 73	24
SECT. I. Opening of the Siege	24
SECT. II. Progress of the Siege—Famine—Crucifying before the Walls	41
SECT. III. Capture and Burning of the Temple	46
SECT. IV. The Fall of Jerusalem	58
EARLY CHRISTIANITY	71
OUTLINE HISTORY OF CHRISTIANITY	75
SECT. I. History of Christianity, from its Origin to its Establishment by Constantine the Great	75
SECT. II. History of the Church of Rome from its establishment to the erection of the Pope's Supremacy by Phocas	92
SECT. III. History of the Church of Rome from the erection of the Pope's Supremacy to his assumption of Universal Power..	109
SECT. IV. Account of various Superstitions that prevailed from the Fifth Century to the Reformation	117
EARLY CHRISTIAN MARTYRS	127
THE CRUSADES	138
THE ALBIGENSES	155
THE WALDENSES	156
JOHN WICKLIFFE, THE ENGLISH REFORMER	160
MARTYRDOM OF JOHN HUSS AND JEROME OF PRAGUE	164
THE HUSSITE WAR	172
HISTORY OF THE GREAT REFORMATION OF THE SIXTEENTH CENTURY	181
MARTYRDOM OF LATIMER AND RIDLEY	224

DEATH OF LADY JANE GREY	228
CAREER OF GUSTAVUS ADOLPHUS, KING OF SWEDEN, DEFENDER OF THE PROTESTANT FAITH	234
MASSACRE OF ST. BARTHOLOMEW	257
RELIGIOUS WAR IN FRANCE IN THE REIGN OF HENRY III.	265
DECLINE OF THE PROTESTANT POWER IN FRANCE	289
THE PURITANS	285
THE PURITANS IN ENGLAND	289
THE PURITANS IN AMERICA	291
THE PURITANS IN AMERICA—SETTLEMENT OF MASSACHUSETTS	303
THE PURITANS IN AMERICA—SETTLEMENT OF RHODE ISLAND	308
SIR HENRY VANE	313
MISSIONARY LABOURS OF ELIOT AND MAYHEW	318
GENERAL VIEW OF MISSIONS	321
THE GUNPOWDER PLOT	330
SANDWICH ISLANDS	336
POPERY AND THE BIBLE IN IRELAND	340
THE BIBLE IN FRANCE	349
PROTESTANTISM AND THE REVOLUTIONS OF 1848	351
THE INQUISITION AT ROME IN 1848	359
THE MADIAI	371
THE BIBLE IN MADEIRA	385
CONTRAST BETWEEN JESUIT AND PROTESTANT MISSIONS	406
THE IMMACULATE CONCEPTION OF THE VIRGIN MARY	416

THE COMING AND MINISTRY OF OUR SAVIOUR.

AMONG great events in the history of the world, none can be compared, for magnitude and importance, with the descent upon earth and the ministry of our blessed Lord and Saviour, Jesus Christ. Upon this the whole destiny of the human race depends. All succeeding important events in history take their character and colouring from this; and in giving a series of sketches of leading events in the religious history of the world, the reader will not be surprised that we give to this the first and most prominent place.

To appreciate the astonishing effects of the ministry of our Lord and the diffusion of his religion, in civilizing and humanizing mankind, it may be well to look at the dreadful condition to which the nations of the world had fallen at the time of his coming. A recent learned writer has the following remarks on the social condition of the ancient world:

"In antiquity, human nature, as such, was invested with no sacred character: men were divided into two classes—masters and slaves; and according as they belonged to the one or to the other, they ranked as demigods or as brute beasts. The former held possessions, had a family, a religion, a country, and a name; the slaves were looked upon as things, not men, and were by the laws of the times declared not only vile, but null. In truth, in antiquity, liberty meant nothing more than the exclusive rights of the smaller number, who were alone considered as constituting the people and representing the state, while all others were looked upon as strangers or enemies—these terms being synonymous. In the domestic relation the same spirit prevailed. The father of the family alone possessed rights: wife and children were held in a state of subordination differing little from bondage, their life even being at the mercy of him who, though husband and father, recognized no duties incumbent upon him as such. Women, ignorant of their own dignity and their peculiar duties, and having no higher standard by which to form their opinion of themselves than that of the other sex, looked upon themselves as beings created for no higher purpose than the gratification of man and the propagation of the species. By the laws of the state they were treated as goods and chattels. They might be bought and sold; their life was taken for the smallest offence. Polygamy everywhere prevailed, either openly or in disguise. Prostitution was sanctioned by religion. The sanctity of the conjugal, the paternal, and the filial relation, of course nowhere existed. There were no homes, no domestic affections, no family life: the state absorbed every feeling of those individuals, who were happy enough to count for something in its organization; the interests and glory of the state, as a political, not a social body, was considered the end of existence. Public life absorbed private life; and while the intellect had attained a degree of development and cultivation never surpassed, the heart remained a desert waste in which no tender feelings could take root, no delicate sentiments could germinate. Even the religions of antiquity were systems of state machinery used for purposes of government, but exercising no influence over the heart and the conscience, and in nowise contributing to the moral development of society.

" At the period of the birth of Christ these systems of antiquity had worked their worst. The sceptre of Rome was extended over all the countries of the west; her race of conquest was spent; her mission was accomplished; with her tranquility degenerated into stagnation, and ended in rottenness. 'Humanity incapable of submitting to inactivity, fell back upon itself, and revelled in selfishness, debauchery, and cruelty: the three capital errors of antiquity had reached their apogee: 30,000 gods were enthroned in the Capitol; the slaves of the wealthy citizens were thrown into the fishponds to fatten the murœnas: a decree of the senate declared that all women belonged by right to Cæsar!' But the Saviour was born who was to extricate mankind from the frightful depths of wickedness into which it had sunk."

Our Lord Jesus Christ was born at Bethlehem, a city of Judea, in the days of King Herod. The first chapter of St. Matthew contains the genealogy of Jesus, deduced from Abraham through David to his reputed father Joseph: the third chapter of St. Luke contains his pedigree from Joseph to Adam. From

Joseph to David, the two genealogies are entirely different; but this discrepancy is satisfactorily explained by the commentators. The birth of Jesus was miraculous; " when his mother Mary (according to the words of St. Matthew) was espoused to Joseph, before they came together, she was found with child of the Holy Ghost." Joseph, who intended to put her away privately, being warned in a dream by the Angel of the Lord, that what was 'conceived in her was of the Holy Ghost, took unto him his wife and knew her not, till she had brought forth her first-born son: and he called his name Jesus.' (Matt. i.) Herod was much troubled at the miraculous circumstances which attended the birth of Christ, and at the coincidence of the place of his birth with the prophecies. In order therefore that the infant might with certainty be destroyed, he gave orders that all the male children in Bethlehem and the neighbourhood under two years of age should be put to death; but Jesus was saved by his parents, who were warned by an angel in a dream to take the child into Egypt. This part of the sacred history is recorded by St. Matthew only. According to St. Luke, when the days of the purification of Mary were accomplished, his parents took him from Bethlehem to Jerusalem to present him in the Temple, after which they returned to their own city Nazareth in Galilee. At twelve years of age Christ disputed with the Jewish doctors in the temple at Jerusalem, whom he astonished by his answers and his understanding. Towards his parents his conduct was an example of filial obedience. He was not above following the business of his reputed father, which was that of a carpenter; and until about his thirtieth year he fulfilled the common duties of life in an humble and obscure station. His public ministry was preceded by the warnings and admonitions of John the

OUR LORD INSTRUCTING THE APOSTLES.

Baptist, the son of a Jewish priest, who called upon the people to repent and believe, for the time was fulfilled, and the kingdom of God was at hand. Christ was baptised by John in the river Jordan, and shortly after commenced his ministry, being about thirty years of age. For about the space of three years he was engaged in the work of promulgating his doctrines, and confirming his divine mission by numerous miracles. In order to diffuse that religion which he came to make known, Christ selected a certain number of persons to be his constant companions, to learn his doctrines, to witness their influence, to testify to the miracles by which their truth was demonstrated, and to be prepared to propagate after his death the truths which he had thus made known. The twelve persons whom he chose are called the Twelve Apostles. They were ignorant persons, who possessed neither wealth, rank, nor education, and yet they were called to root out opinions which were deeply implanted in men's minds, and to overturn systems strengthened by all the influence which ancient and venerable authorities exert over the mind. Christ next appointed from among his followers seventy disciples, whom he sent by twos to every place which he himself intended to visit. (Luke x. 1.) This appointment of the seventy disciples is not mentioned by the other evangelists. Many of the Jews being convinced by Christ's preaching, and the miracles which he wrought among them, of his divine mission, the Jewish priesthood were alarmed, and sought some means of accomplishing his death. Being betrayed by Judas, one of the twelve whom he had chosen, Christ was taken before the Jewish court of the Sanhedrim, which had the cognizance of offences against religion, and from thence to the tribunal of Pontius Pilate, the Roman procurator or administrator of the revenues of the province.

Before the former he was accused of blasphemy, a charge which was supported by two false witnesses; and before Pilate, as a seditious person, and a stirrer up of disaffection, a charge which was also totally without foundation. But the Jews clamoured for his death; and though Pilate saw nothing in the accusations brought against him worthy of capital punishment, he was sentenced to death, in compliance with the clamour of the people, and apparently also from fear of some disturbance. In the midst of their scoffing and jeers he was led to the place of execution, and crucified, with circumstances of the greatest cruelty, between two criminals. On the third day Christ rose from the grave, according to his own prediction, (Mark x. 34,) and during forty days previous to his ascension into heaven he appeared among his disciples, whom he instructed more fully concerning the nature of his mission, which he now left in their hands. Fifty days after his ascension, the disciples being assembled in Jerusalem at the feast of Pentecost, (Acts ii.,) were suddenly "all filled with the Holy Ghost," and endowed with the gift of speaking all languages. On this occasion three thousand persons were converted and received baptism. Being thus fitted for disseminating in every part of the world the principles of the new religion, the apostles and disciples whom Christ had appointed, scattered themselves throughout various countries, but principally in the east. Matthias had been chosen to supply the place of Judas, the traitor, and an additional disciple, named Saul, afterwards Paul, a person of education, and though a Jew, a Roman citizen of Tarsus, was especially called to co-operate with them.

The history of Christ has been written by four different individuals, whose accounts are received by

THE CRUCIFIXION OF OUR LORD.

2*

the Christian world, and some of the arguments for the credibility of their testimony are founded upon the mode in which they accomplished their task. Matthew, who had been a collector of customs, wrote his Gospel in Hebrew for the use of the Jews soon after Christ's death; Mark is believed to have written under the direction of Peter, for the use of the Christians at Rome; Luke, whose Gospel was written for the Heathen converts, was a physician, a companion in the labours of St. Paul, and is supposed to have written his account of Christ while travelling with the apostle; John's Gospel was written after all the preceding, and notices circumstances which the other evangelists had passed over. That part of the New Testament which follows the four Gospels was also written by St. Luke, and gives the Acts of the Apostles, and the history of Christianity, for about thirty years after Christ's death.

The primitive assemblies of the converts to Christianity were called Churches. The converts at Jerusalem formed the earliest Christian society. The church of Antioch, which was founded by Paul and Barnabas, was the second; and its members first received the name of Christians, having previously been called Nazarenes, by way of derision. The first churches or Christian communities were those of Jerusalem, Antioch, Ephesus, Smyrna, Athens, Corinth, Rome, and Alexandria. The churches founded by the apostles were regarded with peculiar veneration in after times. Their authority was appealed to on points of discipline and doctrine, as it was conceived that the letter and spirit of the apostolical regulations had been more rigidly adhered to. The church of Jerusalem may be regarded as the mother of all other churches; but the church at Rome, then the capital of the world, subsequently became, with the churches of Antioch and Alexandria, which were respectively capitals of Roman provinces, by far the most important of all the churches. The four churches of Jerusalem, Antioch, Rome, and Alexandria were formed in the order in which they are mentioned, though some doubt exists as to the title of the church of Rome to priority over that of Alexandria. The church of Rome became the metropolitan of the West, while that of Antioch was regarded as the chief of the eastern churches. As the apostles extended their travels, churches were planted in various parts of Asia. Paul and Barnabas visited the islands of Cyprus and Crete, and various parts of Greece, where they made converts to Christianity. In a second visit to the churches which were formed by Paul, he regulated some of the practices into which the converts had fallen. At Corinth he remained eighteen months, during which period he exerted himself to establish firmly the faith of the Christian believers, which in that church was exposed to peculiar dangers. When unable to visit distant churches, he addressed them in 'Epistles.' Paul next directed his attention to the West of Europe, to nations ' that were yet rude and barbarous.' There is no certain record of this portion of his travels. The writings and labours of St. Paul, who is emphatically called the Apostle of the Gentiles, form the most important part of the history of the second period of Christianity. In less than forty years after the death of Christ, the Gospel had been preached in every country of the then civilized world, and in some countries which were in a state of barbarism. In the year 68, that is 37 years after Christ's death, Peter and Paul suffered martyrdom at Rome.

The records as to the other apostles do not afford an adequate idea of the extent of their labours.

John was banished to the island of Patmos by Domitian, and there wrote the Revelation. He was subsequently permitted to return to Ephesus, where he wrote his Gospel and Epistles. He was the last survivor of the apostles, and died a natural death at the close of the first century, about the year 98. The seven churches mentioned by John in the Revelation are Ephesus, Smyrna, Pergamus, Thyatira, Sardis, Philadelphia, and Laodicea.

The Christian religion, as founded by Jesus Christ, and as accepted by all Christians, whatever differences there may be in their opinions, rests for its historical authority upon the proofs of his divine mission. The history of Jesus Christ, as given in the Four Gospels, presents us with a series of miracles wrought by him from the commencement of his ministry to the crowning miracle of all—his resurrection from the dead, and his ascent into heaven. Whether the miracles recorded in the Gospels actually took place, or not, is a matter of historical inquiry which must be determined from the whole evidence, like any other historical fact. If the miracles are admitted actually to have taken place—if the dead, for instance, were actually raised to life, there are very few who will not allow that He who performed these miracles must have had a particular power which other men have not. It has sometimes been said that the miracles, if true, do not prove a divine mission. But if a man proclaim his divine mission, and perform miracles in confirmation of it; if he predict his own death and resurrection, and actually do die and rise from the dead in accordance with his prediction—this will ever seem to the mass of mankind sufficient proof of a divine mission, and indeed it would be difficult to say what other proof can be asked for. The second proof of the divine mission of Christ to which Christians appeal, is contained in the types and prophecies of the Old Testament, which, under various figures, and in a great variety of expressions, of different ages, refer to the future coming of the Messiah, and to his kingdom. A comparison of the passages of the prophets with the passages in the history of Christ, and the application of many of these passages of the prophets by the Evangelists, and even by Christ himself on several occasions, are considered by all Christians to be a proof of the divine mission of Christ, and also a collateral evidence for the truth of those Gospels in which those prophecies are thus fulfilled. The predictions of Christ himself as to his own death, the destruction of Jerusalem, and the condition of his followers after his death, are also appealed to as evidence of his divine mission. The predictions of the prophets were accomplished in Jesus, and the prophecies of Jesus were accomplished in the subsequent history of the religion which he founded.

The diffusion of the Gospel, after the ascension of Jesus, by means at first apparently so insufficient for the purpose, is also viewed by all believers as a proof that his doctrines were not of man. And further, that the early preachers of Christianity sincerely believed what they taught, is shown by their inflexible zeal in diffusing the Gospel amidst sufferings and persecutions even unto death; and this strong conviction in the minds of those who had the best opportunity of learning the genuine doctrines of Christianity must be taken as confirmatory evidence of their divine origin.

The religion which Christ came to teach has for its great sanction, the resurrection of the dead, and the doctrine of future rewards and punishments. In the Mosaic law there is no declaration of the doctrine of

EVIDENCES OF CHRISTIANITY. 23

the resurrection, and of course the sanction of rewards and punishments in a future life forms no part of the law. Before the coming of Christ indeed there was a partial belief of a resurrection among some of the Jewish sects, (Matt. xxii. 23; Acts xxiv. 15:) but the preaching of Jesus proclaimed in the clearest terms a general resurrection, and rewards and punishments in a future life for all. It is this firm belief in a future state, which gave to the primitive Christians their inflexible courage and their readiness to suffer death; and which, as it was one of the main causes of the success which attended the preaching of Christianity in its early history, so is it now the vital spirit of the Christian religion.

During our Lord's ministry on earth he predicted the destruction of Jerusalem and the temple. The succeeding articles refer to the fulfilment of his prophecy.

JOSEPHUS.

SCENES IN THE SIEGE OF JERUSALEM BY THE ROMANS, A. D., 73.

OPENING OF THE SIEGE.

Quite exhausted as the Jews had already been by dissensions, the last winter of Jerusalem passed away in the same ferocious civil contests; her streets ran with the blood of her own children; and, instead of organizing a regular defence against the approaching enemy, each faction was strengthening its own position against the unintermitting assaults of its antagonists. According to Josephus, the Jewish historian, the city was now divided into three distinct garrisons, at fierce

CHRIST PREDICTING THE DESTRUCTION OF THE TEMPLE.

and implacable hostility with each other. Eleazar the son of Simon, the man who was the first cause of the war, by persuading the people to reject the offerings of the Roman emperors, and who afterwards had set himself at the head of the Zealots, and seized the temple, saw, with deep and rankling jealousy, the superiority assumed by John of Gischala. He pretended righteous indignation at his sanguinary proceedings, and, at length, with several other men of influence, Judas the son of Hilkiah, Simon the son of Ezron, and Hezekiah the son of Chobar, he openly seceded from the great band of Zealots who remained true to John, and seized the inner court of the temple. And now the arms of savage men, reeking with the blood of their fellow-citizens, were seen to rest upon the gates and walls of the Holy of Holies; the sacred songs of the Levites gave place to the ribald jests of a debauched soldiery; instead of the holy instruments of music, were heard the savage shouts of fighting warriors: and among the appointed victims, men, mortally wounded by the arrows of their own brethren without, lay gasping upon the steps of the altar. The band of Eleazar was amply supplied with provisions; for the stores of the temple were full, and they were not troubled with religious scruples. But they were few, and could only defend themselves from within, without venturing to sally forth against the enemy. The height of their position gave them an advantage over John, whose numbers were greatly superior—yet, though he suffered considerable loss, John would not intermit his attacks; clouds of missiles were continually discharged into the upper court of the temple, and the whole sacred pavement was strewn with dead bodies.

Simon the son of Gioras, who occupied the upper city, attacked John the more fiercely, because his strength was divided, and he was likewise threatened by Eleazar from above. But John had the same advantage over Simon, which Eleazar had over John. It was a perilous enterprise to scale the ascent to the temple, and on such ground the Zealots had no great difficulty in repelling the incessant assaults of Simon's faction. Against Eleazar's party they turned their engines, the scorpions, catapults, and balistas, with which they slew not a few of their enemies in the upper court, and some who came to sacrifice; for it was a strange feature in this fearful contest, that the religious ceremonies still went on upon the altar, which was often encircled with the dead. Beside the human victims which fell around, the customary sacrifices were regularly offered. Not only the pious inhabitants of Jerusalem constantly entreated and obtained permission to offer up their gifts and prayers before the altar of Jehovah, but even strangers from distant parts would still arrive, and, passing over the pavement slippery with human blood, make their way to the temple of their fathers; where they fondly thought, the God of Abraham, Isaac, and Jacob, still retained his peculiar dwelling within the Holy of Holies. Free ingress and egress were granted; the native Jews were strictly searched, the strangers were admitted with less difficulty; but often in the very act of prayer, or sacrifice, the arrows would come whizzing in, or the heavy stone fall thundering on their heads; and they would pay with their lives the price of kneeling and worshipping in the sacred place.

The contest raged more and more fiercely, for the abundant stores within the temple so unsparingly supplied the few adherents of Eleazar, that, in their drunkenness, they would occasionally sally out against John. When these attacks took place, John stood on the defensive, from the outer porticoes repelled Simon, and with his engines within harassed Eleazar. When the drunken or overwearied troops of Eleazar gave him repose, he would sally forth against Simon, and waste the city. Simon in his turn would drive him back; and thus the space around the temple became a mass of ruin and desolation; and in these desultory conflicts, the granaries, which, if carefully protected and prudently husbanded, might have maintained the city in plenty for years, were either wantonly thrown to waste or set on fire by Simon, lest they should be seized by John.

The people, in the mean time, particularly the old men and the women, groaned in secret; some uttered their prayers, but not aloud, for the speedy arrival of the Romans to release them from the worse tyranny of these fierce strangers. In one point the three parties concurred, the persecution of the citizens, and in the condign punishment of every individual whom they suspected of wishing well to the Roman army, as their common enemy. It was dreadful to witness the deep and silent misery of the people: they dared not utter their griefs; their very groans were watched, and stifled in their hearts. But it was even more dreadful to see the callous hard-heartedness which had seized all ranks—all were alike become reckless from desperation; there was no feeling for the nearest kindred; their very burial was neglected: all the desires, the hopes, the interests of life were extinguished, death was so near it was scarcely worth while to avoid it. Men went trampling over dead bodies as over the common pavement; and this familiarity with murder, as it deadened the hearts of the citizens, so it increased the ferocity of the soldiers. Yet, even in the midst of all this, the old religious prejudices were the last to yield. Among the atrocities of John, the promiscuous spoliations and murders, one act made still a deep impression upon the public mind—his seizing some

3*

sacred timbers, of great size and beauty, which Agrippa had brought from Lebanon, for the purpose of raising the temple twenty feet, and his converting them to the profane use of raising military towers, to annoy the factions of Eleazar in the inner temple. He erected these towers on the west side, where alone there was an open space, the others being occupied by flights of steps. The force of the three factions was as follows: Simon had ten thousand men, and five thousand Idumeans; John, six thousand; Eleazar, two thousand four hundred.

At length, after this awful interval of suspense, the war approached the gates of Jerusalem. Titus, having travelled from Egypt, arrived at Cæsarea, and began to organize his forces. In addition to the three legions which Vespasian had commanded, the twelfth returned to Syria, burning with revenge for its former disgraceful defeat under Cestius Gallus. The Syrian king sent large contingents. The legions were full; the men who had been drafted off by Vespasian having been replaced by two thousand picked troops from Alexandria, and three thousand of those stationed on the Euphrates. Tiberius Alexander, who was distinguished not only by his wisdom and integrity, but by the intimate friendship of Titus, was appointed to a high command. He had been the first, in the recent political changes, to espouse the party of Vespasian; and his experience in arms and knowledge of the country, which he had once governed, added weight to his counsels. The army advanced in its customary order of march; first the allies, then the pioneers; the baggage of the principal officers strongly guarded; then Titus himself, with a select guard of spearmen; then the horse attached to the legions. The military engines next, strongly guarded. The eagles and the trumpeters followed; then the legionaries in their

TITUS ESCAPING FROM THE JEWS.

phalanx, six deep; the slaves with the baggage; last of all, the mercenaries, with the rear-guard to keep order.

The host moved slowly through Samaria into Gophna, and encamped in the valley of Thorns, near a village called Gaboth Saul, the hill of Saul, about three miles and three quarters from Jerusalem. Titus himself, with six hundred horse, went forward to reconnoitre.

As they wound down the last declivities which sloped towards the walls, the factious and turbulent city seemed reposing in perfect peace. The gates were closed; not a man appeared. The squadron of Titus turned to the right, filed off, and skirted the wall towards the tower Psephina. On a sudden, the gate behind him, near the tower of the Women, towards the monument of Helena, burst open, and countless multitudes threw themselves, some across the road on which Titus was advancing, some right through his line, separating those who had diverged from the rest of the party. Titus was cut off with only a few followers—to advance was impossible. The ground was covered with orchards and gardens, divided by stone walls and intersected by deep trenches and watercourses, which reached the city walls. To retreat was almost as difficult, for the enemy lay in thousands across his road. Titus saw that not a moment was to be lost: he wheeled his horse round, called to his men to follow him, and charged fiercely through. Darts and javelins fell in showers around him; he had rode forth to reconnoitre, not to battle, and had on neither helmet nor breastplate. Providentially, not an arrow touched him: clearing his way with his sword on both sides, and trampling down the enemy with his fiery steed, he continued to cleave his passage through the dense masses. The Jews shouted with astonishment at the bravery of Cæsar, but exhorted each other to secure the inestimable prize. Yet still they shrank and made way before him: his followers formed round him as well as they could, and at length they reached their camp in safety. One man had been surrounded and pierced with a thousand javelins. Another, having dismounted, was slain, and his horse led away into the city. The triumph of the Jews was unbounded—Cæsar himself had been seen to fly—it was the promise and presage of more glorious and important victories.

The legion from Emmaus now joined the camp, and advanced to Scopos, within a mile of the city, from which all its extent could be surveyed. A level plain lay between the army and the northern wall; the Romans encamped, two legions in front, the fifteenth three stadia behind. The tenth legion now likewise arrived from Jericho, and occupied a station at the foot of the Mount of Olives.

Each from his separate watch-tower—Eleazar from the summit of the temple, John from the porticoes of the outer courts, and Simon from the heights of Sion, beheld three camps forming immediately under the walls of the city. For the first time they felt the imperious necessity of concord. They entered into negotiations, and agreed on a simultaneous attack: their mutual animosity turned to valiant emulation: they seized their arms, and rushing along the Valley of Jehoshaphat, fell with unexpected and irresistible impetuosity upon the tenth legion at the foot of the Mount of Olives. The legionaries were at work on their intrenchments, and many of them unarmed. They fell back overpowered by the suddenness of the onset: many were killed before they could get to their arms. Still more and more came swarming out of the city: and the consternation of the Romans yet further multiplied their numbers. Accustomed to fight in array, they were astonished at this wild and desultory warfare: they occasionally turned and cut off some of the Jews who exposed themselves in their blind fury: but, overborne by numbers, they were on the verge of total and irreparable defeat, when Titus, who had received intelligence of the assault, with some picked men, fell as unexpectedly on the flank of the Jews, and drove them up the valley with great loss. Still the battle raged the whole day. Titus, having planted the troops who came with him in front across the valley, sent the rest to seize and fortify the upper part of the hill. The Jews mistook this movement for flight; their watchmen on the walls shook their garments violently as a signal; it seemed as if the whole city poured forth, roaring and raging like wild beasts. The ranks of the Romans were shattered by the charge, as if by military engines; they fled to the mountain. Titus was again left, with but a few followers, on the declivity. With the advantage of the ground, he defended himself resolutely, and at first drove his adversaries down; but, like waves broken by a promontory, they went rushing up on both sides, pursuing the other fugitives, or turning and raking his party on both flanks. Those on the mount, as they saw the enemy swarming up the hill, were again seized with a panic, and dispersed on all sides, until a few, horror-struck at the critical situation of their commander, by a loud outcry raised an alarm among the whole legion, and bitterly reproaching each other for their base desertion of their Cæsar, with the resolute courage of men ashamed of their flight, rallied their scattered forces, made head, and drove the Jews down the hill into the valley. The Jews contested every foot of ground, till at length they were completely repulsed: and Titus again having established a strong line of outposts, dismissed his wearied men to their works.

It was now the Passover, the period during which, in the earlier days of Mosaic polity, or during the splendour of their monarchy, the whole people used to come up with light and rejoicing hearts to the hospitable city, where all were welcome; where every house was freely opened and without reward; and the united voices of all the sons of Abraham blessed the Almighty for their deliverance from Egypt. Even in these disastrous days the festival retained its reverential hold upon the hearts of the people. Not merely multitudes of Jews from the adjacent districts, but even from remote quarters, were assembled to celebrate the last public Passover of the Jewish nation. Dio Cassius states, that many Jews came even from beyond the Euphrates to join in the defence of the city; probably he meant those strangers who had come to the festival. These numbers only added to the miseries of the inhabitants, by consuming the stores, and hastening the general distress and famine. Yet, even the day of sacrifice was chosen by John of Gischala, for an act of treachery and bloodshed. When Eleazar opened the gates of the court to admit the worshippers, some of John's most desperate adherents, without having performed their ablutions, (Josephus adds this as a great aggravation of the crime,) stole in among the rest with their swords under their cloaks. No sooner were they within, than they threw away their cloaks, and the peaceful multitude beheld the swords of these dauntless ruffians flashing over their heads. The worshippers apprehended a general massacre. Eleazar's Zealots knew well on whom the attack was made. They leaped down and took refuge in the subterranean chambers of the temple. The multitude cowered around the altar; some were slain out of wantonness, or from private animosity; others trampled to death. At length, having glutted their vengeance upon those with whom they had no feud, the partizans of John came to terms with their real enemies. They were permitted to come up out of their hiding places, even to resume their arms, and Eleazar was still left in command; but one faction became thus absorbed in another, and two parties instead of three divided the city.

In the mean time, Titus was cautiously advancing his approaches. The whole plain from Scopos to the outward wall was levelled. The blooming gardens, with their bubbling fountains and cool water-courses, in which the inhabitants of Jerusalem had enjoyed sweet hours of delight and recreation, were ruthlessly swept away. The trees, now in their spring flower, fell before the axe; the landmarks were thrown down, the water-courses destroyed; even the deep and shady glens were levelled and filled up with the masses of, rugged and picturesque rocks which used to overshadow them. A broad and level road led from Scopos to the tomb of Herod, near the pool of Serpents.

While this work was proceeding, one day a considerable body of the Jews were seen to come, as if driven out from the gate near the tower of the Women. They stood cowering under the wells, as if dreading the attack of the Romans. It seemed as if the peace party had expelled the fiercer insurgents, for many at the same time were seen upon the walls, holding out their right hands in token of surrender, and making signs that they would open the gates: at the same time they began to throw down stones on those without. The latter appeared at one moment to endeavour to force their way back, and to supplicate the mercy of those on the walls; at another to advance towards the Romans, and then retreat as if in terror. The unsuspecting soldiers were about to charge in a body, but the more wary Titus ordered them to remain in their position. A few, however, who were in front of the workmen, seized their arms and advanced towards the gates. The Jews fled till their pursuers were so close to the gates as to be within the flanking towers; they then turned; others sallied forth and surrounded the Romans, while those on the walls hurled down stones and every kind of missile on their heads. After suffering great loss in killed and wounded, some of them effected their retreat, and were pursued by the Jews to the monument of Helena.

The Jews, not content with their victory, stood and laughed at the Romans for having been deceived by so simple a stratagem, clashed their shields, and assailed them with every ludicrous and opprobrious epithet. Nor was this the worst; they were received with stern reproof by their tribunes, and Cæsar himself addressed them in language of the strongest rebuke; "The Jews," he said, "who have no leader but despair, do every thing with the utmost coolness and precaution; lay ambushes, and plot stratagems; while the Romans, who used to enslave fortune by their steady discipline, are become so rash and disorderly as to venture into battle without command." He then threatened, and was actually about to put into execution the military law, which punished such a breach of order with death, had not the other troops surrounded him, entreating mercy for their fellow soldiers, and pledging themselves to redeem the blow by their future regularity and discipline. Cæsar was with difficulty appeased.

The approach to the city was now complete, and the army took up a position along the northern and western wall. They were drawn up, the foot in front, seven deep, the horse behind, three deep, with the archers behind them. The Jews were thus effectually blockaded;

CRUCIFYING BEFORE THE WALLS.

THE NEW YORK
PUBLIC LIBRARY

ASTOR, LENOX AND
TILDEN FOUNDATIONS
R   L

and the beasts of burden which carried the baggage, came up to the camp in perfect security. Titus himself encamped about a quarter of a mile from the wall, near the tower Psephi; another part of the army near the tower called Hippicus, at the same distance; the tenth legion kept its station near the Mount of Olives.

PROGRESS OF THE SIEGE—FAMINE—CRUCIFYING BEFORE THE WALLS.

LATER in the progress of the siege two walls had fallen, but still the precipitous heights of Sion, the impregnable Antonia and the stately temple, lowered defiance on the invaders. Titus determined to suspend the siege for a few days, in order to allow time for the terror of his conquests to operate on the minds of the besieged, and for the slow famine to undermine their strength and courage. He employed the time in making a magnificent review of all his troops, who were to receive their pay in view of the whole city. The troops defiled slowly, in their best attire, with their arms taken out of their cases, and their breast-plates on, the cavalry leading their horses, accoutred in their most splendid trappings. The whole suburbs gleamed with gold and silver. The Romans beheld the spectacle with pride, the Jews with consternation. The whole length of the old wall, the northern cloisters of the temple, every window, every roof, was crowded with heads, looking down, some with stern and scowling expressions of hate and defiance; others in undisguised terror; some emaciated with famine, others heated with intemperance. The sight might have appalled the boldest but the insurgents knew that they had offended too deeply to trust to Roman mercy, and that nothing remained but still to contend with the stubborn obstinacy of desperation. For four days this procession continued defiling beneath the walls: on the fifth, as no overtures for capitulation were made, Titus gave orders to recommence the siege: one part of the army was employed to raise embankments against the Antonia, where John and his followers fought; the rest against the monument of John, the high priest, on the other part of the wall defended by Simon. The Jews had now learned, by long practice, the use of their military engines, and plied them from their heights with tremendous effect. They had three hundred scorpions for the discharge of darts, and forty balistas which threw enormous stones. Titus used every means to induce them to surrender, and sent Josephus to address them in their native language.

Josephus with some difficulty found a place whence he might be heard, and, at the same time be out of arrow-shot. Whether his prudence marred the effect of his oratory or not, by his own statement, he addressed to them a long harangue. He urged their own interest in the preservation of the city and temple, the unconquerable power of the Romans, their mercy in offering them terms of capitulation, and he dwelt on the famine which had begun to waste their strength. Neither the orator himself, nor his topics were very acceptable to the fierce zealots. They scoffed at him, reviled him, and hurled their darts against his head. Josephus then reverted to the ancient history of the nation: he urged that the Jewish people had never yet relied on such defenders, but ever on their God. Such was the trust of Abraham, who did not resist, when Necho, the Pharaoh of Egypt, took away his wife Sarah! The orator seems here to have reckoned on the ignorance of his audience. He then recounted, first, the great deliverances, then the great calamities of the nation; and proceeded in a strain of vehement invective little calculated to excite to any thing but furious indignation in the minds of the zealots. They, as might be expected, were only more irritated. The people, by his account, were touched by his expostulations; probably their miseries and the famine argued more powerfully to their hearts: they began to desert in numbers. Some sold their property at the lowest price: others swallowed their more valuable articles, gold and jewels, and when they fled to the Romans, unloaded themselves of their precious burthens. Titus allowed them to pass unmolested. The news of their escape excited many others to follow their example, though John and Simon watched every outlet of the city, and executed without mercy all they suspected of a design to fly. This, too, was a convenient charge, by which they could put to death as many of the more wealthy as they chose.

In the meantime the famine increased, and with the famine the desperation of the insurgents. No grain was exposed for public sale; they forced open and searched the houses; if they found any, they punished the owners for their refusal; if none was discovered, they tortured them with greater cruelty, for concealing it with such care. The looks of the wretched beings were the marks by which they judged whether they had any secret store or not: those who were hale and strong were condemned as guilty of concealment: they passed by only the pale and emaciated. The wealthy secretly sold their whole property for a measure of wheat—the poorer for one of barley, and, shrouding themselves in the darkest recesses of their houses, devoured it unground. Others made bread, snatched it half-baked from the embers, and tore it with their teeth. The misery of the weaker was aggravated by seeing the plenty of the stronger. Every kind feeling—love, respect, natural affection—were extinct through the all-absorbing want. Wives would snatch the last morsel from husbands, children from parents, mothers from children; they would intercept even their own milk from the lips of their pining babes. Even the most scanty supply of food was consumed in terror and peril. The marauders were always prowling about. If a house was closed, they supposed that eating was going on; they burst in, and squeezed the crumbs from the mouths and the throats of those who had swallowed them. Old men were scourged till they surrendered the food to which their hands clung desperately, and even were dragged about by the hair till they gave up what they had. Children were seized as they hung upon the miserable morsels they had got, whirled around and dashed upon the pavement. Those who anticipated the plunderers by swallowing every atom, were treated still more cruelly, as if they had wronged those who came to rob them. Tortures, which cannot be related with decency, were employed against those who had a loaf, or a handful of barley. Nor did their own necessities excuse these cruelties; sometimes it was done by those who had abundance of food, with a deliberate design of husbanding their own resources. If any wretches crept out near the Roman posts to pick up some miserable herbs or vegetables, they were plundered on their return; and if they entreated, in the awful name of God, that some portion, at least, might be left them of what they had obtained at the hazard of their lives, they might think themselves well off if they escaped being killed as well as pillaged.

Such were the cruelties exercised on the lower orders by the satellites of the tyrants; the richer and more distinguished were carried before the tyrants themselves. Some were accused of treasonable correspondence with the Romans; others with an intention to desert. He that was plundered by Simon was sent to John; he that had been stripped by John was sent to Simon; so that, by turns, they, as it were, shared the bodies, and drained the blood of the citizens. Their ambition made them enemies; their common crimes united them in friendship: they were jealous if either deprived the other of his share in some flagrant cruelty, and complained of being wronged if excluded from some atrocious iniquity.

The blood runs cold, and the heart sickens at these unexampled horrors, and we take refuge in a kind of desperate hope that they have been exaggerated by the historian; those which follow, perpetrated under his own eyes, by his Roman friends, and justified under the all-extenuating plea of necessity, admit of no such reservation. They must be believed in their naked and unmitigated barbarity.

Many poor wretches, some few of them insurgents, but mostly the poorest of the people, would steal down the ravines by night to pick up whatever might have served for food. They would, most of them, willingly have deserted, but hesitated to leave their wives and children to be murdered. For these, Titus laid men in ambush: when attacked, they defended themselves: as a punishment, they were scourged, tortured, and crucified before the walls; and in the morning sometimes five hundred, sometimes more, of these miserable beings were seen writhing on crosses before the walls. This was done because it was thought unsafe to let them escape, and to terrify the rest. The soldiers added ridicule to their cru-city: they would place the bodies in all sorts of ludicrous postures; and this went on till room was wanting for the crosses, and crosses for the bodies.

These executions produced a contrary effect to that which was contemplated. The zealots dragged the relatives of the deserters, and all they suspected as inclined towards peace, up to the walls, and bade them behold those examples of Roman mercy. This checked the desertion, excepting in those who thought it better to be killed at once than to die slowly of hunger. Titus sent others back to Simon and John, with their hands cut off, exhorting them to capitulate, and not to force him to destroy the city and the temple. It cannot be wondered, that as Titus went round the works he was saluted from all parts, in contempt of the imperial dignity, with the loudest and bitterest execrations against his own name and that of his father.

The extract which follows relates to a much later period of the siege.

CAPTURE AND BURNING OF THE TEMPLE.

PROCEEDING by gradual approaches and successive assaults, the Romans had now captured the tower of Antonia, and were threatening the temple itself. In the mean time, the famine continued its fearful ravages: men would fight even the dearest friends for the most miserable morsel: the very dead were searched, as though they might conceal some scrap of food. Even the robbers began to suffer severely:

they went prowling about like mad dogs, or reeling, like drunken men, from weakness, and entered and searched the same house twice or thrice in the same hour. The most loathsome and disgusting food was sold at an enormous price; they gnawed their belts, shoes, and even the leathern coats of their shields: chopped hay and shoots of trees sold at high prices. Yet what were all these horrors to that which followed?

There was a woman of Perea, from the village of Bethzob, Mary, the daughter of Eleazar. She possessed considerable wealth when she took refuge in the city. Day after day she had been plundered by the robbers, whom she had provoked by her bitter imprecations. No one, however, would mercifully put an end to her misery, and her mind maddened with wrong, her body preyed upon by famine, she wildly resolved on an expedient which might gratify at once her vengeance and her hunger. She had an infant that was vainly endeavouring to obtain some moisture from her dry bosom: she seized it, cooked it, ate one half, and set the other aside. The smoke and the smell of food quickly reached the robbers: they forced her door, and, with horrible threats, commanded her to give up what she had been feasting on. She replied, with horrible indifference, that she had carefully reserved her good friends a part of her meal. She uncovered the remains of her child! The savage men stood speechless, at which she cried out, with a shrill voice, "Eat, for I have eaten: be ye not more delicate than a woman—more tender-hearted than a mother! or, if ye are too religious to touch such food, I have eaten half already—leave me the rest." They retired, pale and trembling with horror: the story spread rapidly through the city, and reached the Roman camp, where it was first heard with incredulity—afterward with the deepest commisseration.

How dreadfully must the recollection of the words of Moses have fixed themselves upon the minds of all those Jews who were not entirely unread in their holy writings:—" The tender and delicate woman among you, which would not adventure to set the sole of her foot upon the ground for delicateness and tenderness, her eye shall be evil towards the husband of her bosom, and toward her son, and toward her daughter; and toward her young one that cometh out from between her feet, and toward her children which she shall bear: for she shall eat them for want of all things, secretly, in the siege and straitness wherewith thine enemy shall distress thee in thy gates."

The destruction of the outer cloisters had left the Romans masters of the great court of the Gentiles. On the eighth of August, the engines began to batter the eastern chambers of the inner court. For six previous days the largest and most powerful of the battering rams had played upon the wall; the enormous size and compactness of the stones had resisted all its efforts; other troops at the same time endeavoured to undermine the northern gate, but with no better success; nothing therefore remained but to fix the scaling ladders, and storm the cloisters. The Jews made no resistance to their mounting the walls; but as soon as they reached the top hurled them down headlong, or slew them before they could cover themselves with their shields. In some places they thrust down the ladders, loaded with armed men, who fell back and were dashed to pieces on the pavement. Some of the standard bearers had led the way; they also were repelled, and the Jews remained masters of the eagles. On the side of the Romans fell many distinguished soldiers; on that of the Jews, Eleazar, the nephew of Simon. Repulsed on all hands from the top of the wall, Titus commanded fire to be set to the gates.

In the mean time, Ananus of Emmaus, the bloody executioner of Simon, and Archelaus son of Magadat, deserted to the Romans. Titus at first intended to put them to death, but afterwards relented. No sooner had the blazing torches been applied to the gates, than the silver plates heated, the wood kindled, the whole flamed up and spread rapidly to the cloisters. Like wild beasts environed in a burning forest, the Jews saw the awful circle of fire hem them in on every side; their courage sank; they stood, gasping, motionless, and helpless; not a hand endeavoured to quench the flames, or stop the silent progress of the conflagration. Yet still fierce thoughts of desperate vengeance were brooding in their hearts. Through the whole night and the next day the fire went on, consuming the whole range of cloisters. Titus at length gave orders that it should be extinguished, and the way through the gates levelled for the advance of the legionaries. A council of war was summoned, in which the expediency of destroying the magnificent building was solemnly discussed. It consisted of six of the chief officers of the army; among the rest, of Tiberius Alexander, whose offerings had formerly enriched the splendid edifice. Three of the council insisted on the necessity of destroying for ever this citadel of a mutinous people; it was no longer a temple, but a fortress, and to be treated like a military stronghold. Titus inclined to milder counsels; the magnificence of the building had made a strong impression upon his mind, and he was reluctant to destroy what might be considered as one of the wonders of the Roman empire. Alexander, Fronto, and Cerealis concurred in this opinion, and the soldiers were ordered to do all they could to quench the flames. But higher counsels had otherwise decreed, and the Temple of Jerusalem was to be for ever obliterated from the face of the earth. The whole of the first day after the fire began, the Jews, from exhaustion and consternation, remained entirely inactive. The next, they made a furious sally from the eastern gate against the guards who were posted in the outer court. The legionaries locked their shields together, and stood the brunt of the onset: but the Jews still came pouring forth in such overbearing multitudes, that Titus himself was forced to charge at the head of some cavalry, and with difficulty drove them back into the temple.

It was the 10th of August, the day already darkened in the Jewish calendar by the destruction of the former temple by the king of Babylon: it was almost passed. Titus withdrew again into the Antonia, intending the next morning to make a general assault. The quiet summer evening came on; the setting sun shone for the last time on the snow-white walls and glistening pinnacles of the temple roof. Titus had retired to rest, when, suddenly, a wild and terrible cry was heard, and a man came rushing in, announcing that the temple was on fire. Some of the besieged, notwithstanding their repulse in the morning, had sallied out to attack the men who were busily employed in extinguishing the fires about the cloisters. The Romans not merely drove them back, but, entering the sacred space with them, forced their way to the door of the temple. A soldier, without orders, mounting on the shoulders of one of his comrades, threw a blazing brand into a gilded small door on the north side of the chambers, in the outer building or porch. The flames sprang up at once. The Jews uttered one simultaneous shriek, and grasped their

THE NEW YORK
PUBLIC LIBRARY

ASTOR, LENOX AND
TILDEN FOUNDATIONS
R   L

ROMAN SOLDIER SETTING FIRE TO THE TEMPLE.

SIEGE OF JERUSALEM.

swords, with a furious determination of revenging and perishing in the ruins of the temple. Titus rushed down with the utmost speed: he shouted: he made signs to his soldiers to quench the fire: his voice was drowned and his signs unnoticed in the blind confusion: the legionaries either could not or would not hear; they rushed on, trampling each other down in their furious haste, or, stumbling over the crumbling ruins, perished with the enemy: each exhorted the other, and each hurled his blazing brand into the inner part of the edifice, and then hurried to his work of carnage. The unarmed and defenceless people were slain in thousands; they lay heaped, like sacrifices, round the altar: the steps of the temple ran with streams of blood, which washed down the bodies that lay about.

Titus found it impossible to check the rage of the soldiery; he entered with his officers, and surveyed the interior of the sacred edifice. The splendour filled them with wonder; and as the flames had not yet penetrated to the holy place, he made a last effort to save it, and, springing forth, again exhorted the soldiers to stay the progress of the conflagration. The centurion, Liberalis, endeavoured to force obedience with his staff of office; but even respect for the emperor gave way to the furious animosity against the Jews, to the fierce excitement of battle, and to the insatiable hope of plunder. The soldiers saw every thing around them radiant with gold, which shone dazzlingly in the wild light of the flames; they supposed that incalculable treasures were laid up in the sanctuary. A soldier, unperceived, thrust a lighted torch between the hinges of the door—the whole building was in flames in an instant. The blinding smoke and fire forced the officers to retreat, and the noble edifice was left to its fate.

It was an appalling spectacle to the Roman—what was it to the Jew! The whole summit of the hill which commanded the city blazed like a volcano. One after another the buildings fell in with a tremendous crash, and were swallowed up in the fiery abyss. The roofs of cedar were like sheets of flame: the gilded pinnacles shone like spikes of red light: the gate towers sent up tall columns of flame and smoke: the neighbouring hills were lighted up; and dark groups of people were seen watching in horrible anxiety the progress of the destruction: the walls and heights of the upper city were crowded with faces, some pale with the agony of despair, others scowling unavailing vengeance. The shouts of the Roman soldiery, as they ran to and fro, and the howlings of the insurgents who were perishing in the flames, mingled with the roaring of the conflagration and the thundering sound of falling timbers. The echoes of the mountains replied, or brought back the shrieks of the people on the heights: all along the walls resounded screams and wailings: men, who were expiring with famine, rallied their remaining strength to utter a cry of anguish and desolation.

The slaughter within was even more dreadful than the spectacle from without. Men and women, old and young, insurgents and priests, those who fought and those who entreated mercy, were hewn down in indiscriminate carnage. The number of the slain exceeded that of the slayers. The legionaries had to clamber over heaps of dead to carry on the work of extermination. John, at the head of some of his troops, cut his way through, first into the outer court of the temple, afterward into the upper city. Some of the priests upon the roof wrenched off the gilded spikes, with their sockets of lead, and used them as missiles against the Romans below. Afterward they fled to a

ROMAN SOLDIERS IN THE TEMPLE.

THE NEW YORK
PUBLIC LIBRARY

ASTOR, LENOX AND
TILDEN FOUNDATIONS
R   L

part of the wall about fourteen feet wide; they were summoned to surrender; but two of them, Mair, son of Belga, and Joseph, son of Dalai, plunged headlong into the flames.

No part escaped the fury of the Romans. The treasuries, with all their wealth of money, jewels, and costly robes—the plunder which the zealots had laid up—were totally destroyed. Nothing remained but a small part of the outer cloister, in which about six thousand unarmed and defenceless people, with women and children, had taken refuge. These poor wretches, like multitudes of others, had been led up to the temple by a false prophet, who had proclaimed that God commanded all the Jews to go up to the temple, where he would display his Almighty power to save his people. The soldiers set fire to the building—every soul perished.

For during all this time, false prophets, suborned by the zealots, had kept the people in a state of feverish excitement, as though the appointed Deliverer would still appear. They could not, indeed, but remember the awful, the visible signs which had preceded the siege: the fiery sword, the armies fighting in the air; the opening of the great gate; the fearful voice within the sanctuary, "Let us depart;" the wild cry of Jesus, son of Ananus—*Wo, wo to the city*, which he had continued from the government of Albinus to the time of the siege, when he suddenly stopped, shrieked out—*wo to myself*, and was struck dead by a stone. Yet the undying hopes of fierce fanaticism were kept alive by the still renewed predictions of that Great One, who would at this time arise out of Judea, and assume the dominion of the world. This prophecy the flattering Josephus declared to have been accomplished in the Roman Vespasian; but more patriotic interpreters, still, to the last, expected to see it fulfilled in the person of the conquering Messiah, who would reveal himself in the darkest hour, wither the Roman legions with one word, and then transfer the seat of empire from the Capitol to Sion.

The whole Roman army entered the sacred precincts, and pitched their standards among the smoking ruins: they offered sacrifice for the victory, and, with loud acclamations, saluted Titus as emperor. Their joy was not a little enhanced by the value of the plunder they had obtained, which was so great that gold fell in Syria to half its former value. The few priests were still on the top of the walls to which they had escaped. A boy, emaciated with hunger, came down on a promise that his life should be spared. He immediately ran to drink, filled his vessel, and hurried away to his comrades with such speed that the soldiers could not catch him. Five days afterward the priests were starved into surrender; they entreated for their lives, but Titus answered that the hour of mercy was passed. They were led to execution.

THE FALL OF JERUSALEM.

Untold miseries were heaped on the unfortunate people who fell captives to the Romans. Still the upper city held out; but Simon and John, disheartened by the capture of the temple, demanded a conference. It was granted, and Titus, stationing himself at the western verge of the hill, addressed them through an interpreter. He offered to spare their

SIEGE OF JERUSALEM.

lives on condition of instant surrender. John and
Simon demanded free egress with their wives and
children, promising to evacuate the city, and depart
into the wilderness. The terms were rejected, and
Titus vowed the unsparing extermination of the whole
people; his troops had immediate license to plunder
and burn Acra. The archives, the council house,
the whole of Acra and Ophla were instantly set on
fire. The insurgents took possession of the palace,
where, from its strength, the people had laid up much
of their wealth: they drove the Romans back, and
put to death eight thousand four hundred of the people
who had taken refuge there, and plundered all
the treasures. They took two Roman soldiers alive:
one they put to death and dragged his body through
the city. The other, pretending to have something
to communicate to Simon, was led before him; but as
he had nothing to say, he was made over to one
Ardala to be put to death. He was led forth with
his hands bound and his eyes bandaged, to be killed
in sight of the Romans; but while the Jew was drawing
his sword, he contrived to make his escape. Titus,
unwilling to punish him with death after he had thus
escaped, but wishing to show that it was unworthy of
a Roman soldier to be taken alive, had him stripped
of his armour, and dismissed him with disgrace. The
next day the Romans entirely cleared the lower city,
and set the whole on fire. The insurgents, cooped
up in the upper city, lay in ambush near the outlets,
and slew every one who attempted to desert; their
great trust was in the subterranean passages in which
they hoped to lie hid.

On the 20th of August, Cæsar at length raised his
mounds against the steep cliffs of the upper city: he
had the greatest difficulty in obtaining timber: but
at last his works were ready in two places—one oppo-

site to the palace, the other near the Xystus. The Idumean chieftains now endeavoured secretly to make their terms. Titus reluctantly consented; but the vigilant John detected the plot, threw the leaders into prison, and intrusted the defence of the wall to more trusty soldiers. Still the guards could not prevent desertion: though many were killed, yet many escaped. The Romans, weary of the work of slaughter, spared the people, but sold all the rest as slaves, though they brought but a low price, the market being glutted, and few purchasers found. Forty thousand were thus spared: the number sold as slaves was incalculable. About the same time, a priest, named Jesus, son of Thebuth, obtained his life on condition of surrendering some of the treasure of the temple which he had secured—two candlesticks, tables, goblets, and vessels of pure gold, as well as the curtains and robes of the high priests. Another, who had been one of the treasurers, showed a place where the vests and girdles of the priests were concealed, with a great quantity of purple and scarlet thread, and an immense store of cinnamon, cassia, and other spices.

Eighteen days elapsed before the works were completed: on the seventh of September, the engines were advanced to batter down the last bulwark of the besieged. Some did not await the conflict, but crept down into the lower city; others shrunk into the subterranean passages; others more manfully endeavoured to beat down the engineers. The Romans advanced in the pride of victory; the Jews were weary, famine-stricken, disheartened. A breach was speedily made; some of the towers fell; the leaders did not display their customary valour and conduct; they fled on all sides. Some who were accustomed to vaunt the most loudly, now stood pale, trembling,

JERUSALEM.

THE NEW YORK
PUBLIC LIBRARY

ASTOR, LENOX AND
TILDEN FOUNDATIONS
R   L

inactive: others endeavoured to break through the Roman works and make their escape. Vague rumours were spread abroad that the whole western wall had fallen—that the Romans were in the city. The men looked round for their wonted leaders: they neither saw their active figures hurrying about in the thickest of the fray, nor heard their voices exciting them to desperate resistance. Many threw themselves on the ground and bitterly lamented their fate. Even John and Simon, instead of remaining in their three impregnable towers, where nothing but famine could have reduced them, descended into the streets, and fled into the valley of Siloam. They then made an attempt to force their way through the wall; but their daring and strength seemed alike broken; they were repulsed by the guard, dispersed, and at length crept down into the subterranean vaults. The Romans ascended the wall with shouts of triumph at a victory so much beyond all hope easy and bloodless; they spread through the streets slaying and burning as they went. In many houses where they expected rich plunder, they found nothing but heaps of putrid bodies—whole families who had died of hunger: they retreated from the loathsome sight and insufferable stench. But they were not moved to mercy towards the living; in some places the flames were actually retarded or quenched with streams of blood: night alone put an end to the carnage.

When Titus entered the city, he gazed with astonishment at the massy towers, and recognized the hand of God in a victory which had thus made him master of such fortresses without a struggle. The multitudes of prisoners who pined in the dungeons, where they had been thrown by the insurgents, were released. The city was ordered to be razed, excepting the three towers, which were left as standing monuments of the victory.

The soldiers themselves were weary of the work of slaughter, and orders were issued to kill only those who resisted. Yet the old and infirm, as unsaleable, were generally put to death: the rest were driven into a space of the temple, called the Court of the Women. There a selection was made: the noted insurgents were put to death, except some of the tallest and most handsome, who were reserved to grace the triumph of Titus. Of the rest, all above seventeen years old were sent to Egypt to work in the mines, or distributed among the provinces to be exhibited as gladiators in the public theatres, and in combats against wild beasts. Twelve thousand died of hunger, part from want or neglect of supplies—part obstinately refusing food. During the whole siege, the number killed was one million one hundred thousand; that of prisoners, ninety-seven thousand. In fact, the population, not of Jerusalem alone, but that of the adjacent districts—many who had taken refuge in the city, more who had assembled for the feast of unleavened bread—had been shut up by the sudden formation of the siege.

Yet the chief objects of their vengeance, the dauntless Simon, son of Gioras, and John the Gischalite, still seemed to baffle all pursuit. The Roman soldiers penetrated into the subterranean caverns; wherever they went they found incalculable treasures, and heaps of dead bodies—some who had perished from hunger, others from their wounds, many by their own hands: the close air of the vaults reeked with the pestilential effluvia. Most recoiled from these pits of death; the more rapacious went on, breathing death for the sake of plunder. At length, reduced by famine, John and his brethren came forth upon

SIMON APPEARING FROM THE VAULT.

terms of surrender. His life was spared—a singular instance of lenity, if indeed his conduct had been so atrocious as it is described by his rival Josephus. He was condemned to perpetual imprisonment, and finally sent to Italy.

Many days after, towards the end of October, when Titus had left the city, as some of the Roman soldiers were reposing amid the ruins of the temple, they were surprised by the sudden apparition of a man in white raiment, and with a robe of purple, who seemed to rise from the earth in silent and imposing dignity. At first they stood awe-struck and motionless: at length they ventured to approach him; they encircled him and demanded his name. He answered, "Simon the son of Gioras; call hither your general." Terentius Rufus was speedily summoned, and to him the brave though cruel defender of Jerusalem surrendered himself.

On the loss of the city, Simon had leaped down into one of the vaults, with a party of miners, hewers of stone, and iron workers. For some distance they had followed the natural windings of the cavern, and then attempted to dig their way out beyond the walls. But their provisions, however carefully husbanded, soon failed, and Simon determined on the bold measure of attempting to overawe the Romans by his sudden and spectral appearance. News of his capture was sent to Titus: he was ordered to be set apart for the imperial triumph.

Thus fell, and for ever, the metropolis of the Jewish state. Other cities have risen on the ruins of Jerusalem, and succeeded as it were, to the inalienable inheritance of perpetual siege, oppression and ruin. Jerusalem might almost seem to be a place under a peculiar curse: it has probably witnessed a far greater portion of human misery than any other spot upon the earth.

Nothing could equal the splendour of the triumph which Vespasian shared with his son Titus for their common victories. Besides the usual display of treasures, gold, silver, jewels, purple, vases, the rarest wild beasts from all quarters of the globe; there were extraordinary pageants, three or four stories high, representing to the admiration and delight of those civilized savages, all the horrors and miseries of war, beautiful countries laid waste; armies slain, routed, led captive; cities breached by military engines, stormed, laid waste with fire and sword; women wailing; houses overthrown; temples burning; and rivers of fire flowing through regions no longer cultivated or peopled, but blazing far away into the long and dreary distance. Among the spoils, the golden table, the seven-branched candlestick, and the book of the law from the Temple of Jerusalem, were conspicuous.

The triumph passed on to the Capitol, and there paused to hear that the glory of Rome was completed by the insulting and cruel execution of the bravest general of the enemy. This distinction fell to the lot of Simon, the son of Gioras. He was dragged along to a place near the Forum, with a halter round his neck, scourged as he went, and there put to death.

EARLY DIFFUSION OF CHRISTIANITY.

 THE spread of the gospel was aided chiefly by the easy means of communication throughout the Roman empire and the constant and close relation the dispersed Jews maintained with Jerusalem. As a general rule, Christianity first gained ground in the cities; for as it was needful above all to obtain fixed seats for the propagation of the gospel, its first preachers, passing rapidly over the country, published the glad tidings first of all in the cities, from which it might afterwards be easily diffused through the country by native teachers. In this manner, that fanaticism, obstinacy and ignorance which prevailed among the peasantry was avoided until the intelligent citizens were won to the cause of righteousness. Yet, in many districts, country churches were formed very early.

In the New Testament, we find accounts of the dissemination of Christianity in Syria, Cilicia, the Parthian empire, Arabia, Lesser Asia and the countries adjacent, Greece and the neighbouring countries as far as Illyricum, and Italy. But authentic accounts on the subject are greatly deficient. We confine ourselves to what may be safely credited. It is certain that Christianity was early diffused in Mesopotamia, though the story of a correspondence between a prince of Abgari and our Saviour is not to be trusted as true. Between the years 160–170, the

Abgar Bar Manu is mentioned as a Christian. As early as 202, the Christians of Edessa had a church which was built after the model of the temple at Jerusalem. Bardesanes, who wrote in the time of the Emperor Marcus Aurelius, notices the spread of Christianity in Parthia, Media, Persia and Bactria. After the restoration of the independent empire of Persia, the Persian Mani attempted to form a new religious doctrine by a union of the ancient oriental systems with Christianity.

In Arabia, there were Jews residing in great numbers, who may have afforded an opening for the preaching of the gospel in that country. It is clear from his own words, that the apostle Paul, soon after his conversion, retired from Damascus to Arabia. But how he employed himself and with what results, remains uncertain. If the country called India in tradition is to be taken for part of Arabia, it would appear that St. Bartholomew preached the gospel to the Jews there. On this supposition, too, the learned Pantænus was teacher of a portion of this people in the latter half of the second century. In the early part of the third century, Origen, the great father of the Alexandrian church, laboured in the same field. Most probably, however, this was that part of Arabia which was in subjection to the Roman Empire. At a somewhat later period, we find Christian churches in Arabia, standing in immediate connection with Origen.

The ancient Syro-Persian church whose remains survive to the present day on the coast of Malabar in the East Indies, boasts as its founder the Apostle St. Thomas, and professes to be able to point out the place of his burial. The earliest notice of this church is found in the reports of Cosmas Indicopleustes, about the middle of the sixth century. The traditions in regard to the propagation of the gospel in these regions are not reliable, and it is extremely doubtful to what countries they particularly refer. In the time of the emperor Constantine, a missionary, Theophilus Indicus is spoken of as coming from the island Diu, by which is to be understood the island Zocotara. In his native land and in many other districts of India, he found Christianity already planted.

Egypt was the first African country where Christianity was disseminated. Among the first zealous preachers of the gospel we find men of Alexandrian education, as for instance, Apollos of Alexandria, and probably, also, Barnabas of Cyprus. An ancient tradition mentions the Evangelist Mark as the founder of the Alexandrian Church. A persecution of the Christians in Thebais under the Emperor Septimius Severus proves that Christianity had as early as the closing years of the second century made some progress in Upper Egypt.

There are no credible accounts of the diffusion of Christianity in Ethiopia in these centuries. History gives no account of the consequences which resulted from the conversion of the chamberlain of Candace, Queen of Meroe, which is narrated in the Acts. The first certain indications of the conversion of a part of Abyssinia is that through the instrumentality of Frumentius in the fourth century. The gospel early found its way to Carthage and the whole of the Roman proconsular Africa. In the second century, the church at Carthage was in a very flourishing condition. Tertullian, the presbyter, mentions a persecution of the Christians in Mauritania.

Passing over to Europe, we have Rome, the chief but not the only seat of the propagation of Christianity. Flourishing communities at Lugdunum (Lyons) and Vienne, became known during a bloody persecution in 177

In the greater part of Gaul, the pagan superstition long withstood the further spread of Christianity. Even as late as the middle of the third century there were few Christian communities to be found there. At that time, seven missionaries went from Rome to Gaul, and founded churches in seven cities. Irenæus, who became bishop of the church at Lyons, some time after the persecution of 177, speaks of the spread of the gospel in Germany, among the barbarians as well as among the inhabitants of Roman Germany. Irenæus is also the first to speak of the diffusion of Christianity in Spain. The apostle Paul visited that country, it is believed, and by his labours, gave the words of life a wide circulation.

Of the early propagation of Christianity in Britain, Tertullian is a witness. A later tradition given by Bede, in the eighth century, reports that Lucius, a British king, requested the Roman bishop, Eleutherus, in the latter part of the second century, to send missionaries to that country. But the peculiarities of the British Church are evidence against its owing its origin to Rome. Neander conjectures that the Britons received Christianity through Gaul from Asia Minor, a thing quite possible and easy by commercial intercourse. The later Anglo-Saxons, who opposed the ecclesiastical independence maintained by the Britons, and endeavoured to establish the supremacy of Rome were uniformly disposed to trace back the church to a Roman origin. From such an attempt many false legends may have arisen.

OUTLINE HISTORY OF CHRISTIANITY
TO THE TIME OF THE REFORMATION.

SECTION I.
HISTORY OF CHRISTIANITY, FROM ITS ORIGIN TO ITS ESTABLISHMENT BY CONSTANTINE THE GREAT.

WHEN the true religion was preached by the Saviour of mankind, it is not to be wondered at, if he became on that account obnoxious to a people so deeply sunk in corruption and ignorance as the Jews then were. It is not here requisite to enter into the particulars of the doctrine advanced by him, or of the opposition he met with from the Jews, as a full account of these things, and likewise of the preaching of the Gospel by the apostles, may be found in the New Testament. The rapid progress of the Christian religion under these faithful and inspired ministers soon alarmed the Jews, and raised various persecutions against its followers. The Jews, indeed, seemed at first to have been everywhere the chief promoters of persecution; for we find that they officiously went from place to place, wherever they heard of the increase of the Gospel, and by their calumnies and false sug-

CHRISTIANITY IN THE REIGN OF NERO.

ROME SET ON FIRE BY ORDER OF NERO.

gestions endeavoured to stir up the people against the apostles.

The Heathens, though at first they showed no very violent spirit of persecution against the Christians, soon came to hate them as much as the Jews themselves. Tacitus acquaints us with the causes of this hatred, when speaking of the first general persecution under Nero. That inhuman tyrant having set fire to the city of Rome, to avoid the imputation of this wickedness, transferred it on the Christians. Our author informs us, that they were already abhorred on account of their many and enormous crimes. "The author of this name, (*Christians*,)" says he, "was CHRIST, who, in the reign of Tiberius, was executed under Pontius Pilate, procurator of Judea. The pestilent superstition was for a while suppressed: but it revived again, and spread, not only over Judea, where this evil was first broached, but reached Rome, whither from every quarter of the earth is constantly flowing whatever is hideous and abominable amongst men, and is there readily embraced and practised.

First, therefore, were apprehended such as openly avowed themselves to be of that sect; then by them

ROME.

were discovered an immense multitude; and all were convicted, not of the crime of burning Rome, but of hatred and enmity to mankind. Their death and tortures were aggravated by cruel derision and sport; for they were either covered with the skins of wild beasts and torn in pieces by devouring dogs, or fastened to crosses, or wrapped up in combustible garments, that, when the day-light failed, they might, like torches, serve to dispel the darkness of the night. Hence, towards the miserable sufferers, however guilty and deserving the most exemplary punishment, compassion arose; seeing they were doomed to perish, not with a view to the public good, but to gratify the cruelty of one man."

That this account of Tacitus is downright misrepresentation and calumny, must be evident to every one who reads it. It is impossible that any person can be convicted of hatred and enmity to mankind, without specifying a number of facts by which this hatred showed itself. The burning of Rome would indeed have been a very plain indication of enmity to mankind, but of this Tacitus himself clears them, and mentions no other crime of which they were guilty. It is probable, therefore, that the only reason of this charge against the Christians was their absolute refusal to have any share in the Roman worship, or to countenance the absurd superstitions of Paganism in any degree.

The persecution under Nero was succeeded by another under Domitian: during which the apostle John was banished to Patmos, where he saw the visions, and wrote the book called *Revelation*, which completes the canon of Scripture. This persecution commenced the ninety-fifth year of the Christian era; and John is supposed to have written his Revelation the year after, or in the following one.

During the *first century*, the Christian religion spread over a great number of different countries; but as we have now no authentic records concerning the travels of the apostles, or the success which attended them in their ministry, it is impossible to determine how far the Gospel was carried during this period. We are, however, assured that even during this early period many corruptions were creeping in, the progress of which was with difficulty prevented even by the apostles themselves. Some corrupted their profession by a mixture of Judaism; others by mixing it with the oriental philophy; while others were already attempting to deprive their brethren of liberty, setting themselves up as eminent pastors, in opposition even to the apostles, as we learn from the epistles of St. Paul, and the third epistle of St. John. Hence arose the sects of the Gnostics, Cerinthians, Nicolaitans, Nazarenes, Ebionites, &c., with which the church was agitated during this century.

TRAJAN. FROM A COIN.

The *second century* commences with the third year of the emperor Trajan. The Christians were still persecuted; but as the Roman emperors were for the most part of this century princes of a mild and moderate turn, they persecuted less violently than formerly.

MARCUS AURELIUS. FROM A COIN.

Yet Marcus Aurelius, notwithstanding the clemency and philosophy for which he is so much celebrated, treated the Christians worse than Trajan, Adrian, or even Severus himself, who was noted for his cruelty. This respite from rigorous persecution proved a very favourable circumstance for the spreading of the Christian religion; yet it is by no means easy to point out the particular countries through which it was diffused. We are, however, assured, that in the second century, Christ was worshipped as God almost through the whole east; as also among the Germans, Spaniards, Celts, and many other nations: but which of them received the Gospel in the first century, and which in the second, is a question unanswerable at this distance of time. The writers of this century attribute the rapid progress of Christianity chiefly to the extraordinary gifts that were imparted to the first Christians, and the miracles which were wrought at their command; without supposing that any part of the success ought to be ascribed to the intervention of human means, or secondary causes. Many of the moderns, however, are so far from being of this opinion, that they either deny the authenticity of all miracles said to have been wrought since the days of the apostles, or ascribe them to the power of the devil. To enter into the particulars of this controversy is foreign to our present purpose; for which reason we must refer to the writers of polemical divinity, who have largely treated of this and other points of a similar nature.

The corruptions which had been introduced in the first century, and which were almost coeval with Christianity itself, continued to gain ground in the second. Ceremonies, in themselves futile and useless, but which must be considered as highly pernicious when joined to a religion incapable of any other ornament than the upright and virtuous conduct of its professors, were multiplied for no other purpose than to please the ignorant multitude. The immediate consequence of this was, that the attention of Christians was drawn aside from the important duties of morality; and they were led to imagine, that a careful observance of the ceremonies might make amends for the neglect of moral duties. This was the most pernicious opinion that could possibly be entertained; and was indeed the very foundation of that enormous system of ecclesiastical power which afterwards took place, and held the whole world in slavery and barbarism for many ages.

Another corruption was the introduction of *mysteries*, as they were called, into the Christian religion; that is, insinuating that some parts of the worship in common use had a hidden efficacy and power, far superior to the plain and obvious meaning assigned to them by the vulgar: and by paying peculiar respect to these mysteries, the pretended teachers of the religion of Jesus accommodated their doctrines to the taste of their heathen neighbours, whose religion consisted in a heap of mysteries of which nobody knew the meaning.

By these, and other means of a similar kind, the

USURPATIONS OF THE CLERGY. 83

Christian pastors greatly abridged the liberty of their flock. Being masters of the ceremonies and mysteries of the Christian religion, they had it in their power to make their followers worship and believe whatever they thought proper; and this they did not fail to make use of for their own advantage. They persuaded the people, that the ministers of the Christian church succeeded to the character, rights, and privileges of the Jewish priesthood; and accordingly the bishops considered themselves as invested with a rank and character similar to those of the high-priest among the Jews, while the presbyters represented the priests, and the deacons the Levites. This notion, which was first introduced in the reign of Adrian, proved a source of very considerable honour and profit to the clergy.

The form of ecclesiastical government was in this century rendered permanent and uniform. One inspector or bishop presided over each Christian assembly, to which office he was elected by the voices of the whole people. To assist him in his office, he formed a council of presbyters, which was not confined to any stated number. To the bishops and presbyters the ministers, or *deacons*, were subject; and the latter were divided into a variety of classes, as the different exigencies of the church required. During a great part of this century, the churches were independent of each other; nor were they joined together by association, confederacy, or any other bonds but those of charity. Each assembly was a little state governed by its own laws; which were either enacted, or at least approved of, by the society. But in process of time all the Christian churches of a province were formed into one large ecclesiastical body, which, like confederate states, assembled at certain times, in order to deliberate about the common interests of the whole. This institution had its origin among the Greeks; but in a short time it became universal, and similar assemblies were formed in all places where the Gospel had been planted. These assemblies, which consisted of the deputies or commissioners from several churches, were called SYNODS by the Greeks, and COUNCILS by the Latins; and the laws enacted in these general meetings were called *Canons,* i. e. *rules.*

These councils, of which we find not the smallest trace before the middle of this century, changed the whole face of the church, and gave it a new form; for by them the ancient privileges of the people were considerably diminished, and the power and authority of the bishops greatly augmented. The humility, indeed, and prudence, of these pious prelates hindered them from assuming all at once the power with which they were afterwards invested. At their first appearance in these general councils, they acknowledged that they were no more than the delegates of their respective churches, and that they acted in the name and by the appointment of their people. But they soon changed this humble tone; imperceptibly extended the limits of their authority; turned their influence into dominion, their counsels into laws; and at length openly asserted, that Christ had empowered them to prescribe to his people *authoritative rules* of *faith* and *manners.*

Another effect of these councils was the gradual abolition of that perfect equality which reigned among all bishops in the primitive times; for the order and decency of these assemblies required that some one of the provincial bishops met in council should be invested with a superior degree of power and authority; and hence the rights of metropolitans derive their origin. In the mean time, the bounds of the church were enlarged; the custom of holding councils was followed wherever the sound of the Gospel had reached; and the universal church had now the appearance of one vast republic formed by a combination of a great number of little states. This occasioned the creation of a new order of ecclesiastics, who were appointed in different parts of the world as heads of the church, and whose office it was to preserve the consistence and union of that immense body, whose members were so widely dispersed throughout the nations. Such was the nature and office of the *patriarchs;* among whom, at length, ambition, being arrived at its most insolent period, formed a new dignity, investing the bishop of Rome with the title and authority of the *prince of the patriarchs.*

During the second century, all the sects continued which had sprung up in the first, with the addition of several others; the most remarkable of which were the *Ascetics.* These owed their rise to an error propagated by some doctors of the church, who asserted that Christ had established *a double rule of sanctity and virtue* for two different orders of Christians. Of these rules, one was ordinary, the other extraordinary; the one of a lower dignity, the other more sublime: the first for persons in the active scenes of life; the other for those who, in a sacred retreat, aspired after the glory of a celestial state. In consequence of this system, they divided into two parts all those moral doctrines and instructions which they had received either by writing or tradition. One of these divisions they called *precepts,* and the other *counsels.* They gave the name of *precepts* to those laws that were universally obligatory upon all orders of men; and that of *counsels* to those which related to Christians of a more sublime rank, who proposed to themselves great and glorious ends, and breathed after an intimate communion with the Supreme Being.

Thus were produced all at once a new set of men, who made pretensions to an uncommon sanctity and virtue, and declared their resolution of obeying all the *precepts* and *counsels* of Christ, in order to their enjoyment of communion with God here; and also that, after the dissolution of their mortal bodies, they might ascend to him with the greater facility, and find nothing to retard their approach to the centre of happiness and perfection. They looked upon themselves as prohibited from the use of things which it was lawful for other Christians to enjoy; such as wine, flesh, matrimony, and commerce. They thought it their indispensable duty to extenuate their body by watchings, abstinence, labour, and hunger. They looked for felicity in solitary retreats, and desert places; where by severe and assiduous efforts of sublime meditation, they raised the soul above all external objects, and all sensual pleasures. They were distinguished from other Christians, not only by their titles of *Ascetics*, and philosophers, but also by their garb. In this century, indeed, those, who embraced such an austere kind of life, submitted themselves to all these mortifications in private, without breaking asunder their social bands, or withdrawing themselves from mankind; but in process of time they retired into deserts, and, after the example of the Essenes and Therapeutæ, formed themselves into select companies.

This austere sect arose from an opinion, which has been more or less prevalent in all ages and in all countries; namely, that religion consists more in prayers, meditations, and a kind of secret intercourse with God, than in fulfilling the social duties of life in acts of benevolence and humanity to mankind.

THE ASCETICS.

Nothing can be more evident, than that the Scripture reckons the fulfilling of these infinitely superior to the observance of all the ceremonies that can be imagined: yet it somehow happens that almost every body is more inclined to observe the ceremonial part of devotion than the moral; and hence, according to the different humours or constitutions of different persons, there have been numberless forms of Christianity, and the most virulent contentions among those who professed themselves followers of the Prince of Peace. It is obvious, that if the moral conduct of Christians was to be made the standard of faith, instead of speculative opinions, all these divisions must cease in a moment; but while Christianity, or any part of it, is made to consist in speculation, or the observance of ceremonies, it is impossible there can be an end of sects or heresies. No opinion whatever is so absurd, but some people have pretended to argue in its defence; and no ceremony so insignificant, but it has been explained and sanctified by hot-headed enthusiasts; and hence ceremonies, sects, and absurdities, have been multiplied without number, to the prejudice of society and of the Christian religion. This short relation of the rise of the Ascetic sect will also serve to account for the rise of any other; so that it is needless to enter into particulars concerning the rest, as they all took their origin from the same general principle, variously modified, according to the different dispositions of mankind.

The Ascetic sect began first in Egypt, from whence it passed into Syria and the neighbouring countries. At length it reached the European nations: and hence that train of austere and superstitious vows and rites which totally obscured, or almost annihilated Christianity; the celibacy of the clergy, and many other absurdities of the like kind. The errors of the Ascetics, however, did not stop here. In compliance with the doctrines of some Pagan philosophers, they affirmed, that it was not only lawful, but even praiseworthy, to deceive, and to use the expedient of a lie, in order to advance the cause of piety and truth; and hence the *pious frauds* for which the church of Rome hath been so notorious, and with which she hath been so often and justly reproached.

As Christians thus deviated more and more from the true practice of their religion, they became more zealous in the external profession of it. Anniversary festivals were celebrated in commemoration of the death and resurrection of Christ, and of the effusion of the Holy Ghost on the apostles. Concerning the days on which these festivals were to be kept, there arose violent contests. The Ascetic churches in general differed in this point from those of Europe: and towards the conclusion of the second century, Victor, bishop of Rome, took it into his head to force the eastern churches to follow the rules laid down by the western ones. This they absolutely refused to comply with: upon which Victor cut them off from communion with the church of Rome; though by means of the intercession of some prudent people, the difference was made up for a time.

During most of the third century, the Christians were allowed to enjoy their religion, such as it was, without molestation. The emperors Maximinus and Decius, indeed, made them feel all the rigours of a severe persecution; but their reigns were short, and from the death of Decius to the time of Diocletian the church enjoyed tranquillity. Thus vast multitudes were converted: but at the same time the doctrine grew daily more corrupt, and the lives of professed Christians more wicked and scandalous. New ceremonies were invented in great numbers, and an unaccountable passion now prevailed for the oriental superstitions concerning demons; whence proceeded the whole train of exorcisms, spells, and fears for the apparition of evil spirits, which to this day are nowhere quite eradicated. Hence also the custom of avoiding all connection with those who were not baptized, or who lay under the penalty of excommunication, as persons supposed to be under the dominion of some evil spirit. And hence the rigour and severity of that discipline and penance imposed upon those who had incurred, by their immoralities, the censures of the church.

Several alterations were now made in the manner of celebrating the Lord's supper. The prayers used on this occasion were lengthened, and the solemnity and pomp with which it was attended were considerably increased. Gold and silver vessels were used in the celebration; it was thought essential to salvation, and for that reason administered even to infants.— Baptism was celebrated twice a year to such as, after a long course of trial and preparation, offered themselves candidates. The remission of sins was thought to be its immediate consequence; while the bishop, by prayer and imposition of hands, was supposed to confer those sanctifying gifts of the Holy Ghost, that are necessary to a life of righteousness and virtue. An evil demon was supposed naturally to reside in every person, who was the author and source of all the corrupt dispositions and unrighteous actions of that person. The driving out of this demon was therefore an essential property of baptism; and, in consequence of this opinion, the baptized persons returned home clothed in white garments, and adorned with crowns, as sacred emblems, the former of their inward purity and innocence, and the latter of their victory over sin and the world.

Fasting began now to be held in more esteem than formerly. A high degree of sanctity was attributed to this practice; it was even looked upon as indispensably necessary, from a notion that the demons directed their force chiefly against those who pampered themselves with delicious fare, and were less troublesome to the lean and hungry who lived under the severities of a rigorous abstinence. The sign of the cross also was supposed to administer a victorious power over all sorts of trials and calamities; and was more especially considered as the surest defence against the snares and stratagems of malignant spirits: for which reason no Christian undertook any thing of moment, without arming himself, as he imagined, with the power of this triumphant sign. The heresies which troubled the church during this century, were the Gnostics, (whose doctrines were newmodelled and improved by Manes, from whom they were afterwards chiefly called *Manicheans*,) the Hieracites, Noetians, Sabellians, and Novatians.

The fourth century is remarkable for the establishment of Christianity by law in the Roman empire; which, however, did not take place till the year 324. In the beginning of the century, the empire was governed by four chiefs, viz. Diocletian, Maximian, Constantius Chlorus, and Galerius, under whom the church enjoyed a perfect toleration. Diocletian, though much addicted to superstition, had no ill-will against the Christians; and Constantius Chlorus, having abandoned polytheism, treated them with condescension and benevolence. This alarmed the Pagan priests, whose interests were so closely connected with the continuance of the ancient superstitions; and who justly apprehended that the Christian religion would at length prevail throughout the empire. To prevent the downfall of the Pagan superstition, therefore, they appealed to Diocletian and Galerius Cæsar; by whom a most bloody persecution was commenced A. D. 303, and continued till 311. An asylum, however, was opened for the Christians in the year 304. Galerius having dethroned Diocletian and Maximian, declared himself emperor in the east; leaving all the western provinces, to which great numbers of Christians resorted to avoid the cruelty of the former, to Constantius Chlorus. At length Galerius being afflicted with an incurable and dreadful disease, published an edict ordering the persecution to cease, and restoring freedom to the Christians, whom he had most inhumanly oppressed for eight years. Galerius died the same year; and in a short time after, when Constantine the Great ascended the throne, the Christians were freed from any farther uneasiness, by his abrogating all the penal laws against them, and afterwards issuing edicts, by which no other religion than the Christian was tolerated throughout the empire.

SECTION II.

HISTORY OF THE CHURCH OF ROME FROM ITS ESTABLISHMENT TO THE ERECTION OF THE POPE'S SUPREMACY BY PHOCAS.

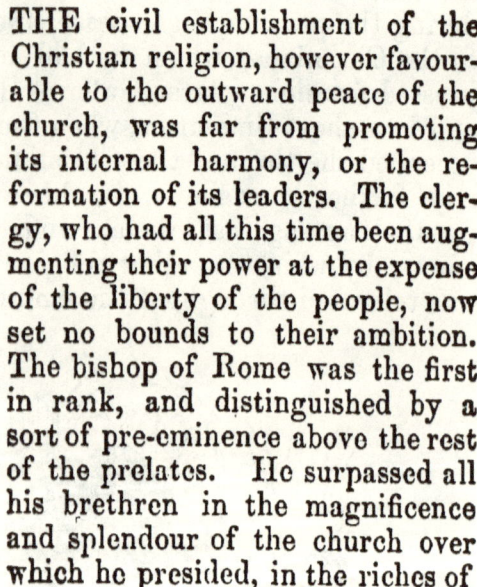

THE civil establishment of the Christian religion, however favourable to the outward peace of the church, was far from promoting its internal harmony, or the reformation of its leaders. The clergy, who had all this time been augmenting their power at the expense of the liberty of the people, now set no bounds to their ambition. The bishop of Rome was the first in rank, and distinguished by a sort of pre-eminence above the rest of the prelates. He surpassed all his brethren in the magnificence and splendour of the church over which he presided, in the riches of his revenues and possessions, in the number and variety of his ministers, in his credit with the people, and in his sumptuous and splendid manner of living. Hence it happened, that when a new pontiff was to be chosen

THE AMPHITHEATRE OF TITUS, IN WHICH THE EARLY CHRISTIAN MARTYRS WERE THROWN TO THE WILD BEASTS.

by the presbyters and people, the city of Rome was generally agitated with dissensions, tumults, and cabals, which often produced fatal consequences. The intrigues and disturbances which prevailed in that city in the year 366, when, upon the death of Liberius, another pontiff was to be chosen in his place, are a sufficient proof of this. Upon that occasion, one section elected Damasus to that high dignity; while the opposite party chose Ursicinus, a deacon of the vacant church, to succeed Liberius. This double election gave rise to a dangerous schism, and to a sort of civil war within the city of Rome; which was carried on with the utmost barbarity and fury, and produced the most cruel massacres and desolations. The inhuman contest ended in the victory of Damasus; but whether his cause was more just than that of Ursicinus, is not easily to be determined.

Notwithstanding the pomp and splendour which surrounded the Roman see, the bishops of Rome had not yet acquired that pre-eminence of power and jurisdiction which they afterwards enjoyed. In the ecclesiastical commonwealth, indeed, they were the most eminent order of citizens: but still they were citizens as well as their brethren, and subject, like them, to the laws and edicts of the emperors. All religious causes of extraordinary importance, were examined and determined, either by judges appointed by the emperors, or in councils assembled for that purpose; while those of inferior moment were decided in each district by its respective bishop. The ecclesiastical laws were enacted either by the emperor or councils. None of the bishops acknowledged that they derived their authority from the permission and appointment of the bishop of Rome, or that they were created bishops by the favour of the *apostolic see*. On the contrary, they all maintained that they were the ambassadors and ministers of Jesus Christ, and that their authority was derived from above.

It must, however, be observed, that even in this century several of those steps were laid, by which the bishops of Rome mounted afterwards to the summit of ecclesiastical power and despotism. This happened partly by the imprudence of the emperors, partly by the dexterity of the Roman prelates themselves, and partly by the inconsiderate zeal and precipitate judgment of certain bishops. The imprudence of the emperor, and the precipitancy of the bishops, were both remarkably obvious in the following circumstance, which favoured extremely the ambition of the Roman pontiff. About A. D. 372, Valentinian enacted a law, empowering the bishop of Rome to examine and judge other bishops, that religious disputes might not be decided by any profane or secular judges. The bishops assembled in council at Rome in 378, not considering the fatal consequences that must arise from this imprudent law, both to themselves and to the church, declared their approbation in the strongest terms, and recommended the execution of it in their address to the emperor Gratian. Some think, indeed, that this law empowered the Roman bishop to judge only the bishops within the limits of his jurisdiction; others, that his power was given only for a certain time, and for a particular purpose. This last notion seems the most probable: but still this privilege must have been an excellent instrument in the hands of sacerdotal ambition.

By removing the seat of empire to Constantinople, the emperor raised up, in the bishop of this new metropolis, a formidable opponent to the bishop of Rome, and a bulwark which threatened a vigorous opposition to his growing authority. For as the emperor, to render Constantinople a second Rome, enriched it

ST. AMBROSE REFUSING THE COMMUNION TO THE EMPEROR THEODOSIUS.

THEODOSIUS THE GREAT.

with all the rights and privileges, honours and ornaments, of the ancient capital of the world; so its bishop, measuring his own dignity and rank by the magnificence of the new city, and its eminence as the residence of the emperor, assumed an equal degree of dignity with the bishop of Rome, and claimed a superiority over the rest of the episcopal order. Nor did the emperors disapprove of these high pretensions; as they considered their own dignity as connected in a certain measure with that of the bishop of their imperial city. Accordingly, in a council held at Constantinople in 381, by the authority of Theodosius the Great, the bishop of that city was, during the absence of the bishop of Alexandria, and against the consent of the Roman prelate, placed, by the third canon of that council, in the first rank after the Bishop of Rome, and consequently above those of Alexandria and Antioch.

An incident in the reign of Theodosius the Great illustrates the height to which the power of the clergy had arisen in his time.

In 390, a sedition took place in Thessalonica, the result of which has branded the name of Theodosius with great odium. The origin of the catastrophe was in itself very trivial, being simply the imprisonment of a favourite charioteer of the circus. This provocation, added to some former disputes, so inflamed the populace, that they murdered their governor and several of his officers, and dragged their mangled bodies through the mire. The resentment of Theodosius was natural and merited; but the manner in which he displayed it was in the highest degree detestable and inhuman. An invitation was given, in the emperor's name, to the people of Thessalonica, to an exhibition at the circus, and when a great concourse of spectators had assembled, they were massacred by a body of barbarian soldiery, to the number, according to the lowest computation, of 7,000, and to the highest, 15,000. For this atrocious proceeding, Ambrose, with great courage and propriety, refused him communion for eight months; and the docile, and, it is to be hoped, repentant Theodosius humbly submitted.

Nectarius was the first bishop who enjoyed the new honours accumulated upon the see of Constantinople. His successor, the celebrated John Chrysostom, extended still farther the privileges of that see, and included within its jurisdiction all Thrace, Asia, and Pontus; nor were the succeeding bishops of that imperial city deficient in equal zeal to augment their privileges and extend their dominion. By this unexpected promotion, the most disagreeable effects were produced. The bishops of Alexandria were not only filled with the most inveterate hatred against those of Constantinople, but a contention was excited between the bishops of Rome and the latter; which, after being carried on for many ages, concluded at last in the separation of the Greek and Latin churches.

Constantine the Great, to prevent civil commotions and to fix his authority on a stable and solid foundation, made several changes not only in the laws of the empire, but also in the form of the Roman government. And as he had many reasons to suit the administration of the church to these changes in the civil constitution, this necessarily introduced among the bishops new degrees of eminence and rank. The four bishops of Rome, Constantinople, Antioch, and Alexandria, were distinguished by a certain degree of preeminence over the rest. These four prelates answered to the four prætorian prefects created by Constantine; and it is probable, that even in this century they were distinguished by the Jewish title of *patriarchs*. After these followed the *exarchs*, who had the inspection of several provinces, and answered to the appointment of certain civil officers who bore the same title. In a lower class were the *metropolitans*, who had only the government of one province; under whom were the *archbishops*, whose inspection was confined to certain districts. In this gradation the *bishops* brought up the rear; but the sphere of their authority was not in all places equally extensive; being in some considerably ample, and in others confined within narrow limits. To these various ecclesiastical orders we might add that of the *chorepiscopi*, or superintendents of the country churches; but this last order was in most places suppressed by the bishops, with a design to extend their own authority, and enlarge the sphere of their power and jurisdiction.

The administration of the church was divided by Constantine into an *external* and *internal* inspection. The latter, which was committed to bishops and councils, related to religious controversies, the forms of divine worship, the offices of the priests, the vices of the ecclesiastical orders, &c. The external administration of the church the emperor assumed to himself. This comprehended all those things which related to the outward state and discipline of the church; it likewise extended to all contests that should arise between the ministers of the church, superior as well as inferior, concerning their possessions, their reputation, their rights and privileges, their offences against the laws, &c.; but no controversies that related to matters purely spiritual were cognizable by this external inspection. In consequence of this artful division of the ecclesiastical government, Constantine and his successors called councils, presided in them, appointed the judges of religious controversies, terminated the differences which arose between the bishops and the people, fixed the limits of the ecclesiastical provinces, took cognizance of the civil causes that subsisted between the ministers of the church, and punished the crimes committed against the laws by the ordinary judges appointed for that purpose; giving over all causes purely ecclesiastical to the bishops and councils. But this famous division of the administration of the church was never explained with sufficient accuracy; so that both in the fourth and fifth centuries, there are frequent instances of the emperors determining matters purely ecclesiastical, and likewise of bishops and councils determining matters which related merely to the external form and government of the church.

After the time of Constantine many additions were made by the emperors and others to the wealth and honours of the clergy; and these additions were followed by a proportionable increase of their vices and luxury, particularly among those who lived in great and opulent cities. The bishops, on the one hand, contended with each other in the most scandalous manner concerning the extent of their respective ju-

CONSTANTINOPLE.

risdictions: while, on the other, they trampled on the rights of the people, violated the privileges of the inferior ministers, and imitated in their conduct and in their manner of living, the arrogance, voluptuousness, and luxury of magistrates and princes. This pernicious example was soon followed by the several ecclesiastical orders. The presbyters, in many places, assumed an equality with the bishops in point of rank and authority. Many complaints are also made by authors in this century about the vanity and effeminacy of the deacons. Those more particularly of the presbyters and deacons who filled the first stations of these orders, carried their pretensions to an extravagant length, and were offended at the notion of being placed on an equality with their colleagues. For this reason they not only assumed the titles of *arch-presbyters* and *arch-deacons*, but also claimed a degree of authority and power, much superior to that which was vested in the other members of their respective orders.

In the fifth century, the bishops of Constantinople having already reduced under their jurisdiction all the Asiatic provinces, began to grasp at still further accessions of power. By the twenty-eighth canon of the council held at Chalcedon in 451, it was resolved, that the same rights and honours which had been conferred on the bishop of Rome were due to the bishop of Constantinople, on account of the equal dignity and lustre of the two cities in which these prelates exercised their authority. The same council confirmed also, by a solemn act, the bishop of Constantinople in the spiritual government of those provinces over which he had usurped the jurisdiction. Leo the Great, bishop of Rome, opposed with vehemence the passing of these laws: and his opposition was seconded by that of several other prelates. But their efforts were vain, as the emperors threw their weight into the balance, and thus supported the decisions of the Grecian bishops. In consequence, then, of the decisions of this famous council, the bishop of Constantinople began to contend obstinately for the supremacy with the Roman pontiff, and to crush the bishops of Antioch and Alexandria.

About this time, Juvenal, bishop of Jerusalem, attempted to withdraw himself and his church from the jurisdiction of the bishop of Cæsarea, and aspired after a place among the first prelates of the Christian world. The high degree of veneration and esteem in which the church of Jerusalem was held among all other Christian societies (on account of its rank among the apostolical churches, and its title to the appellation of *mother-church*, as having succeeded the first Christian assembly formed by the apostles,) was extremely favourable to the ambition of Juvenal, and rendered his project much more practicable than it would otherwise have been. Encouraged by this, and likewise by the protection of Theodosius the younger, this aspiring prelate not only assumed the dignity of patriarch of all Palestine, a right which rendered him independent of all spiritual authority, but also invaded the rights of the bishop of Antioch, and usurped his jurisdiction over the provinces of Phœnicia and Arabia. Hence arose a warm contest between Juvenal and Maximus, bishop of Antioch; which the council of Chalcedon decided, by restoring to the latter the provinces of Phœnicia and Arabia, and confirming the former in the spiritual possession of all Palestine, and in the high rank which he had assumed in the church.

In 588, John, bishop of Constantinople, surnamed the *Faster*, either by his own authority or that of the emperor Mauritius, summoned a council at Constantinople to inquire into an accusation brought against Gregory, bishop of Antioch; and upon this occasion assumed the title of *œcumenical* or *universal bishop.* This title had been formerly enjoyed by the bishops of Constantinople without any offence; but now, Gregory the Great, then bishop of Rome, suspecting that John was aiming at the supremacy over all the churches, opposed his claim with the greatest vigour. For this purpose he wrote to the emperor, and others whom he thought capable of assisting him in his opposition; but all his efforts were without effect; and the bishops of Constantinople were allowed to enjoy the disputed title, though not in the sense which had alarmed the Roman pontiff.

Gregory, however, adhered tenaciously to his purpose, raised new tumults and dissensions among the clergy, and aimed at nothing less than an unlimited supremacy over the Christian church. This ambitious design succeeded in the west; while, in the eastern provinces, his arrogant pretensions were scarcely respected by any but those who were at enmity with the bishop of Constantinople. How much the people were at this time deluded by the Roman pontiffs, appears from the expressions of Ennodius, one of the flatterers of Symmachus, (who was a prelate of but ambiguous fame,) that the Roman pontiff was constituted *judge in the place of God*, which he filled as the *vice-gerent of the Most High.* On the other hand, it is certain, from a variety of the most authentic records, that both the emperors and the nations in general were far from being disposed to bear with patience the yoke of servitude which the see of Rome was arrogantly imposing on the whole church.

In the beginning of the seventh century, according to the most learned historians, Boniface III. engaged

SEVENTH CENTURY.

Phocas, emperor of Constantinople, to take from the bishop of that metropolis the title of *œcumenical* or *universal bishop*, and to confer it upon the Roman pontiff; and thus was first introduced the supremacy of the pope. The Roman pontiffs used all methods to maintain and enlarge this authority and pre-eminence which they had acquired from one of the most odious tyrants that ever disgraced the annals of history.

SECTION III.

HISTORY OF THE CHURCH OF ROME FROM THE ERECTION OF THE POPE'S SUPREMACY TO HIS ASSUMPTION OF UNIVERSAL POWER.

IN the eighth century, the power of the bishop of Rome, and of the clergy in general, increased prodigiously. The chief cause of this, besides the superstition of the people, was the method at that time used by the European princes to secure themselves on their thrones. All these princes being then employed either in usurpation or in self-defence, and the whole continent being in the most unsettled and barbarous condition, they endeavoured to attach warmly to their interests those whom they considered as their friends and clients. For this purpose they distributed among them extensive territories, cities, and fortresses, with the various rights and privileges belonging to them; reserving only to themselves the supreme dominion and the military service of these powerful vassals. For this reason it was by the European princes reckoned a high instance of political prudence to distribute among the bishops and other Christian doctors the same sort of donations which had formerly been given to their generals and clients. By means of the clergy, they hoped to check the seditious and turbulent spirits of their vassals; and to maintain them in their obedience by the influence and authority of their bishops, whose commands were highly respected, and whose spiritual thunderbolts, rendered formidable by ignorance, struck terror into the boldest and most resolute hearts.

This prodigious accession to the opulence and authority of the clergy in the west, began at their head, viz., the Roman pontiff; from whence it spread gradually among the inferior sacerdotal orders. The barbarous nations, who had received the gospel, looked upon the bishop of Rome as the successor of their chief druid or high-priest: and as this tremendous druid had enjoyed, under the darkness of Paganism, a kind of boundless authority; so these barbarous nations thought proper to confer upon the chief bishop the same authority which had belonged to the chief druid. The pope received the same august privileges with great pleasure; and lest, upon any change of affairs, attempts should be made to deprive him of them, he strengthened his title to these extraordinary honours by a variety of passages drawn from ancient history, and, what is still more astonishing, by arguments of a religious nature. This swelled the Roman druid to an enormous size; and gave to the see of Rome that high pre-eminence and despotic authority in civil and political matters, that were unknown in former ages. Hence, among other unhappy circumstances, arose that monstrous and pernicious opinion, that such persons as were excluded from the communion of the church by the pontiff himself, or any of the bishops, forfeited thereby, not only their civil rights and advantages as citizens, but even the common claims and privileges of humanity. This horrid opinion, which was a fatal source of wars, massacres, and rebellions, without number, and which contributed more than any thing else to confirm and augment the papal authority, was borrowed by the clergy from the Pagan superstitions.

Though excommunication, from the time of Constantine the Great, was in every part of the Christian world attended with many disagreeable effects; yet its highest terrors were confined to Europe, where its aspect was truly formidable and hideous. It acquired also, in the eighth century, new accessions of terror; so that from that period the excommunication practised in Europe differed entirely from that which was in use in other parts of Christendom. Excommunicated persons were indeed considered in all places as objects of hatred both to God and man: but they were not, on that account, robbed of the privileges of citizens, nor of the rights of humanity; much less were those kings and princes, whom an insolent bishop had thought proper to exclude from the communion of the church, supposed to forfeit, on that account, their crowns or their territories. But from this century it was quite otherwise in Europe. Excommunication received that infernal power which dissolved all connections; so that those whom the bishops, or their chief, excluded from church communion, were degraded to a level with the beasts.

The origin of this unnatural and horrid power was as follows. On the conversion of the barbarous nations to Christianity, these ignorant proselytes confounded the excommunication in use among Christians with that which had been practised in the times of Paganism, and which was attended with all the dreadful effects above mentioned. The Roman pontiffs, on the other hand, were too artful not to encourage this error; and therefore employed all sorts of means to gain credit to an opinion so well calculated to gratify their ambition, and to aggrandize in general the episcopal order. The annals of the French nation furnish us with the following instance of the enormous power which was at this time vested in the Roman pontiff.

Pepin, who was mayor of the palace to Childeric III., king of France, and who in the exercise of that high office was possessed in reality of the royal power and authority, aspired to the titles and honours of majesty also, and formed a scheme of dethroning his sovereign. For this purpose he assembled the states in 751; and though they were devoted to the interests of this ambitious usurper, they gave it as their opinion, that the bishop of Rome was previously to be consulted, whether the execution of such a scheme was lawful or not. In consequence of this, ambassadors were sent by Pepin to Zachary, the reigning pontiff, with the following question, "Whether the divine law did not permit a valiant and warlike people to dethrone a pusillanimous and indolent prince, who was incapable of discharging any of the functions of royalty; and to substitute in his place one more worthy to rule, and who had already rendered most important services to the state?" The situation of Zachary, who stood much in need of the succours of Pepin against the Greeks and Lombards, rendered his answer such as the usurper desired: and when this favourable decision of the Roman oracle was published in France, the unhappy Childeric was stripped of his royalty without the least opposition; and Pepin, without the smallest resistance, stepped into the throne of his master and his sovereign. This decision was solemnly confirmed by Stephen II., the successor of Zachary; who undertook a journey into France in

754, to solicit assistance against the Lombards. The pontiff at the same time dissolved the obligations of the oath of fidelity and allegiance which Pepin had sworn to Childeric, and violated by his usurpation in 751; and to render his title to the crown as sacred as possible, Stephen anointed and crowned him, with his wife and two sons, for the second time. This complaisance of the pope was rewarded with the exarchate of Ravenna and all its dependencies.

In the succeeding centuries, the Roman pontiffs continued to increase their power by every kind of artifice and fraud; and, by continually taking advantage of the civil dissensions which prevailed throughout Italy, France, and Germany, their influence in civil affairs arose to an enormous height. The increase of their authority in religious matters was not less rapid. The wisest and most impartial among the Roman Catholic writers acknowledge that from the time of Lewis the Meek, the ancient rules of ecclesiastical government were gradually changed in the courts of Europe by the counsels and instigation of the church of Rome, and new laws substituted in their place. The European princes suffered themselves to be divested of the supreme authority in religious matters, which they had derived from Charlemagne; the power of the bishops was greatly diminished, and even the authority of both provincial and general councils began to decline.

The Popes, elated with their overgrown prosperity, and become arrogant beyond measure by the daily accessions that were made to their authority, were eagerly bent upon establishing the maxim, That the bishop of Rome was constituted and appointed by Jesus Christ supreme legislator and judge of the church universal; and that therefore the bishops derived all their authority from him. This opinion, which they inculcated with the utmost zeal, was opposed in vain by such as were acquainted with the ancient ecclesiastical constitutions, and the government of the church in the earlier ages. To gain credit to this new ecclesiastical code, and to support the pretensions of the popes to supremacy, it was necessary to produce the authority of ancient deeds, in order to stop the mouths of such as were disposed to set bounds to their usurpations. The bishops of Rome were aware of this; and as those means were looked upon as the most lawful, that tended best to the accomplishment of their purposes, they employed some of their most ingenious and zealous partizans in forging conventions, acts of councils, epistles, and such like records, by which it might appear, that in the first ages of the church, the Roman pontiffs were clothed with the same spiritual majesty and supreme authority which they now assumed. There were, however, among the bishops some men of prudence and sagacity, who saw through these impious frauds, and perceived the chains that were forging both for them and the church. The French bishops distinguished themselves eminently in this respect; but their opposition was soon quashed; and as all Europe was sunk in the grossest ignorance and darkness, none remained who were capable of detecting those odious impostures, or disposed to support the expiring liberty of the church. This may serve as a general specimen of the character and behaviour of the pretended vicegerents of Jesus Christ to the tenth century.[1]

In the eleventh century, their power seems to have risen to its utmost height. They now received the pompous titles of *Masters of the world, and popes*, i.e. *universal fathers*. They presided over every council, by their legates, assumed the authority of supreme arbiters in all controversies that arose concerning religion or church discipline, and maintained the pretended rights of the church against the encroachments and usurpations of kings and princes. Their authority, however, was confined within certain limits; for, on the one hand, it was restrained by sovereign princes, that it might not arrogantly aim at civil dominion; and, on the other, it was opposed by the bishops themselves, that it might not arise to a spiritual despotism, and utterly destroy the privileges and liberty of synods and councils.

From the time of Leo IX. the popes employed every method which the most artful ambition could suggest, to remove those limits, and to render their dominion both despotic and universal. They not only aspired to the character of supreme legislators in the church, to an unlimited jurisdiction over all synods and councils whether general or provincial, to the sole distribution of all ecclesiastical honours and benefices, as divinely authorised and appointed for that purpose; but they carried their insolent pretensions so far as to give themselves out for *lords of the universe*, arbiters of the fate of kingdoms and empires, and *supreme rulers of the kings and princes of the earth*. Hence, we find instances of their giving away kingdoms, and loosing subjects from their allegiance to their sovereigns; among which the history of John, king of England, is very remarkable. At last they plainly affirmed the whole earth to be their property, as well where Christianity was preached as where it was not; and therefore, on the discovery of America and the East Indies, the pope, by virtue of this spiritual property, granted to the Portuguese a right to all the countries lying eastward, and to the Spaniards all those lying to the westward of Cape Non in Africa, which they were able to conquer by force of arms;

116 USURPATIONS OF THE POPES.

and that nothing might be wanting to complete their character, they pretended to be lords of the future worlds also; and to have a power of restraining even the divine justice itself, and remitting that punishment which the Deity has denounced against the workers of iniquity.

FIFTH CENTURY.

SECTION IV.

ACCOUNT OF VARIOUS SUPERSTITIONS THAT PREVAILED FROM THE FIFTH CENTURY TO THE REFORMATION.

ALL this time the powers of superstition reigned triumphant over those remains of Christianity which had escaped the corruptions of the first four centuries. In the fifth century commenced the invocation of the happy souls of departed saints. Their assistance was intreated by many fervent prayers, while none stood up to oppose this preposterous kind of worship. The images of those who during their lives had acquired the reputation of uncommon sanctity, were now honoured with a particular worship in several places; and many imagined that this drew into the images the propitious presence of the saints, or celestial beings, which they were supposed to represent. A singular and irresistible efficacy was attributed to the bones of martyrs, and to the figure of the cross, in defeating all the attempts of Satan, removing all sorts of calamities, and in healing not only the diseases of the body, but also those of the mind. The famous Pagan doctrine concerning the *purification of departed souls* by means of a certain kind of fire, *i.e.* purgatory, was also confirmed and explained more fully than it had formerly been; and every one knows of how much consequence this absurd doctrine once was to the wealth and power of the Romish clergy.

In the sixth century, Gregory the Great advanced an opinion, that all the *words* of the sacred writings were *images* of invisible and spiritual things: for which reason he loaded the churches with a multitude of ceremonies the most insignificant and futile that can be imagined; and hence arose a new and most difficult science, namely, the explication of these ceremonies, and the investigation of the causes and circumstances whence they derive their origin. A new method was contrived of administering the Lord's supper, with a magnificent assemblage of pompous ceremonies. This was called the *canon of the mass*. Baptism, except in cases of necessity, was administered only on the great festivals. An incredible number of temples were erected in honour of the saints. The places set apart for public worship were also very numerous; but now they were considered as the means of purchasing the protection and favour of the saints: and the ignorant and barbarous multitude were persuaded, that these departed spirits defended and guarded against evils and calamities of every kind, the provinces, lanes, cities, and villages in which they were honoured with temples. The number of these temples was almost equalled by that of the festivals, which seem to have been invented in order to bring the Christian religion as near the model of Paganism as possible.

In the seventh century, religion seemed to be altogether buried under a heap of superstitious ceremonies; the worship of the true God and Saviour of the world was exchanged for the worship of bones, bits of wood, (said to be of the cross,) and the images of saints. The eternal state of misery threatened in Scripture to the wicked was exchanged for the temporary punishment of purgatory; and the expressions of faith in Christ by an upright and virtuous conduct, for the augmentation of the riches of the clergy by donations to the church, and the observance of a heap of idle ceremonies. New festivals were still added: one in particular was instituted in honour of the *true cross* on which our Saviour suffered: and churches were declared to be sanctuaries to all such as fled to them, whatever their crimes might have been.

Superstition, it would seem, had now attained its highest pitch; nor is it easy to conceive a degree of ignorance and degeneracy beyond what we have already mentioned. If any thing can possibly be imagined more contrary to true religion, it is an opinion which prevailed in the eighth century; viz., that Christians might appease an offended Deity by voluntary acts of mortification, or by gifts and oblations lavished on the church; and that people ought to place their confidence in the works and merits of the saints. The piety in this and some succeeding ages consisted in building and embellishing churches and chapels; in endowing monasteries and basilics; hunting after the relics of saints and martyrs, and treating them with an absurd and excessive veneration; in procuring the intercession of the saints by rich oblations or superstitious rites; in worshipping images; in pilgrimages to those places which were esteemed holy, particularly to Palestine, &c. The genuine religion of Jesus was now utterly unknown both to the clergy and people, if we except a few of its general doctrines contained in the creed. In this century, also, the superstitious custom of *solitary masses* had its origin. These were celebrated by the priest alone in behalf of souls detained in purgatory, as well as upon some other occasions. They were prohibited by the laws of the church, but proved a source of immense wealth to the clergy. Under Charlemagne they were condemned by a synod assembled at Mentz, as criminal effects of avarice and sloth.

A new superstition, however, still sprung up in the tenth century. It was imagined, from Rev. xx. 1, that Antichrist was to make his appearance on the earth, and that soon after the world would be destroyed. An universal panic ensued; vast numbers of people, abandoning all their connections in society, and giving over to the churches and monasteries all their worldly effects, repaired to Palestine, where they imagined that Christ would descend from heaven to judge the world. Others devoted themselves by a solemn and voluntary oath to the service of the churches, convents, and priesthood, whose slaves they became, in the most rigorous sense of that word, performing daily their heavy tasks; and all this from a notion that the supreme judge would diminish the severity of their sentence, and look upon them with a favourable and propitious eye, on account of their having made themselves the slaves of their minister. When an eclipse of the sun or moon happened to be visible, the cities were deserted, and their miserable inhabitants fled for refuge to hollow caverns, and hid themselves among the craggy rocks, and under the bending summits of steep mountains. The opulent attempted to bribe the saints and the Deity himself by rich donations conferred upon the sacerdotal tribe, who were looked upon as the immediate vice-gerents of heaven. In many places, temples, palaces, and noble edifices both public and private, were suffered to decay, nay, were deliberately pulled down, from a notion, that they were no longer of any use, as the final dissolution of all things was at hand.

In a word, no language is sufficient to express the confusion and despair that tormented the minds of miserable mortals upon this occasion. The general delusion was indeed opposed and combated by the discerning few, who endeavoured to dispel these terrors, and to efface the notion from which they arose in the minds of the people. But their attempts were ineffectual; nor could the dreadful apprehensions of the superstitious multitude be removed before the end of the century, and this terror became one of the accidental causes of the CRUSADES. That nothing might now be wanting to complete that antichristian religion which had overspread all Europe, it was in the eleventh century determined that divine worship should be celebrated in the Latin tongue, though now unknown throughout the continent. During the whole of this century, also, Christians were employed in rebuilding and ornamenting their churches, which they had destroyed through the superstitious fear already mentioned.

In much the same way with what is above related, or worse if possible, matters went on till the time of the reformation. The clergy were immersed in crimes of the deepest dye; and the laity imagining themselves able to purchase pardon of their sins for money, followed the example of their pastors without remorse. The absurd principle, that religion consists in acts of austerity, and an unknown mental correspondence with God, produced the most extravagant and ridiculous behaviour in the devotees and reputed saints. They not only lived among the wild beasts, but also after the manner of those savage animals; they ran naked through the lonely deserts with a furious aspect, and all the agitations of madness and phrensy; they prolonged a wretched life by grass and wild herbs, avoided the sight and conversation of men, remained almost motionless in certain places for several years exposed to the rigour and inclemency of the seasons, and towards the conclusion of their lives shut themselves up in narrow and miserable huts; and all this was considered as true piety, the only acceptable method of worshipping the Deity, and attaining a share in his favour.

But of all the instances of superstitious phrensy which disgraced these times, none was held in higher veneration, or excited more the wonder of the multitude, than that of a certain order of men who were called *Stilites* by the Greeks, and *Sancti Columnares*, or Pillar Saints, by the Latins. These were persons of a most singular and extravagant turn of mind, who stood motionless on the tops of *pillars* expressly raised for this exercise of their patience, and remained there for several years amidst the admiration and applause of the stupid populace. The inventor of this strange discipline was one *Simeon*, a Syrian, who began his follies by changing the agreeable employment of a shepherd for the austerities of a monkish life. He began his devotion on the top of a pillar six cubits high; but as he increased in sanctity, he also increased the height of his pillar, till, towards the conclusion of his life, he had got up on the top of a pillar forty cubits in height. Many of the inhabitants of Syria and Palestine, seduced by a false ambition, and an utter ignorance of true religion, followed the example of this fanatic, though not with the same degree of austerity. This superstitious practice began in the fifth century, and continued in the east for six hundred years. The Latins, however, had too much wisdom to imitate the Syrians and Orientals in this whimsical superstition; and when a certain fanatic, or impostor, named *Wulfilaicus*, erected one of these pillars in the county of Trevers, and proposed to live on it after the manner of Simeon, the neighbouring bishops ordered it to be pulled down.

The practices of austere worship and discipline in other respects, however, gained ground throughout all parts of Christendom. Monks of various kinds were to be found in every country in prodigious numbers. But though their discipline was at first exceedingly severe, it became gradually relaxed, and the monks gave into all the prevailing vices of the times. Other orders succeeded, who pretended to still greater degrees of sanctity, and to reform the abuses of the preceding ones; but these in their turn became corrupted, and fell into the same vices which they had blamed in others. The most violent animosities, disputes, and hatred, also reigned among the different orders of monks; and, indeed, between the clergy of all ranks and degrees, whether we consider them as classed in different bodies, or as individuals of the same body.

To enter into a detail of their wranglings and disputes, the methods which each of them took to aggrandize themselves at the expense of their neighbours, and to keep the rest of mankind in subjection, would require many volumes. We shall only observe, therefore, that even the external profession of the austere and absurd piety, which took place in the fourth and fifth centuries, continued gradually to decline. Some, indeed, boldly opposed the torrent of superstition and wickedness which threatened to overflow the whole world; but their opposition proved fruitless, and all these towards the era of the reformation had either been silenced or destroyed; so that, at that time, the pope and clergy reigned over mankind without control; had made themselves masters of almost all the wealth in every country of Europe, and may truly be said to have been the only *sovereigns;* the rest of the human race, even kings and princes, being only their vassals and slaves.

While the Popish superstition reigned thus violently in the west, the absurd doctrines of Mahomet overspread all the east. His successors conquered in order to establish the religion of their apostle; and thus the very name of Christianity was extinguished in many places where it had formerly flourished. The conquests of the Tartars having intermingled them with the Mahometans, they greedily embraced the superstitions of that religion, which thus almost entirely overspread the whole continents of Asia and Africa; and, by the conquest of Constantinople by the Turks in 1453, was likewise established throughout a considerable part of Europe.

About the beginning of the sixteenth century, the Roman pontiffs lived in the utmost tranquillity; nor had they, according to the appearance of things at that time, any reason to fear an opposition to their authority in any respect, since the commotions which had been raised by the Waldenses, Albigenses, &c., were now entirely suppressed. We must not however conclude, from this apparent tranquillity and security of the pontiffs and their adherents, that their measures were universally applauded. Not only private persons, but also the most powerful princes and sovereign states, exclaimed loudly against the tyranny of the popes, and the unbridled licentiousness of the clergy of all denominations. They demanded, therefore, a reformation of the church in its head and members, and a general council to accomplish that necessary purpose. But these complaints and demands were not carried to such a length as to produce any good effect; as they came from persons who never entertained the least doubt about the supreme authority of the pope in religious matters; and who of consequence, instead of attempting themselves to bring about that reformation which was so ardently desired, remained entirely inactive, or looked for redress to the court of Rome, or to a general council.

But while the so much desired reformation seemed to be at a great distance, it suddenly arose from a quarter whence it was not at all expected. MARTIN LUTHER, a monk of the order of St. Augustine, ventured to oppose himself to the whole torrent of papal power and despotism. This bold attempt was first made public on the 30th of September, 1517; and, notwithstanding all the efforts of the pope and his adherents, the doctrines of Luther continued daily to gain ground. Others, encouraged by his success, lent their assistance in the work of the reformation; which, at last, produced new churches, founded upon principles quite different from that of Rome, and which still continue.

THE CONQUEST OF CONSTANTINOPLE BY THE TURKS.

EARLY CHRISTIAN MARTYRS.

BEFORE proceeding to notice the leading events of the reformation of the sixteenth century, we must pause to record some examples of Christian heroism in the early days of Christianity. While the usurpations of the clergy, and the corruptions in faith and worship were going on, which we have noticed in the last article, the Lord in his providence was preserving a true church among the people. Here the Bible was always making its conquests. The simple good, the unlearned in all learning but the best, namely, the Holy Scriptures, were at all times ready to seal their faith with their blood.

In the primitive ages of Christianity the people had free access to the Scriptures, and in those times we find the most noble examples of martyrdom for the truth. Our limits will not permit us to cite many examples of this kind. Under several of the Roman emperors the Christians were visited with terrible persecutions. Paganism resisted the light of truth with most envenomed malignity. Martyrs of all ages and both sexes were burned, decapitated, exposed in the arena of the amphitheatre to wild beasts and tortured with a fiendish cruelty and ingenuity, which makes one shudder at the bare recital.

We will quote from Dean Milner's History of the Church a portion of the narrative of the persecution of the Christians under the emperor Severus; and this will serve as a sufficient indication of the spirit in which all those persecutions were conducted, and of the noble Christian heroism with which they were borne.

Dean Milner says,—

"If the ancient martyrologies had been preserved uncorrupted, they would, doubtless afford us useful materials, and illustrate much the spirit and genius of real Christianity in its primitive professors. But frauds, interpolations, and impostures, are endless: The papal and monastic superstitions, in after-ages, induced their supporters to corrupt these martyrologies, and indeed the writings of the fathers in general. The difficulty of procuring materials for a well-connected credible history of real Christians, is hence increased exceedingly. What I cannot believe, I shall not take the trouble to transcribe; what I can, where the matter appears worthy of memory, shall be exhibited. This is the case of the martyrs of Scillita, a city of Africa, in the province of Carthage. The narration is simple, credible throughout, and worthy of the purest ages of the Gospel.—The facts belong to the times of Severus.

"Twelve persons were brought before Saturninus, the proconsul at Carthage, the chief of whom were Speratus, Narzal, and Cittin; and three women, Donata, Secunda, and Vestina. When they came before him, he said to them all, 'You may expect the emperor our master's pardon, if you return to your senses, and observe the ceremonies of our gods.' To which Speratus replied, 'We have never been guilty of any thing that is evil, nor been partakers of injustice: We have even prayed for those who persecute us unjustly; in which we obey OUR EMPEROR, who prescribed to us this rule of behaviour.' Saturninus answered, 'We have also a religion that is simple: We swear by the genius of the emperors, and we offer up vows for their health, which you ought also to do.' Speratus answered, 'If ye will hear me patiently, I will declare unto you the mystery of Christian simplicity.' The proconsul said, 'Shall I hear you speak ill of our ceremonies? Rather swear, all of you, by the genius of the emperors our masters, that you may enjoy the pleasures of life.' Speratus answered, 'I know not the genius of the emperors. I serve God who is in heaven, whom no man hath seen nor can see. I have never been guilty of any crime punishable by the public laws; if I buy any thing, I pay the duties to the collectors: I acknowledge my God and Saviour to be the Supreme Governor of all nations: I have made no complaints against any person; and therefore they ought to make none against me.' The proconsul, turning to the rest, said, 'Do not ye imitate the folly of this mad wretch; but rather fear our prince and obey his commands.' Cittin answered, 'We fear only the Lord our God, who is in heaven.' The proconsul then said,—'Let them be carried to prison, and put in fetters till tomorrow.'

"The next day the proconsul, seated on his tribunal, caused them to be brought before them, and said to the women,—'Honour our prince, and do sacrifice to the gods.' Donata replied, 'We honour Cæsar as Cæsar, but to God we offer prayer and worship.' Vestina said, 'I also am a Christian.' Secunda said, 'I also believe in my God, and will continue steadfast to him; and, in regard to your gods, we will not serve and adore them.' The proconsul ordered them to be separated; then, having called for the men, he said to Speratus, 'Perseverest thou in being a Christian?' Speratus answered, 'Yes, I do persevere:—Let all give ear, I am a Christian;' which being heard by the rest, they said, 'We also are Christians.' The proconsul said, 'You will neither consider your danger, nor receive mercy.' They replied, 'Do what you please, we shall die joyfully for the sake of Jesus Christ.' The proconsul asked, 'What books are those which you read and revere?' Speratus replied, 'The four Gospels of our Lord and Saviour Jesus Christ; the Epistles of the Apostle St. Paul, and all the Scripture that is inspired of God.' The proconsul said, 'I will give you three days to reflect and to come to yourselves.' Upon which Speratus answered, 'I am a Christian, and such are all those who are with me; and we will never quit the faith of our Lord Jesus. Do, therefore, what you think fit.'

"The proconsul, seeing their resolution, pronounced sentence against them,—that they should die by the hands of the executioner, in these terms:—'Speratus and the rest, having acknowledged themselves to be Christians, and having refused to pay due honour to the emperor, I command their heads to be cut off.' This sentence having been read, Speratus and his fellow-sufferers said, 'We give thanks to God, who honoureth us this day with being received as martyrs in heaven, for confessing his name.' They were carried to the place of punishment, where they fell on their knees all together, and having again given thanks to Jesus Christ, they were beheaded."*

†At Carthage itself four young catechumens were seized, Revocatus and Felicitas,—slaves to the same master,—with Saturninus and Secundulus; and also Vivia Perpetua, a lady of quality. She had a father, a mother, and two brothers, of whom one was a catechumen; she was about twenty-two years of age; was married, and was then pregnant; and moreover, she had a young child at her breast. To these five, by an excess of zeal too common at that time, Satur, voluntarily, joined himself. While they were in the hands of the persecutors, the father of Perpetua, himself a Pagan, but full of affection to his favourite offspring, importuned her to fall from the faith. His intreaties were vain. Her pious constancy appeared to him an absurd obstinacy, and enraged him so much as to induce him to give her very rough treatment. For a few days while these catechumens were under guard, but not confined in the prison, they found means to be baptized; and Perpetua's prayers were directed particularly for patience under bodily pains. They were then put into a dark prison. To the rest, who had been more accustomed to hardships, this change of scene had not any thing in it very terrible. To her, who had experienced nothing but the delicacies of genteel life, it was peculiarly formidable and distressing: her concern for her infant was extreme. —Tertius and Pomponius, two deacons of the church, obtained by money, that the prisoners might go out of the dark dungeon, and for some hours refresh

* Henry, B. 5, p. 77.   † Acta sincera, p. 86.

themselves in a more commodious place, where Perpetua gave the breast to her infant, and then recommended him carefully to her mother. For some time her mind was oppressed with concern for the misery she had brought on her family; though it was for the sake of a good conscience; but she grew more composed, and her prison became a palace.

Her father, some time after, came to the prison overwhelmed with grief; which, in all probability, was augmented by the reflections he had made on his own rough and angry behaviour to her at their last interview. "Have pity, my daughter," says he, "on my gray hairs; have pity on your father, if I was ever worthy of that name: if I myself have brought you up to this age; if I have preferred you to all your brethren, make me not a reproach to mankind: respect your father and your aunt"—these, it seems, were joined in the interests of paganism, while the mother appears to have been a Christian, otherwise his silence concerning her seems scarcely to be accounted for;—"have compassion on your son, who cannot survive you: lay aside your obstinacy, lest you destroy us all: for if you perish we must all of us shut our mouths in disgrace." The old gentleman, with much tenderness, kissed her hands, threw himself at her feet, weeping and calling her no longer his daughter, but his mistress—the mistress of his fate! He was the only person of the family who did not rejoice at her martyrdom. Perpetua, though inwardly torn with filial affection, could offer him no other comfort than to desire him to acquiesce in the Divine disposal.

The next day they were all brought into the court, and examined in the presence of vast crowds. There the unhappy old man appeared with his little grandson, and taking Perpetua aside, conjured her to have some pity on her child. The procurator, Hilarian, joined in the suit, but in vain. The old man then attempted to draw his daughter from the scaffold. Hilarian ordered him to be beaten; and a blow, which he received with a staff, was felt by Perpetua very severely.

Hilarian condemned them to be exposed to the wild beasts. They then returned cheerfully to their prison. Perpetua sent the deacon, Pomponius, to demand her child of her father, which he refused to return. The health of the child, we are told, suffered not; nor did Perpetua feel any bodily inconvenience.

Secondulus died in prison. Felicitas was eight months gone with child; and seeing the day of the public shows to be near, she was much afflicted lest her execution should take place before her delivery. Her companions joined in prayer for her three days before the spectacles; and she was, with great difficulty, delivered of a child. One of the doorkeepers, who, perhaps, expected to have found in her a stoical insensibility, and heard her cries, said, "Do you complain of THIS? what will you do when you are exposed to the beasts?" Felicitas answered, with a sagacity truly Christian, "It is I that suffer now, but then there will be another with me, that will suffer for me, because I shall suffer for his sake."— Her new-born daughter was delivered to a Christian woman, who nursed it as her own.

The tribune appears to have credited a report, that the prisoners would free themselves by magical practices; and in consequence, to have treated them roughly. "Why don't you," says Perpetua, "give us some relief? Will it not be for your honour that we should appear well fed at the spectacles?"

This address of hers had the desired effect: It

procured a very agreeable alteration in their treatment. On the day before the shows, they were supplied with their last meal; and the martyrs did their utmost to convert it into a love-feast: they eat in public; their brethren and others were allowed to visit them; and the keeper of the prison himself, by this time, was converted to the faith: they talked to the people, and warned them to flee from the wrath to come; they pointed out to them their own happy lot, and smiled at the curiosity of those who ran to see them. "Observe well our faces," cries Satur, with much animation, "that ye may know them at the day of judgment."

The Spirit of God was much with them on the day of trial; joy, rather than fear, was painted on their looks. Perpetua, cherished by Jesus Christ, went on with a composed countenance and an easy pace, holding down her eyes, lest the spectators might draw wrong conclusions from their vivacity. Some idolatrous garments were offered them by the Pagans: "We sacrifice our lives," said they, "to avoid every thing of this kind."—The tribune desisted from his demand.

Perpetua sang, as already victorious: and Revocatus, Saturninus, and Satur, endeavoured to affect the people with the fear of the wrath to come. Being come into Hilarian's presence, "Thou judgest us," said they, "and God shall judge thee." The mob was enraged, and insisted on their being scourged before they were exposed to the beasts. It was done, and the martyrs rejoiced in being conformed to their Saviour's sufferings.

Perpetua and Felicitas were stripped, and put into the nets, and exposed to a wild cow. The spectators were shocked at the sight: for the one was an accomplished beauty, and the other had been recently delivered of a child.—The assisting executioner drew them back and covered them with loose garments. Perpetua was the first attacked; and falling backwards she put herself into a reclining posture; and seeing her habit torn by her side, she retired to cover herself: she then gathered up her hair, that she might seem less disordered: she raised herself up, and seeing Felicitas bruised, she gave her her hand and lifted her up: then they went toward the gate, where Perpetua was received by a catechumen, called Rusticus, who attended her; "I wonder," said she, "when they will expose us to the cow;"—She had been, it seems, insensible of what had passed, nor could believe it till she saw on her body and clothes the marks of her sufferings. She caused her brother to be called, and addressing herself to him and Rusticus, she said, "Continue firm in the faith; love one another; and be neither frightened nor offended at our sufferings."

The people insisted on having the martyrs brought into the midst of the amphitheatre, that they might have the pleasure of seeing them die; some of them rose up and went forward of their own accord, after having given one another the kiss of charity: others received the last blow without speaking or stirring. Perpetua fell into the hands of an unskilful gladiator, who pierced her between the ribs so as to give her much unnecessary pain. She cried out; and then she herself guided his trembling hand to her throat: —and thus with the rest she slept in Jesus.

Augustine, in his exposition of the forty-seventh Psalm, takes notice of the victorious strength of divine love prevailing over all natural affections, and produces this same Perpetua as an example:*—

* Tom. v. 3.

"We know and read thus in the sufferings of the blessed Perpetua."—He mentions the same story also in three other places in his treatise of the Soul.* But it is evident that he doubts whether Perpetua herself wrote what is ascribed to her. If so, we may well doubt; and more than doubt the truth of the visions with which this excellent narrative has been intermixed; and with which I have not thought it worth while to trouble the reader. Yet the general history has every mark of authenticity.—Augustine himself published three sermons on the anniversary of the martyrs. It is much to be regretted that the finest monuments of ecclesiastical antiquity have been thus tarnished by mixtures of fraud or superstition.— The authority of Augustine has enabled me to distinguish with some degree of precision the truth from the falsehood. My business does not call me to recite the frauds; and it will be needless to add further remarks: The pious reader sees, with pleasure, that God was yet present with his people.—Indeed the power of God appeared evidently displayed during the course of this dreadful persecution, by the sudden and amazing conversions of several persons who voluntarily suffered death for that doctrine which they before detested. Of this we have the very respectable testimony of Origen, who, whatever other defects he be justly charged with, is certainly allowed to be of unquestionable veracity.†

Severus would naturally extend his persecution to Gaul, the scene of his former cruelties. In fact, it was now that Irenæus suffered: and many more suffered with him; and Lyons was once more dyed with the blood of the martyrs of Jesus. Vivarius and

---

* L. 1. c. 10. L. 3. c. 9. L. 4. c. 18. Tom. vii.
† Contra Celsum, L. 1.

Androlus, who had been sent by Polycarp there to preach the Gospel, were put to death. At Comana, in Pamphylia, Zoticus, the bishop, who had distinguished himself by writing against the Montanists, obtained the crown of martyrdom.

At this trying season it was that some churches purchased their peace and quiet by paying money, not only to the magistrates, but also to the informers and soldiers who were appointed to search them out. The pastors of the churches approved of this proceeding, because it was only suffering the loss of their goods, and preferring that to the endangering of their lives. However casuists may decide this question, it is easily conceivable that the practice might take place with many in real uprightness of heart.

It is usual with God to moderate the sufferings of his people, and not to suffer them to be tried by persecution at once very long and very violent.—In the year two hundred and eleven, after a reign of eighteen years, the tyrant Severus died: and the Church found repose and tranquillity under his son and successor Caracalla, though a monster of wickedness.

THE CRUSADES.

HESE expeditions commenced A. D. 1096. The foundation of them was a superstitious veneration for those places where our Saviour performed his miracles and accomplished the work of man's redemption. Jerusalem had been taken and Palestine conquered by Omar. This proved a considerable interruption to the pilgrims, who flocked from all quarters to perform their devotions at the holy sepulchre.

THE FIRST CRUSADERS SETTING OUT FOR PALESTINE.

They had, however, still been allowed this liberty, on paying a small tribute to the Saracen caliphs, who were not much inclined to molest them. But, in 1064, this city changed its masters. The Turks took it from the Saracens; and being much more fierce and barbarous, the pilgrims now found they could no longer perform their devotions with the same safety.

An opinion was about this time also prevalent in Europe, which made these pilgrimages much more frequent than formerly: it was imagined that the 1000 years mentioned in Rev. xx. were fulfilled; that Christ was soon to make his appearance in Palestine to judge the world; and consequently that journeys to that country were in the highest degree meritorious, and even absolutely necessary. The multitudes of pilgrims who now flocked to Palestine, meeting with a very rough reception from the Turks, filled all Europe with complaints against those infidels, who profaned the holy city, and derided the sacred mysteries of Christianity even in the place where they were fulfilled. Pope Gregory VII. had formed a design of uniting all the princes of Christendom against the Mahometans; but his exorbitant encroachments upon the civil power of princes had created him so many enemies, and rendered his schemes so suspicious, that he was not able to make great progress in his undertaking. The work was reserved for a meaner instrument.

Peter, commonly called the Hermit, a native of Amiens, in Picardy, had made the pilgrimage to Jerusalem; and being deeply affected with the dangers to which that act of piety now exposed the pilgrims, as well as with the oppression under which the eastern Christians now laboured, formed the bold, and, in all appearance, impracticable design of leading into Asia, from the farthest extremities of the West, armies sufficient to subdue those potent and warlike nations that now held the holy land in slavery. He proposed his scheme to pope Martin II., who, prudently resolving not to interpose his authority till he saw a probability of success, summoned at Placentia a council of 4000 ecclesiastics, and 30,000 seculars. As no hall could be found large enough to contain such a multitude the assembly was held in a plain. Here the pope himself, as well as Peter, harangued the people, representing the dismal situation of their brethren in the East, and the indignity offered to the Christian name in allowing the holy city to remain in the hands of the infidels. These speeches were so agreeable to those who heard them, that the whole multitude suddenly and violently declared for the war, and solemnly devoted themselves to perform this service, which they believed so meritorious in the sight of God. But though Italy seemed to have embraced the design with ardour, Martin thought it necessary, in order to obtain perfect success, to engage the greater and more warlike nations in the same enterprise. Having, therefore, exhorted Peter to visit the chief cities and sovereigns of Christendom, he summoned another council at Clermont, in Auvergne.

The fame of this great and pious design being now universally diffused, procured the attendance of the greatest prelates, nobles, and princes: and when the pope and the hermit renewed their pathetic exhortations, the whole assembly, as if impelled by immediate inspiration, exclaimed with one voice, "It is the will of God!" These words were deemed so much the effect of divine impulse, that they were employed as the signal of rendezvous and battle in all future exploits of these adventurers. Men of all ranks now flew to arms with the utmost ardour, and a cross was

BATTLE OF ASCALON.

affixed to their right shoulder by all who enlisted in this holy enterprise.

At this time Europe was sunk in the most profound ignorance and superstition. The ecclesiastics had gained the greatest ascendency over the human mind; and the people, who committed the most horrid crimes and disorders, knew of no other expiation than the observances imposed on them by their spiritual pastors. But amidst the abject superstition which now prevailed, the military spirit had also universally diffused itself; and, though not supported by art or discipline, was become the general passion of the nations governed by the feudal law. All the great lords possessed the right of peace and war. They were engaged in continual hostilities with one another: the open country was become a scene of outrage and disorder: the cities, still mean and poor, were neither guarded by walls nor protected by privileges. Every man was obliged to depend for safety on his own force, or his private alliances; and valour was the only excellence which was held in esteem, or gave one man the pre-eminence above another. When all the particular superstitions, therefore, were here united in one great object, the ardour for private hostilities took the same direction; "and all Europe," as the princess Anna Comnena expresses it, "torn from its foundations, seemed ready to precipitate itself in one united body upon Asia."

All ranks of men now deeming the crusades the only road to heaven, were impatient to open the way with their swords to the holy city. Nobles, artizans, peasants, even priests, enrolled their names; and to decline this service, was branded with the reproach of impiety or cowardice. The nobles were moved, by the romantic spirit of the age, to hope for opulent establishments in the East, the chief seat of arts and commerce at that time. In pursuit of these chimerical projects, they sold at low prices their ancient castles and inheritances, which had now lost all value in their eyes. The infirm and aged contributed to the expedition by presents and money, and many of them attended it in person; being determined, if possible, to breathe their last in sight of that city where their Saviour died for them. Even women, concealing their sex under the disguise of armour, attended the camp; and often forgot their duty still more by prostituting themselves to the army. The greatest criminals were forward in a service which they considered as an expiation for all crimes; and the most enormous disorders were, during the course of these expeditions, committed by men inured to wickedness, encouraged by example, and impelled by necessity.

The adventurers were at last so numerous, that their sagacious leaders became apprehensive lest the greatness of the armament would be the cause of its own disappointment. For this reason they permitted an undisciplined multitude, computed at 300,000 men, to go before them under the command of Peter the hermit, and Gauthier or Walter, surnamed the *Moneyless*, from his being a soldier of fortune. These took the road towards Constantinople through Hungary and Bulgaria; and trusting that Heaven, by supernatural assistance, would supply all their necessities, they made no provision for subsistence in their march. They soon found themselves obliged to obtain by plunder what they vainly expected from miracles; and the enraged inhabitants of the countries through which they passed attacked the disorderly multitude, and slaughtered them without resistance. The more disciplined armies followed after; and, passing the straits of Constantinople,

RICHARD I. IN PALESTINE.

were mustered in the plains of Asia, and amounted in the whole to 700,000 men.

The princes engaged in this first crusade were, Hugo, count of Vermandois, brother to Philip I., king of France; Robert, duke of Normandy; Robert, earl of Flanders; Raimond, earl of Toulouse and St. Giles; the celebrated Godfrey of Bouillon, duke of Lorrain, with his brothers Baldwin and Eustace; Stephen, earl of Chartres and Blois; Hugo, count of St. Paul; with many other lords. The general rendezvous was at Constantinople. In this expedition, Godfrey besieged and took the city of Nice. Jerusalem was taken by the confederated army, and Godfrey chosen king. The Christians gained the famous battle of Ascalon against the sultan of Egypt, which put an end to the first crusade, but not to the spirit of crusading. The rage continued for near two centuries.

The second crusade, in 1144, was headed by the emperor Conrad III., and Louis VII., king of France. The emperor's army was either destroyed by the enemy, or perished through the treachery of Manuel, the Greek emperor; and the second army, through the unfaithfulness of the Christians of Syria, was forced to break up the siege of Damascus.

The third crusade, 1188, immediately followed the taking of Jerusalem by Saladin, the sultan of Egypt. The princes engaged in this expedition were, the emperor Frederic Barbarossa; Frederic, duke of Suabia, his second son; Leopold, duke of Austria; Berthold, duke of Moravia; Herman, marquess of Baden; the counts of Nassau, Thuringia, Missen, and Holland; and above sixty other princes of the empire; with the bishops of Besançon, Cambray, Munster, Osnaburg, Missen, Passau, Visburg, and several others.

In this expedition the emperor Frederic defeated the sultan of Iconium; his son Frederic, joined by Guy Lusignan, king of Jerusalem, in vain endeavoured to take Acre or Ptolemais. During these transactions Philip Augustus, king of France, and Richard I., king of England, joined the crusade: by which means the Christian army consisted of 300,000 fighting men; but great disputes happening between the kings of France and England, the former quitted the holy land, and Richard concluded a peace with Saladin.

The fourth crusade was undertaken in 1195, by the emperor Henry VI. after Saladin's death. In this expedition the Christians gained several battles against the infidels, took a great many towns, and were in the way of success, when the death of the emperor obliged them to quit the holy land, and return into Germany.

The fifth crusade was published by pope Innocent III., in 1198. Those engaged in it made fruitless efforts for the recovery of the holy land; for, though John de Neule, who commanded the fleet equipped in Flanders, arrived at Ptolemais a little after Simon of Montfort, Renard of Dampierre, and others, yet the plague destroyed many of them, and the rest either returning or engaging in the petty quarrels of the Christian princes, there was nothing done; so that the sultan of Aleppo easily defeated their troops in 1204.

The sixth crusade began in 1228; in which the Christians took the town of Damietta, but were forced to surrender it again. In 1229, the emperor Frederic made peace with the sultan for ten years. About 1240, Richard, earl of Cornwall, brother to Henry III., king of England, arrived at Palestine, at the head of the English crusade; but finding it most ad

THE NEW YORK
PUBLIC LIBRARY

ASTOR LEN
TILDEN FO
R

BATTLE OF PTOLEMAIS.

vantageous to conclude a peace, he re-embarked, and steered towards Italy.

In 1244, the Karasmians being driven out of Turkey by the Tartars, broke into Palestine, and gave the Christians a general defeat near Gaza.

The seventh crusade was headed, in 1249, by St. Lewis, who took the town of Damietta; but a sickness happening in the Christian army, the king endeavoured a retreat; in which, being pursued by the infidels, most of his army were miserably butchered, and himself and the nobility taken prisoners. A truce was agreed upon for ten years, and the king and lords set at liberty.

The eighth crusade, in 1279, was headed by the same prince, who made himself master of the port and castle of Carthage in Africa; but dying a short time after, he left his army in a very ill condition. Soon after, the king of Sicily coming up with a good fleet, and joining Philip the Bold, son and successor of Lewis, the king of Tunis, after several engagements with the Christians, in which he was always worsted, desired peace, which was granted upon conditions advantageous to the Christians; after which both princes embarked for their own kingdoms.

Prince Edward, of England, who arrived at Tunis at the time of this treaty, sailed towards Ptolemais, where he landed a small body of 300 English and French, and hindered Bendochar from laying siege to Ptolemais; but being obliged to return to take possession of the crown of England, this crusade ended without contributing any thing to the recovery of the holy land.

In 1291, the town of Acre or Ptolemais was taken and plundered by the sultan of Egypt, and the Christians quite driven out of Syria. There has been no crusade since that period, though several

154 THE CRUSADES.

popes have attempted to stir up the Christians to such an undertaking; particularly Nicholas IV., in 1292, and Clement V. in 1311.

Though these crusades were effects of the most absurd superstition, they tended greatly to promote the good of Europe. Multitudes, indeed, were destroyed. M. Voltaire computes the people who perished in the different expeditions at upwards of two millions. Many there were, however, who returned; and these having conversed so long with the people who lived in a much more magnificent way than themselves, began to entertain some taste for a refined and polished way of life. Thus the barbarism in which Europe had been so long immersed began to wear off soon after.

CRUSADERS ON THEIR MARCH TO JERUSALEM.

THE ALBIGENSES.

HE Albigenses were a party of reformers about Toulouse and the Albigeois, in Languedoc, who sprung up in the twelfth century, and distinguished themselves by their opposition to the church of Rome. They were charged with many errors by the monks of those days; but from these charges they are generally acquitted by the Protestants, who consider them only as the inventions of the Romish church to blacken their character. The Albigenses grew so formidable, that the Catholics agreed upon a holy league or crusade against them. Pope Innocent III., desirous to put a stop to their progress, stirred up the great men of the kingdom to make war upon them. After suffering from their persecutors, they dwindled by little and little, till the time of the Reformation; when such of them as were left, fell in with the Vaudois, and conformed to the doctrine of Zuinglius, and the disciples of Geneva. The Albigenses have been frequently confounded with the Waldenses; from whom it is said they differ in many respects, both as being prior to them in point of time, as having their origin in a different country, and as being charged with divers heresies, particularly Manicheism, from which the Waldenses were exempt.

THE WALDENSES.

THE Waldenses, or Valdenses, were a sect of reformers, who made their first appearance about the year 1160. They were most numerous about the vallies of Piedmont; and hence, some say, they were called Valdenses, or Vaudois, and not from Peter Valdo, as others suppose. Mosheim, however, gives this account of them: he says, that Peter, an opulent merchant of Lyons, surnamed *Valdensis*, or *Validisius*, from Vaux, or Waldum, a town in the marquisate of Lyons, being extremely zealous for the advancement of true piety and Christian knowledge, employed a certain priest, called *Stephanus de Evisa*, about the year 1160, in translating from Latin into French, the four Gospels, with other books of holy Scripture, and the most remarkable sentences of the ancient doctors, which were so highly esteemed in this century. But no sooner had he perused these sacred books with a proper degree of attention, than he perceived that the religion which was now taught in the Roman church differed totally from that which was originally inculcated by Christ and his apostles. Struck with this glaring contradiction between the doctrines of the pontiffs and the truths of the Gospel, and animated with zeal, he abandoned his mercantile vocation, distributed his riches among the poor, (whence the Waldenses were called *poor men of Lyons*,) and, forming an association with other pious men, who had adopted his sentiments and his turn of devotion, he began, in the year 1180, to assume the quality of a public teacher, and to instruct the multitude in the doctrines and precepts of Christianity.

Soon after Peter had assumed the exercise of his ministry, the archbishop of Lyons, and the other rulers of the church in that province, vigorously opposed him. However, their opposition was unsuccessful; for the purity and simplicity of that religion which these good men taught, the spotless innocence that shone forth in their lives and actions, and the noble contempt of riches and honours which was conspicuous in the whole of their conduct and conversation, appeared so engaging to all such as had any sense of true piety, that the number of their followers daily increased. They accordingly formed religious assemblies, first in France, and afterwards in Lombardy; from whence they propagated their sect throughout the other provinces of Europe with incredible rapidity, and with such invincible fortitude, that neither fire nor sword, nor the most cruel inventions of merciless persecution, could damp their zeal, or entirely ruin their cause.

The attempts of Peter Waldus and his followers were neither employed nor designed to introduce new doctrines into the church, nor to propose new articles of faith to Christians. All they aimed at was, to reduce the form of ecclesiastical government, and the manners both of the clergy and people, to that amiable simplicity and primitive sanctity that characterized the apostolic ages, and which appear so strongly recommended in the precepts and injunctions of the Divine Author of our holy religion. In consequence of this design, they complained that the Roman church had degenerated, under Constantine the Great, from its primitive purity and sanctity. They denied the supremacy of the Roman pontiff, and maintained that the rulers and ministers of the church were obliged, by their vocation, to imitate the poverty of the apostles, and to procure for themselves a subsistence by the work of their hands. They considered every Christian as, in a certain measure, qualified and authorized to instruct, exhort, and confirm the brethren in their Christian course; and demanded the restoration of the ancient penitential discipline of the church, i. e. the expiation of transgressions by prayer, fasting, and alms, which the new-invented doctrine of indulgences had almost totally abolished. They at the same time affirmed, that every pious Christian was qualified and entitled to prescribe to the penitent the kind or degree of satisfaction or expiation that their transgressions required; that confession made to priests was by no means necessary, since the humble offender might acknowledge his sins and testify his repentance to any true believer, and might expect from such counsel and admonition which his case demanded. They maintained that the power of delivering sinners from the guilt and punishment of their offences belonged to God alone; and that indulgences, of consequence, were the criminal inventions of sordid avarice. They looked upon the prayers and other ceremonies that were instituted in behalf of the dead, as vain, useless, and absurd, and denied the existence of departed souls in an intermediate state of purification; affirming, that they were immediately, upon the separation from the body, received into heaven, or thrust down to hell. These and other tenets of a like nature, composed the system of doctrine propagated by the Waldenses. It is also said, that several of the Waldenses denied the obligation of infant baptism, and that others rejected water baptism entirely; but Wall has laboured to prove that infant baptism was generally practised among them.

Their rules of practice were extremely austere; for they adopted as the model of their moral discipline the sermon of Christ on the mount, which they interpreted and explained in the most rigorous and literal manner; and consequently prohibited and condemned in their society all wars, and suits of law, and all attempts towards the acquisition of wealth; the inflicting of capital punishments, self-defence against unjust violence, and oaths of all kinds.

During the greatest part of the seventeenth century, those of them who lived in the valleys of Piedmont, and who had embraced the doctrine, discipline, and worship of the church of Geneva, were oppressed and persecuted in the most barbarous and inhuman manner by the ministers of Rome. This persecution was carried on with peculiar marks of rage and enormity in the years 1655, 1656, and 1696. The most horrid scenes of violence and bloodshed were exhibited in this theatre of papal tyranny; and the few Waldenses that survived were indebted for their existence and support to the intercession made for them by the English and Dutch governments, and also by the Swiss cantons, who solicited the clemency of the duke of Savoy on their behalf.

JOHN WICKLIFFE,
THE ENGLISH REFORMER.

JOHN WICKLIFFE was born about the year 1324, near Richmond, in Yorkshire. He seems first to have distinguished himself, during his residence at the university of Oxford, by a controversy with the mendicant friars, who claimed the right of appointment to all academical offices. In the year 1365 he published a defence of the king's refusal to pay the tribute commonly called "Peter's pence," a service which obtained for him the friendship and protection of the famous John of Gaunt, to whose influence he was more than once indebted for escape from the machinations of his enemies. On his return from Bruges, whither he had been sent by the king in 1374, to discuss the question of tribute with the pope's legate, he published his "Trialogue," in which the abuses of the papacy are powerfully attacked. His views respecting the divine presence in the eucharist seem not to have been very different from those of Luther. He held also that deadly sin in a bishop or priest absolved the people from their spiritual allegiance, and made the sacraments which they administered of none effect; that the possession of worldly goods was not permitted to the clergy; and that con-

WICKLIFFE.

fession to a priest was unnecessary, provided men sincerely repented of their sins, and sought forgiveness from God. In the year 1384 he was suddenly seized with mortal sickness, whilst performing mass in his church at Lutterworth. Many years after Wickliffe's death his bones were disinterred and burnt by his enemies. Wickliffe's most important work was a translation of the Bible into English, which the authority of John of Gaunt prevented the bishops from suppressing. His doctrine was carried into Bohemia by one of his disciples, a nobleman, who had come to England in the suite of Richard II.'s first wife, Anne of Bohemia. The followers of Wickliffe were called Lollards: a name derived from the old Flemish verb *lollen* or *lullen*,* (to sing softly,) and given originally to a brotherhood established at Antwerp, for the purpose of visiting the sick and burying the dead. It seems subsequently to have been a common term of reproach for all who resisted the authority of Rome. One of these early reformers, Sir John Oldcastle, Lord Cobham, suffered death for his religious opinions in 1417.

* Hence the English word "lullaby."

MARTYRDOM OF JOHN HUSS AND JEROME OF PRAGUE.

THE university of Prague had been celebrated ever since its establishment in 1348 for the learning and talent of its professors, of whom the one party, termed Realists, maintained that what are called universal or general ideas of things were *objective*, that is to say, existent independently of the human understanding; whilst the other, the Nominalists, held that those ideas were *subjective*, or existent only in the mind of man: of these two parties the latter was especially cherished by the priesthood as being favourable to the sophisms of the Romish theology, but the former was more popular among the students in general. Among the realists was JOHN HUSS, who had read the writings of Wickliffe, and as early as the year 1401 had maintained that the pope was no greater than any other bishop, that useless holidays ought to be abolished, that the doctrine of purgatory had no foundation in Scripture, that confirmation and extreme unction were not sacraments, that auricular confession was a vain thing, that altars, priestly vestments, images and consecrated vessels were useless, and that prayer needed not be offered up in churches, for the whole earth being the Lord's any spot of it might be used as his temple. He also contended that the sacrament of the Lord's supper ought to be received in both kinds by the laity, and that the bread and wine in the eucharist were not transubstantiated into the body and blood of Christ, but that the real body and blood were received after a spiritual and mysterious fashion. In the dissemination of these doctrines he was assisted by his friend and pupil Jerome Faulfisch, commonly called Jerome of Prague; and, in spite of opposition, these two courageous men continued to lecture and preach at Prague and elsewhere, until they were summoned to appear before the council at Constance and give an account of their doctrine, a safe-conduct from the emperor being at the same time promised to them. Immediately after the assembling of the council the bishops of Augsburg and Trent and the burgomaster of Constance were sent to require the attendance of Huss, who had already been some days in the city. As he entered the council-hall and respectfully saluted the company, one of the cardinals said, "Master Huss, we have manifold complaints against you, that you have taught and propagated gross, palpable, fearful errors against the orthodox church, for which cause we have summoned you before us, that we may hear from your own mouth how the matter standeth." To this address Huss replied, "Reverend father, rather would I die than avow myself guilty of one, much less of so many acts of heresy; wherefore I appear before you this day with the determination, whatever errors can be proved against me, to retract and abjure the same." Huss was then removed into an ante-chamber, and the council adjourned, but assembled again in the afternoon, and before night decided on arresting him: this resolution was announced to Huss by his enemy Philip Palitz, in the following words: "We have thee now, and verily I say unto thee, thou shalt not come out thence until thou hast paid the uttermost farthing." He was then thrown into a narrow and filthy dungeon, the pestilential air of which soon brought on a raging fever. In spite of repeated petitions he could not obtain a hearing until the 7th June 1415, and even then was so often interrupted by the outcries of the assembly, that at last he said, "I had hoped that you would have heard me; but inasmuch as this clamour is raised to drown my voice, it remaineth only for me to be silent." The articles of accusation were then read; some of them were absurd enough; and even Huss himself could not forbear smiling at the charge brought against him of maintaining the existence of four Gods, but he was not allowed to reply to this or any other of the articles. This mock enquiry lasted until the 6th of July, when

Huss was condemned to the flames, the emperor Sigismund pronouncing sentence in these words: "If John Huss will not abjure his heresies, we condemn him to be burnt; if he will abjure them, he shall nevertheless be forbidden again to preach or return to Bohemia. His followers, and especially Jerome, shall also be severely punished." Against this sentence the friends of Huss vehemently protested as inconsistent with the safe-conduct which the accused had received from the hands of the emperor himself; but Sigismund coldly replied that such a safe-conduct could have no reference to a heretic, since neither the laws of God nor of man required that faith should be kept with one who obstinately opposed himself to the true belief. Day was just beginning to dawn on the morning of the 6th of July, when the bishop of Riga, attended by four men-at-arms, entered the prison, and commanded Huss to follow him to the cathedral, where he was detained a long time at the door, lest his presence should desecrate the mass which they were performing within. The church had been prepared for the occasion; on a magnificent throne sat the emperor with the imperial sceptre in his hand and the crown on his head, surrounded by princes of the empire, cardinals, and bishops. In the midst of this assembly, on a high table, lay a surplice and other robes, which were to be employed in the ceremony of degrading Huss from the priesthood. The business of the day was opened by a bishop, who preached a long sermon from Romans vi. 1: "What shall we say then? Shall we continue in sin that grace may abound?" Another bishop then mounted the steps of the reading-desk and read from a paper the articles of accusation; but whenever Huss attempted to speak, he was silenced by cries of "Peace, heretic!" When, however, in conclusion, he was charged with having treated the ban of the pope with contempt, he raised his voice, exclaiming, "That is false; I publicly appealed to a higher tribunal, and came before this council to defend myself, trusting to the emperor's promise that no evil should befal me;" —here he fixed his eyes sternly on Sigismund, whose face was instantly covered with the blush of conscious guilt. The papal commissary, an old bald-headed man, then read the sentence by which John Huss was condemned to the flames; and the martyr, kneeling down, prayed that God would forgive his murderers. Seven bishops, who were to perform the ceremony of degradation, next advanced, and put the robes on him, as if he were about to celebrate mass, placing at the same time the chalice in his hands. The first act of degradation was the taking from him the chalice with these words, " Thou accursed Judas! we take from thee this cup, wherein the blood of Christ is offered up for the forgiveness of sins, because thou hast abandoned the counsel of peace." To which Huss meekly replied, " I trust that to-day I shall drink of this cup in the kingdom of God." Then they took from him the priestly vestments one by one, pronouncing a curse as each portion was removed. When they were about to destroy his tonsure, a difference of opinion arose among the bishops, whether it should be done with a razor or scissors.—" See," said Huss, "they cannot even settle how I am to be mocked." These ceremonies being completed, the bishops recommended his soul to the devil; to which Huss rejoined, "And *I* commend it to my Lord Jesus Christ." He was then delivered over to the secular authorities, who placed on his head a paper cap, half an ell in height, ornamented in front with a representation of three devils, and the inscription, "This is an arch heretic." On arriving at the place of execution, where a stake had already been fixed in the ground, Huss fell on his knees, and lifting up his eyes to heaven, recited the 30th and 50th Psalms, often repeating the words, "Into thy hands I commend my spirit, for thou hast redeemed me, O Lord, thou God of truth." Many of the spectators who heard this exclaimed, "What this man's former doctrine may have been we know not, but surely these which we hear are holy words." Others said, "Why is not a confessor allowed him?" This last question was addressed more particularly to a priest who sat close to the stake, feasting his eyes on the preparations for execution. Starting as if from a dream, the churchman stared angrily at the crowd, and raising his voice to a pitch which made him distinctly audible even to those who stood farthest from the prisoner, shouted out, "Listen not to the heretic, there is no need to send him a confessor." The paper cap having fallen from Huss's head during his prayer, this man replaced it, saying, "Let the devils and the devil's servant burn together." The executioner then bound him with an old rusty chain and several cords: but the faggots had yet to be brought: and Huss stood chained to the stake whilst the attendants piled them around him. All being at length ready, and the executioner about to apply his torch to the pile, the duke of Bavaria rode up and promised the prisoner that his life should be spared, if he would recant his errors. To this Huss replied in a loud voice, "I call God to witness that I have never either taught or written those things with which false men have charged me; but in all my teachings I have sought only how best I might turn the people from their sins, and lead them to the kingdom of God. The truth which I have taught I am now ready to seal with my blood." The executioner then set fire to the pile, which was instantly enveloped in flames: and the martyr, standing in the midst, was distinctly heard to say, "O Christ, thou Son of God, have mercy upon me." This he repeated twice, but at the third attempt the flames caught his face, and only the words, "Christ—Son of God," were distinguishable. His lips continued in movement a few seconds longer, and then he bowed his head and died. As the fire declined, the executioner and his men raked out his heart, which was still entire, from the midst of the ashes, and fixing it on a stake, held it in the flame until it was consumed. That nothing might remain to be used as a relic by his disciples in Bohemia, the duke of Bavaria ordered his cloak, girdle, and other garments to be burnt, and the ashes of the whole pile, and even the soil on which it stood, to be scraped together and thrown into the Rhine. The putrid carcass of a mule was also buried on the spot, and the vulgar taught to believe that the soul of the arch heretic had parted from the body in a cloud of sulphur, leaving this unsavoury odour behind it. Thus died John Huss on his forty-second birth-day.—His disciple, Jerome of Prague, had fled from Constance as soon as he found that there was no hope of saving his friend; but was soon arrested and thrown into prison, where the pangs of hunger and sickness so wrought upon his spirit that he recanted. When brought before the council, however, his courage returned, and he boldly declared that he would not retract a tittle of what he had taught. So heroic was his bearing, that cardinal Poggio called him a second Cato. "I will not abjure my belief," continued Jerome, "for my sainted master hath with reason and justice written against your false doctrines, your shameless lives and evil practices. Slay me, if ye list, but in this belief will I live and die." When the executioner was proceeding to light the faggots behind him, he called out, "Light them before my face: for if I had been afraid of fire, I had not stood here this day."

JOHN ZISKA.

THE HUSSITE WAR.

HEN the ashes of John Huss were thrown into the Rhine, the rulers of the church believed that his name had perished with his body. But the people thought far otherwise. In Bohemia, the spirit of his teaching had spread far and wide, and would probably have extended into Germany, had not its progress been checked by the estrangement between the two nations, which the unhappy partiality of Wenceslaus had produced some years before, and by the inability of Huss to preach in the German language. The states of Bohemia, having protested in strong terms against the monstrous acts of the council, proceeded to pass a law, authorizing all landed proprietors to permit the preaching of Huss's doctrines on their estates. Many availed themselves of this permission, and gave public encouragement to the followers of the martyr, who were now called Hussites and "brethren of the chalice," because their master had taught that the laity ought to receive the communion in both kinds. Pope Martin, immediately after the breaking up of the council, had issued a bull of excommunication against all who should adhere to the heretical doctrines of John Huss. This proceeding, which was intended to silence effectually those who were discontented with the abuses in the church, had a directly contrary effect. Scarcely had the bull reached Prague, when crowds of men were seen parading the streets in gloomy silence, or collected in groups discussing, in low murmurs, some subject of deep interest, whilst their fierce countenances and menacing gestures showed that they contemplated deeds of violence. They had not long to wait for an opportunity. At the court of Wenceslaus there lived a tried warrior, named John Ziska, who had fought with distinction in Poland, and was now chief favourite with the king. To this knight the priesthood were particularly hateful, because one of them had seduced and abandoned his favourite sister. As a true Bohemian, too, he detested the Germans. Since the execution of Huss, the man's demeanour had undergone a total change: his frank, blunt manner had given place to moody silence; or he would wander for hours about the palace with eyes fixed on the ground, muttering from time to time words which were but imperfectly understood by those who heard them. At length Wenceslaus himself enquired the cause. "They have burnt

Huss," he replied, in a hollow tone, "and we have not yet avenged him." "I cannot help it," said the king; "you must try yourselves what you can do." These words, which were spoken jestingly, Ziska pretended to understand in sober earnest, and immediately called the Hussites to arms. This was going further than Wenceslaus had intended; and, terrified at the prospect of an insurrection, he ordered the citizens to bring all their weapons into the castle of Wisherad, where he was then residing. The injunction was literally obeyed, except that, instead of bringing their weapons in piles for the purpose of depositing them in the castle, the burghers appeared, armed to the teeth, and marching in military order, headed by Ziska, who thus addressed the king:— "Here we are, most illustrious and gracious sovereign, waiting to know against what enemy it is your royal will that we should march." The whole city was now in confusion. The Hussites, bearing a chalice as their standard, marched in procession through the streets. As they passed the town-hall, a stone was thrown at them: enraged at this affront, they burst into the council-chamber, and threw thirteen German counsellors out at the windows. Ziska at the same time gave orders for storming the house of a priest, (probably the seducer of his sister,) and hanging him up at his own door. Amidst these horrors the unfortunate king sat listening to the roar of the enraged multitude; and when it seemed to approach the castle, was seized with a fit of apoplexy, which put an end to his life on the 16th August, 1418. His death removed the only restraint on the fury of the mob. They burst into convents and churches, dashed the images in pieces, and tore the clerical vestments into shreds, of which they made flags. Meanwhile a priest, named Matthias Toczenicza, had erected in the middle of one of the streets a sort of rude altar or table, and employed himself the whole of the day in administering the communion in both kinds to all who chose to receive it. But the more substantial burgesses of Prague soon recollected how much they had to lose, and how little prospect there was of any advantage adequate to the danger incurred. They therefore treated with the widow of Wenceslaus, queen Sophia, who still held out in the castle of Wisherad, and sent a deputation to the emperor to propose an accommodation; but Sigismund dismissed the envoys with insult, and swore a bloody revenge. Ziska, meanwhile, far from countenancing these pacific measures, had led out the more determined men of his party into the country, in order to raise the peasantry. He called on all who could only throw a stone or wield a staff, to unite and arm themselves against the enemies of God. This appeal was answered by the assembling of an immense crowd at Whitsuntide, 1419. They called themselves God's people, named the hill on which they assembled Mount Tabor, and pledged themselves to exterminate the Moabites and Amalekites; for by this name they designated the adherents of the pope. Ziska was chosen their leader, and thenceforth assumed the title of "John Ziska of the chalice, commander in the hope of God of the Taborites." At the head of an irregular rabble of men, women, and children, he marched through the land, plundering and burning churches and monasteries, and committing the most wanton aggressions. Among other acts of cruelty, he is said to have confined several priests in pitched barrels, and setting them on fire, to have exclaimed, as the unfortunate wretches screamed in the agonies of death, "Hark to my sister's bridal song!" The widow of Wenceslaus despatched a force to destroy the insurgent army before the numbers should increase; but Ziska ordered the women who followed his camp to take off their petticoats and veils, and throw them on the ground, by which manœuvre the feet of the horses became so entangled, that the insurgents gained an easy victory. In the month of June, 1420, the emperor entered Prague, threw twenty-four Hussites into the river, and being reinforced by an army under Frederick of Austria, attacked with 100,000 men a high hill near the city, on which Ziska had intrenched himself. Here the passage of the army was for a long time disputed by three heroic Bohemian maidens, who refused to give way until they were borne down by numbers. After a long and fierce engagement the Germans were compelled to retire, leaving the enemy in possession of their camp. This success of the Taborites drew crowds to their standard. In all parts of the country, the peasants armed with flails, which they wielded with terrible force and effect, were formed into companies, and constructed a temporary barricade wherever they halted by chaining their waggons together. A fresh rabble also appeared in a mountain near Ledecz, which they named Mount Horeb, and themselves Horebites. In Moravia a sect arose, who professed to emulate the simplicity of paradise, walking about stark naked, and committing such gross acts of folly as contributed not a little to bring the Hussite doctrines into contempt. In the year 1421 Ziska made a progress through the country, burning all the convents, and putting to death hundreds of these fanatics, who were known by the title of Adamites. The discipline of his army was cruelly severe. It was forbidden to quit the ranks, on pain of death, to plunder or burn without orders, or to appropriate even the smallest portion of booty before the general distribution. The same punishment was inflicted on liars, gamblers, and unchaste persons. "We swear," thus ran the oath taken by the confederates, "all evil and vicious men to prosecute, to scourge, to smite, to head, to hang, to burn, to drown, and to visit with all punishments which the law of God awardeth unto sin." One John Czapko also wrote a curious book, in which the faithful were exhorted not to lay down their arms until they had exterminated all the sinners in the world. Ziska, who had many years before lost an eye in the Polish wars, was this year reduced to total blindness by an accident which befell him as he was besieging the town of Raby. He had climbed a tree, the better to observe the enemy's operations, when a cannon-ball struck the branches, and forced some of the splinters into his remaining eye. Yet he still commanded his army with as much courage and vigour as before, travelling in a carriage, which was always stationed near the great standard. His progress was like that of the destroying angel; wherever he marched, his course might be tracked by heaps of dead bodies, and the light of blazing towns; for if admittance into any place was refused him, he slew and burnt without mercy. The man's constitution seems, like his heart, to have been of iron. Night and day he compelled his troops to march without taking any rest, until, wearied out and fainting with fatigue, they complained that darkness and light might be the same to him, as he was blind, but that it was not so with them. "What!" exclaimed he, in affected surprise, "cannot you see? Light up a couple of villages, then." Meanwhile the moderate party in Prague, and the nobles of the country, scandalized and terrified at these disorders, and anxiously longing for peace, assembled a diet and agreed on the following articles:—"1. Freedom of preaching; 2. The communion in both kinds; 3. Poverty of the priests, and appropriation of all ecclesiastical property; 4. Extermination of sinners." This last article seems to have been added for the sake of conciliating the Taborites. It was also proposed by the moderate party to offer the crown to Coribut, son of the duke of Lithuania; but the wild Horebites and Taborites, who had been accustomed to live in their waggon-fortresses in a sort of republican equality, had no inclination to become the subjects of a king, or allow the interference of nobles in their affairs. Finding how hopeless their cause was, the nobles abandoned the insurgents, and repaired to Iglan, where the emperor was then residing; whilst the burghers of Prague, seeing no prospect of assistance from any other quarter, were constrained to open their gates to Ziska, who entered the city in solemn procession, the host being borne before him in a golden pyx, and the whole population of Prague falling on their knees as it passed. The following January the emperor put his army in motion against Ziska, who marched out of Prague to meet him. Both parties acted with the greatest circumspection; but the Hussite army was at length surrounded by a skilful manœuvre of the imperialists. With desperate courage the Hussites cut their way by night through the enemy, a great number of whom were drowned in attempting to cross the river Sazeroa, which was imperfectly frozen. Ziska attacked the survivors, overthrew them with great slaughter, and under the shadow of the imperial banners, which he had captured, conferred knighthood on the bravest of the Taborites. The emperor now endeavoured to gain over Ziska by presents and flattering messages; but the veteran leader remained inflexible, and soon afterwards died of the plague in the month of October, 1424. On his death-bed he commanded that his body should be flayed after his decease, and a drum covered with the skin, that his followers might still hear, as it were, the voice of Ziska whenever they went forth to battle. The appearance of this extraordinary man was as remarkable as his actions. A bald bullet head, seamed with a deep crooked furrow across the brow, surmounted a pair of shoulders of preposterous breadth as compared with the shortness of his legs and body; whilst an expression of fierceness was given to the face by a nose like the beak of an eagle, and a fiery red moustache on the upper lip. Many years after his death, when the emperor Ferdinand I. visited his burial place at Cyazlow, and saw the massive iron mace which was Ziska's favourite weapon, he is said to have recoiled in horror, exclaiming, "How terrible must this man have been in life, when even after death the sight of his arms can inspire such dread!"

After Ziska's death the majority of the Horebites chose Procopius Holy for their leader, whilst the minority, styling themselves "Ziska's orphans," vowed never again to submit to the rule of mortal man, or sleep under a roof.

In the year 1431 the imperial army was totally and disgracefully defeated by the Hussites, all their artillery and baggage falling into the hands of the enemy. Sigismund now offered them the right hand of fellowship, but his proposals being received coldly, he left the prosecution of the affair to the council which had lately assembled at Bâsle. To this council the Bohemians were summoned, and on the 9th July, 1433, three hundred of them entered the city on horseback, where they were received with all honour, and the four articles of Prague conceded to them under certain modifications: the Bohemians con-

THE HUSSITE WAR.

senting to receive Sigismund as their king, and he on his part engaging to procure the sanction of the pope to the establishment of their national religion in Bohemia. Still the Taborites and "Orphans" were discontented, but were finally overthrown in a tremendous battle near Prague on the 20th May, 1434.

BOHEMIANS.

PREACHING OF THE REFORMERS.

HISTORY OF THE GREAT REFORMATION OF THE SIXTEENTH CENTURY.

EFORMATION, in general, signifies an act of reforming or correcting an error or abuse in religion, discipline, or the like. By way of eminence, the word is used for that great alteration and reformation in the corrupted system of Christianity, begun by Luther in the year 1517.

THE REFORMATION.

Before the period of the Reformation, the pope had in the most audacious manner declared himself the sovereign of the whole world. All the parts of it which were inhabited by those who were not Christians, he accounted to be inhabited by *nobody;* and if Christians took it into their heads to possess any of those countries, he gave them full liberty to make war upon the inhabitants without any provocation, and to treat them with no more humanity than they would have treated wild beasts. The countries, if conquered, were to be parcelled out according to the pope's pleasure; and dreadful was the situation of that prince who refused to obey the will of the holy pontiff. In consequence of this extraordinary authority which the pope had assumed, he at last granted to the king of Portugal, all the countries to the eastward of Cape Non in Africa, and to the king of Spain all the countries to the westward of it. In this was completed in his person the character of "Antichrist sitting in the temple of God, and showing himself as God." He had long before assumed the supremacy belonging to the Deity himself in spiritual matters; and now he assumed the same supremacy in worldly matters also, giving the extreme regions of the earth to whom he pleased.

Every thing was quiet, every heretic exterminated, and the whole Christian world supinely acquiesced in the enormous absurdities which were inculcated upon them; when, in 1517, in the time of pope Leo X., the empire of superstition began to decline, and has continued to do so ever since. The person who made the first attack on the extravagant superstitions then prevailing was Martin Luther.

The Reformation began in the city of Wittemberg, in Saxony, but was not long confined either to that city or province. In 1520, the Franciscan friars, who had

THE REFORMATION. 183

POPE LEO X.

the care of promulgating indulgences in Switzerland, were opposed by Zuinglius, a man not inferior in understanding and knowledge to Luther himself. He proceeded with the gratest vigour, even at the very beginning, to overturn the whole fabric of popery; but his opinions were declared erroneous by the universities of Cologne and Louvain. Notwithstanding this, the magistrates of Zurich approved of his proceedings; and that whole canton, together with those of Berne, Basil, and Chaffausen, embraced his opinions.

In Germany, Luther continued to make great advances, without being in the least intimidated by the ecclesiastical censures which were thundered against him from all quarters, he being continually protected by the German princes, either from religious or political motives, so that his adversaries could not accomplish his destruction, as they had done that of others. Melancthon, Carlostadius, and other men of eminence, also greatly forwarded the work of Luther; and in all probability the popish hierarchy would have soon come to an end, in the northern parts of Europe at least, had not the emperor Charles V. given a severe check to the progress of reformation in Germany.

During the confinement of Luther in a castle near Warburg, the Reformation advanced rapidly; almost every city in Saxony embracing the Lutheran opinions. At this time an alteration in the established forms of worship was first ventured upon at Wittemberg, by abolishing the celebration of private masses, and by giving the cup, as well as the bread, to the laity in the Lord's supper. In a short time, however, the new opinions were condemned by the university of Paris, and a refutation of them was attempted by Henry VIII. of England. But Luther was not to be thus intimidated. He published his animadversions on both with as much acrimony as if he had been refuting the meanest adversary; and a controversy managed by such illustrious antagonists drew a general attention, and the reformers daily gained new converts both in France and England.

But while the efforts of Luther were thus every where crowned with success, the divisions began to prevail which have since so much agitated the reformed churches. The first dispute was between Luther and Zuinglius concerning the manner in which the body and blood of Christ were present in the eucharist. Both parties maintained their tenets with the utmost obstinacy; and, by their divisions, first gave their adversaries an argument against them, which to this day the Catholics urge with great force; namely, that the Protestants are so divided, that it is impossible to know who are right or wrong; and that there cannot be a stronger proof than these divisions that the whole doctrine is false. To these intestine divisions were added the horrors of a civil war, occasioned by oppression on the one hand, and enthusiasm on the other.

These proceedings, however, were checked.—Luther and Melancthon were ordered by the elector of Saxony to draw up a body of laws relating to the form of ecclesiastical government, the method of public worship, &c., which was to be proclaimed by heralds throughout his dominions.—He, with Melancthon, had translated part of the New Testament in 1522; on the reading of which the people were astonished to find how different the laws of Christ were to those which had been imposed by the pope, and to which they had been subject. The princes and the people saw that Luther's opinions were founded on truth. They openly renounced the papal supremacy, and the happy morn of the Reformation was welcomed by those who had long sat in superstitious darkness.

This open resolution so exasperated the patrons of popery, that they intended to make war on the Lutherans, who prepared for defence. In 1526, a diet was assembled at Spire, when the emperor's ambassadors were desired to use their utmost endeavours to suppress all disputes about religion, and to insist upon the rigorous execution of the sentence which had been pronounced against Luther at Worms. But this opinion was opposed, and the diet proved favourable to the Reformation. But this tranquillity, which they in consequence enjoyed, did not last long. In 1529, a new diet was formed, and the power which had been granted to princes of managing ecclesiastical affairs till the meeting of a general council, was

CHARLES V.

now revoked, and every change declared unlawful that should be introduced into the doctrine, discipline, or worship of the established religion, before the determination of the approaching council was known. This decree was considered as iniquitous and intolerable by several members of the diet; and when they found that all their arguments and remonstrances were in vain, they entered a solemn protest against the decree on the 19th of April, and appealed to the emperor and a future council. Hence arose the denomination of PROTESTANTS, which from that time has been given to those who separate from the church of Rome.

Charles V. was in Italy, to whom the dissenting princes sent ambassadors to lay their grievances before him; but they met with no encouraging reception from him. The pope and the emperor were in close union at this time, and they had interviews upon the business. The pope thought the emperor to be too clement, and alleged that it was his duty to execute vengeance upon the heretical faction. To this, however, the emperor paid no regard, looking upon it as unjust to condemn, unheard, a set of men who had always approved themselves good citizens. The emperor, therefore, set out for Germany, having already appointed a diet of the empire to be held at Augsburg, where he arrived and found there a full assembly of the members of the diet. Here the gentle and pacific Melancthon had been ordered to draw up a confession of their faith, which he did, and expressed his sentiments and doctrine with the greatest elegance and perspicuity; and thus came forth to view the famous *Confession of Augsburg*.

This was attempted to be refuted by the divines of the church of Rome, and a controversy took place, which the emperor endeavoured to reconcile, but without success: all hopes of bringing about a coalition seemed utterly desperate. The votaries of the church of Rome, therefore, had recourse to the powerful arguments of imperial edicts and the force of the secular arm; and, on the 18th of November, a decree was issued by the emperor's orders every way injurious to the reformers. Upon which they assembled at Smalcald, where they concluded a league of mutual defence against all aggressors, by which they formed the Protestant states into one body, and resolved to apply to the kings of France and England, to implore them to patronize their new confederacy. The king of France being the avowed rival of the emperor, determined secretly to cherish those sparks of political discord; and the king of England, highly incensed against Charles, in complaisance to whom the pope had long retarded, and now openly opposed, his long-solicited divorce, was equally disposed to strengthen a league which might be rendered formidable to the emperor. Being, however, so taken up with the scheme of divorce, and of abolishing the papal jurisdiction in England, he had but little leisure to attend to them. Meanwhile Charles was convinced that it was not a time to extirpate heresy by violence; and at last terms of pacification were agreed upon at Nuremberg, and ratified solemnly in the diet at Ratisbon; and affairs so ordered by Divine Providence, that the Protestants obtained terms which amounted almost to a toleration of their religion.

Soon after the conclusion of the peace at Nuremberg, died John, elector of Saxony, who was succeeded by his son John Frederic, a prince of invincible fortitude and magnanimity, but whose reign was little better than one continued train of disappointments and calamities. The religious truce, however, gave new vigour to the Reformation. Those who had hitherto been only secret enemies to the Roman pontiff, now publicly threw off his yoke; and various cities and provinces of Germany enlisted themselves under the religious standards of Luther. On the other hand, as the emperor had now no other hope of terminating the religious disputes but by the meeting of a general council, he repeated his requests to the pope for that purpose. The pontiff, (Clement VII.,) whom the history of past councils filled with the greatest uneasiness, endeavoured to retard what he could not with decency refuse. At last, in 1533, he made a proposal, by his legate, to assemble a council at Mantua, Placentia, or Bologna; but the Protestants refused their consent to the nomination of an Italian council, and insisted that a controversy which had its rise in the heart of Germany should be determined within the limits of the empire. The pope by his usual artifices, eluded the performance of his own promise; and, in 1534, was cut off by death in the midst of his stratagem. His successor, Paul III., seemed to show less reluctance to the assembling a general council, and, in the year 1535, expressed his determination to convoke one at Mantua; and, in the year following, actually sent circular letters for that purpose through all the states and kingdoms under his jurisdiction. This council was summoned by a bull issued out on the 2nd of June, 1536, to meet at Mantua on the following year; but several obstacles prevented its meeting; one of the most material of which was that Frederic, duke of Mantua, had no inclination to receive at once so many guests, some of them very turbulent, into the place of his residence. On the other hand, the Protestants were firmly persuaded, that, as the council was assembled in Italy, and by the authority of the pope alone, the latter must have had an undue influence in that assembly; of consequence, that all things must have been carried by the votaries of Rome. For this reason they assembled at Smalcald in the year 1537, where they solemnly protested against this partial and corrupt council; and, at the same time, had a new summary of their doctrine drawn up by Luther, in order to present it to the assembled bishops, if it should be required of them. This summary, which had the title of *The Articles of Smalcald*, is commonly joined with the creeds and confessions of the Lutheran church.

After the meeting of the general council in Mantua was thus prevented, many schemes of accommodation were proposed both by the emperor and the Protestants; but, by the artifices of the church of Rome, all of them came to nothing. In 1541, the emperor appointed a meeting at Worms on the subject of religion, between persons of piety and learning, chosen from the contending parties. This conference, however, was, for certain reasons, removed to the diet that was to be held at Ratisbon the same year, and in which the principal subject of deliberation was a memorial presented by a person unknown, containing a project of peace. But the conference produced no other effect than a mutual agreement of the contending parties to refer their matters to a general council, or, if the meeting of such a council should be prevented, to the next German diet.

This resolution was rendered ineffectual by a variety of incidents, which widened the breach, and put off to a further day the deliberations which were designed to heal it. The pope ordered his legate to declare to the diet of Spire, assembled in 1542, that he would, according to the promise he had already made, assemble a general council, and that Trent should be the place of its meeting, if the diet had no objection to that city. Ferdinand, and the princes who adhered to the cause of the pope, gave their consent to this proposal; but it was vehemently objected to by the Protestants, both because the council was summoned by the authority of the pope only, and also because the place was within the jurisdiction of the pope; whereas they desired a free council, which should not be biassed by the dictates nor awed by the proximity of the pontiff. But this protestation produced no effect. Paul III. persisted in his purpose, and issued out his circular letters for the convocation of the council, with the approbation of the emperor. In justice to this pontiff, however, it must be observed, that he showed himself not to be averse to every reformation. He appointed four cardinals, and three other persons eminent for their learning, to draw up a plan for the reformation of the church in general,

MARTIN LUTHER.

and of the church of Rome in particular. The reformation proposed in this plan was, indeed, extremely superficial and partial; yet it contained some particulars which could scarcely have been expected from those who composed it.

All this time the emperor had been labouring to persuade the Protestants to consent to the meeting of the council of Trent; but, when he found them fixed in their opposition to this measure, he began to listen to the sanguinary measures of the pope, and resolved to terminate the dispute by force of arms. The elector of Saxony, and landgrave of Hesse, who were the chief supporters of the Protestant cause, upon this took proper measures to prevent their being surprised and overwhelmed by a superior force; but, before the horrors of war commenced, the great reformer Luther died in peace at Aysleben, the place of his nativity, in 1546.

The emperor and the pope had mutually resolved on the destruction of all who should dare to oppose the council of Trent. The meeting of it was to serve as a signal for taking up arms; and accordingly its deliberations were scarcely begun, in 1546, when the Protestants perceived undoubted signs of the approaching storm, and a formidable union between the emperor and pope, which threatened to overwhelm them at once. This year, indeed, there had been a new conference at Ratisbon upon the old subject of accommodating differences in religion; but, from the manner in which the debates were carried on, it plainly appeared that these differences could only be decided in the field of battle. The council of Trent, in the mean time, promulgated their decrees; while the reformed princes, in the diet of Ratisbon, protested against their authority, and were on that account proscribed by the emperor, who raised an army to reduce them to obedience.

The elector of Saxony, and the landgrave of Hesse, led their forces into Bavaria against the emperor, and cannonaded his camp at Ingoldstadt. It was supposed that this would bring on an engagement, which would probably have been advantageous to the cause of the reformed; but this was prevented chiefly by the perfidy of Maurice, duke of Saxony, who invaded the dominions of his uncle. Divisions were also fomented among the confederate princes by the dissimulations of the emperor; and France failed in paying the subsidy which had been promised by its monarch: all of which so discouraged the heads of the Protestant party, that their army soon dispersed, and the elector of Saxony was obliged to direct his march homewards.

But he was pursued by the emperor, who made several forced marches with a view to destroy his enemy before he should have time to recover his vigour. The two armies met near Muhlberg, on the Elbe, on the 24th of April, 1547; and after a bloody action, the elector was entirely defeated, and himself taken prisoner. Maurice, who had so basely betrayed him, was now declared elector of Saxony; and by his entreaties, Philip, landgrave of Hesse, the other chief of the Protestants, was persuaded to throw himself on the mercy of the emperor, and to implore his pardon. To this he consented, relying on the promise of Charles for obtaining forgiveness, and being restored to liberty; but, notwithstanding these expectations, he was unjustly detained a prisoner, by a scandalous violation of the most solemn convention.

The affairs of the Protestants now seemed to be desperate. In the diet of Augsburg, which was soon after called, the emperor required the Protestants to leave the decision of these religious disputes to the wisdom of the council which was to meet at Trent. The greatest part of the members consented to this proposal, being convinced by the powerful argument of an imperial army, which was at hand to dispel the darkness from the eyes of such as might otherwise have been blind to the force of Charles's reasoning. However, this general submission did not produce the effect which was expected from it. A plague which broke out, or was said to do so, in the city, caused the greatest part of the bishops to retire to Bologna, by which means the council was in effect dissolved; nor could all the entreaties and remonstrances of the emperor prevail upon the pope to re-assemble it without delay. During this interval, therefore, the emperor judged it necessary to fall upon some method of accommodating the religious differences, and maintaining peace until the council so long expected should be finally obtained. With this view he ordered Julius Pelagius, bishop of Naumberg, Michael Sidonius, a creature of the pope, and John Agricola, a native of Aysleben, to draw up a formulary which might serve as a rule of faith and worship till the council should be assembled; but, as this was only a temporary expedient, and had not the force of a permanent or perpetual institution, it thence obtained the name of the *Interim*.

This project of Charles was formed partly with a design to vent his resentment against the pope, and partly to answer other political purposes. It contained all the essential doctrines of the church of Rome, though considerably softened by the artful terms which were employed, and which were quite different from those employed before and after this period by the council of Trent. There was even an affected ambiguity in many of the expressions, which made them susceptible of different senses, and applicable to the sentiments of both communions. The consequence of all this was, that the imperial creed was reprobated by both parties.

In the year 1542, the pope (Paul III.) died, and was succeeded by Julius III., who, at the repeated solicitations of the emperor, consented to the re-assembling of a council of Trent. A diet was again held at Augsburg, under the cannon of an imperial army, and Charles laid the matter before the princes of the empire. Most of those present gave their consent to it, and, amongst the rest, Maurice, elector of Saxony; who consented on the following conditions: 1. That the points of doctrine which had already been decided there should be re-examined.—2. That this examination should be made in the presence of the Protestant divines.—3. That the Saxon Protestants should have

MELANCTHON.

a liberty of voting as well as of deliberating in the council.—4. That the pope should not pretend to preside in the assembly, either in person or by his legates. This declaration of Maurice was read in the diet, and his deputies insisted upon its being entered into the registers, which the archbishop of Mentz obstinately refused. The diet was concluded in 1551: and, at its breaking up, the emperor desired the assembled princes and states to prepare all things for the approaching council, and promised to use his utmost endeavours to procure moderation and harmony, impartiality and charity, in the transactions of that assembly.

On the breaking up of the diet, the Protestants took such steps as they thought most proper for their own safety. The Saxons employed Melancthon, and the Wirtembergers, Brengius, to draw up confessions of faith to be laid before the new council. The Saxon divines, however, proceeded no farther than Nuremberg, having received secret orders from Maurice to stop there; for the elector perceiving that Charles had formed designs against the liberties of the German princes, resolved to take the most effectual measures for crushing his ambition at once. He therefore entered with the utmost secrecy and expedition into an alliance with the king of France and several of the German princes, for the security of the rights and liberties of the empire; after which, assembling a powerful army in 1552, he marched against the emperor, who lay with a handful of troops at Inspruck, and expected no such thing. By this sudden and unforeseen accident, Charles was so much dispirited, that he was willing to make peace almost on any terms. The consequence of this was, that he concluded a treaty at Passau, which by the Protestants is considered as the basis of their religious liberty. By the first three articles of this treaty it was agreed that Maurice and the confederates should lay down their arms, and lend their troops to Ferdinand, to assist him against the Turks; and that the landgrave of Hesse should be set at liberty. By the fourth, it was agreed that the rule of faith called the *Interim* should be considered as null and void; that the contending parties should enjoy the free and undisturbed exercise of their religion until a diet should be assembled to determine amicably the present disputes (which diet was to meet in the space of six months;) and that this religious liberty should continue always, in case it should be found impossible to come to an uniformity in doctrine and worship. It was also determined, that all those who had suffered banishment or any other calamity, on account of their having been concerned in the league or war of Smalcald, should be reinstated in their privileges, possessions, and employments; that the imperial chamber at Spire should be open to the Protestants as well as to the Catholics; and that there should always be a certain number of Lutherans in that high court. To this peace,'Albert, marquis of Brandenburgh, refused to subscribe, and continued the war against the Roman Catholics, committing such ravages in the empire, that a confederacy was at last formed against him. At the head of this confederacy was Maurice, elector of Saxony, who died of a wound he received in a battle fought on the occasion in 1553.

The assembly of the diet promised by Charles was prevented by various accidents; however, it met at Augsburg, in 1555, where it was opened by Ferdinand in the name of the emperor, and terminated those deplorable calamities which had so long desolated the empire. After various debates, the following acts were passed, on the 25th of September;—That the Protestants who followed the confession of Augsburg should be for the future considered as entirely free from the jurisdiction of the Roman pontiff, and from the authority and superintendence of the bishops, that they were left at perfect liberty to enact laws for themselves relating to their religious sentiments, discipline, and worship; that all the inhabitants of the German empire should be allowed to judge for themselves in religious matters, and to join themselves to that church whose doctrine and worship they thought the most pure and consonant with the spirit of true Christianity; and that all those who should injure or prosecute any person under religious pretences, and on account of their opinions, should be declared and proceeded against as public enemies of the empire, invaders of its liberty, and disturbers of its peace.

THE REFORMATION.

GUSTAVUS VASA.

Thus was the Reformation established in many parts of the German empire, where it continues to this day; nor have the efforts of the popish powers at any time been able to suppress it, or even to prevent its gaining ground. It was not, however, in Germany alone that a reformation of religion took place. Almost all the kingdoms of Europe began to open their eyes to the truth about the same time. The reformed religion was propagated in Sweden, soon after Luther's rupture with the church of Rome, by one of his disciples, named OLAUS PATRI. The zealous efforts of this missionary were seconded by GUSTAVUS VASA, whom the Swedes had raised to the throne in the place of Christiern, king of Denmark, whose horrid barbarity had lost him the crown. This prince, however, was as prudent as he was zealous ; and as the minds of the Swedes were in a fluctuating state, he wisely avoided all kinds of vehemence and precipitation in spreading the new doctrine. Accordingly the first object of his attention was the instruction of his people in the sacred doctrines of the holy Scriptures ; for which purpose he invited into his dominions several learned Germans, and spread abroad through the kingdom the Swedish translation of the Bible that had been made by Olaus Patri. Some time after this, in 1526, he appointed a conference at Upsal, between the reformer and Peter Gallius, a zealous defender of the ancient superstition, in which each of the champions was to bring forth his arguments, that it might be seen on which side the truth lay. In this dispute Olaus obtained a signal victory, which contributed much to confirm Gustavus in his persuasion of the truth of Luther's doctrine, and to promote its progress in Sweden. The following year another event gave the finishing stroke to its propagation and success. This was the assembly of the states at Westeras, where Gustavus recommended the doctrine of the reformers with such zeal, that, after warm debates, fomented by the clergy in general, it was unanimously resolved that the reformation introduced by Luther should have place in Sweden. This resolution was principally owing to the firmness and magnanimity of Gustavus, who declared publicly, that he would lay down the sceptre, and retire from the kingdom, rather than rule a people enslaved by the orders and authority of the pope, and more controlled by the tyranny of their bishop than by the laws of their monarch. From this time, the papal empire in Sweden was entirely overthrown, and Gustavus declared head of the church.

In *Denmark*, the reformation was introduced as early

as the year 1521, in consequence of the ardent desire discovered by Christiern II. of having his subjects instructed in the doctrines of Luther. This monarch, notwithstanding his cruelty, for which his name has been rendered odious, was nevertheless desirous of delivering his dominions from the tyranny of the church of Rome. For this purpose, in the year 1520, he sent for Martin Reinard, one of the disciples of Carlostadt, out of Saxony, and appointed him professor of divinity at Hasnia; and after his death, which happened in 1521, he invited Carlostadt himself to fill that important place. Carlostadt accepted of this office, indeed, but in a short time returned to Germany; upon which Christiern used his utmost endeavours to engage Luther to visit his dominions, but in vain. However, the progress of Christiern in reforming the religion of his subjects, or rather of advancing his own power above that of the church, was checked, in the year 1523, by a conspiracy, by which he was deposed and banished; his uncle Frederick, duke of Holstein and Sleswic, being appointed his successor.

Frederic conducted the reformation with much greater prudence than his predecessor. He permitted the Protestant doctors to preach publicly the sentiments of Luther, but did not venture to change the established government and discipline of the church. However, he contributed greatly to the progress of the reformation by his successful attempts in favour of religious liberty in an assembly of the states held at Odensee in 1527. Here he procured the publication of a famous edict, by which every subject of Denmark was declared free either to adhere to the tenets of the church of Rome, or to the doctrine of Luther. The papal tyranny was totally destroyed by his successor Christiern III. He began by sup-

FRANCIS I.

THE REFORMATION. 203

pressing the despotic authority of the bishops, and restoring to their lawful owners a great part of the wealth and possessions which the church had acquired by various stratagems. This was followed by a plan of religious doctrine, worship, and discipline, laid down by Bugenhagius, whom the king had sent for from Wittemburg for that purpose; and in 1539 an assembly of the states at Odensee gave a solemn sanction to all these transactions.

In *France*, also, the reformation began to make some progress very early. Margaret, queen of Navarre, sister to Francis I., the perpetual rival of Charles V., was a great friend to the new doctrine; and it appears that as early as the year 1523, there were in several of the provinces of France great numbers of people who had conceived the greatest aversion both to the doctrine and tyranny of the church of Rome; among whom were many of the first rank and dignity, and even some of the episcopal order. But as their number increased daily, and troubles and commotions were excited in several places on account of the religious differences, the authority of the king intervened, and many persons eminent for their virtue and piety were put to death in the most barbarous manner. Indeed, Francis, who had either no religion at all, or, at best, no fixed and consistent system of religious principles, conducted himself towards the Protestants in such a manner as best answered his private views.—Sometimes he resolved to invite Melancthon into France, probably with a view to please his sister, the queen of Navarre, whom he loved tenderly, and who had strongly imbibed the Protestant principles. At other times he exercised the most infernal cruelty towards the reformed; and once made the following mad declaration: That. if he thought the blood of his arm was tainted by the

Lutheran heresy, he would have it cut off; and that he would not even spare his own children, if they entertained sentiments contrary to those of the Catholic church.

About this time the famous Calvin began to draw the attention of the public, but more especially of the queen of Navarre. His zeal exposed him to danger; and the friends of the reformation, whom Francis was daily committing to the flames, placed him more than once in the most perilous situation, from which he was delivered by the interposition of the queen of Navarre.—He therefore retired out of France to Basil in Switzerland, where he published his Christian Institutions, and became afterwards so famous.

Those among the French who first renounced the jurisdiction of the Romish church are commonly called *Lutherans* by the writers of those early times; hence it has been supposed that they had all imbibed the peculiar sentiments of Luther. But this appears by no means to have been the case; for the vicinity of the cities of Geneva, Lausanne, &c., which had adopted the doctrines of Calvin, produced a remarkable effect upon the French Protestant churches; insomuch that, about the middle of this century, they all entered into communion with the church at Geneva.— The French Protestants were called *Huguenots* by their adversaries, by way of contempt. Their fate was very severe, being persecuted with unparalleled fury; and though many princes of the blood, and of the first nobility, had embraced their sentiments, yet in no part of the world did the reformers suffer so much. At last, all commotions were quelled by the fortitude and magnanimity of Henry IV., who, in the year 1598, granted all his subjects full liberty of conscience by the famous edict of Nantes, and seemed to have thoroughly established the reformation through-

THE NEW YORK
PUBLIC LIBRARY

ASTOR LENOX AND
TILDEN FOUNDATIONS
R   L

LOUIS XIV.

out his dominions. During the minority of Louis XIV., however, this edict was revoked by cardinal Mazarin, since which time the Protestants have often been cruelly persecuted; nor was the profession of the reformed religion in France at any time so safe as in most other countries of Europe.

In the other parts of Europe the opposition to the church of Rome was but faint and ambiguous before the diet of Augsburg. Before that period, however, it appears from undoubted testimony, that the doctrine of Luther had made a considerable, though probably secret, progress through Spain, Hungary, Bohemia, Britain, Poland, and the Netherlands; and had in all these countries many friends, of whom several repaired to Wittemburg, in order to enlarge their knowledge by means of Luther's conversation. Some of these countries threw off the Romish yoke entirely, and in others a prodigious number of families embraced the principles of the reformed religion. It is certain, indeed, and the Roman Catholics themselves acknowledge it without hesitation, that the papal doctrines and authority would have fallen into ruin in all parts of the world at once, had not the force of the secular arm been employed to support the tottering edifice. In the Netherlands, particularly, the most grievous persecutions took place, so that by the emperor Charles V. upwards of 100,000 were destroyed, while still greater cruelties were exercised upon the people by his son Philip II.—The revolt of the United Provinces, however, and motives of real policy, at last put a stop to these furious proceedings; and though, in many provinces of the Netherlands, the establishment of the popish religion was still continued, the Protestants have been long free from the danger of persecution on account of their principles.

The reformation made a considerable progress in

Spain and Italy soon after the rupture between Luther and the Roman pontiff. In all the provinces of Italy, but more especially in the territories of Venice, Tuscany, and Naples, the superstition of Rome lost ground, and great numbers of people of all ranks expressed an aversion to the papal yoke. This occasioned violent and dangerous commotions in the kingdom of Naples in the year 1546; which, however, were at last quelled by the united efforts of Charles V. and his viceroy Don Pedro di Toledo. In several places the pope put a stop to the progress of the reformation by letting loose the inquisitors, who spread dreadful marks of their barbarity through the greatest part of Italy. These formidable ministers of superstition put so many to death, and perpetrated such horrid acts of cruelty and oppression, that most of the reformed consulted their safety by a voluntary exile, while others returned to the religion of Rome, at least in external appearance. But the inquisition, which frightened into the profession of popery several Protestants in other parts of Italy, could never make its way into the kingdom of Naples; nor could either the authority or entreaties of the pope engage the Neapolitans to admit even visiting inquisitors.

In *Spain*, several people embraced the Protestant religion, not only from the controversies of Luther, but even from those divines whom Charles V. had brought with him into Germany in order to refute the doctrines of Luther; for these divines imbibed the pretended heresy, instead of refuting it, and propagated it more or less on their return home. But the iniquisition, which could obtain no footing in Naples, reigned triumphant in Spain; and by the most dreadful methods frightened the people back into popery, and suppressed the desire of exchanging their superstition for a more rational plan of religion. It was, indeed, presumed, that Charles himself died a Protestant; and it seems to be certain that, when the approach of death had dissipated those schemes of ambition and grandeur which had so long blinded him, his sentiments became much more rational and agreeable to Christianity than they had ever been. All the ecclesiastics who had attended him, as soon as he expired, were sent to the inquisition, and committed to the flames, or put to death by some other method equally terrible. Such was the fate of Augustine Casal, the emperor's preacher; of Constantine Pontius, his confessor; of Egidius, whom he had named to the bishopric of Tortosa; of Bartholomew de Caranza, a Dominican, who had been confessor to king Philip and queen Mary; with twenty others of less note.

In *England*, the principles of the reformation began to be adopted as soon as an account of Luther's doctrines could be conveyed thither. In that kingdom there were still great remains of the sect called *Lollards*, whose doctrines resembled that of Luther; and among whom, of consequence, the sentiments of the reformer gained great credit. Henry VIII., king of England, at that time was a violent partisan of the church of Rome, and had a particular veneration for the writings of Thomas Aquinas. Being informed that Luther spoke of his favourite author with contempt, he conceived a violent prejudice against the reformer, and even wrote against him, as we have already observed. Luther did not hesitate at writing against his Majesty, overcame him in argument, and treated him with very little ceremony. The first step towards public reformation, however, was not taken till the year 1529. Great complaints had been made in England, and of a very ancient date, of the usurpa-

17*

HENRY VIII

tions of the clergy; and, by the prevalence of the Lutheran opinions, these complaints were now become more general than before. The House of Commons, finding the occasion favourable, passed several bills, restraining the impositions of the clergy: but what threatened the ecclesiastical order with the greatest danger, were the severe reproaches thrown out almost without opposition in the House against the dissolute lives, ambition, and avarice of the priests, and their continual encroachments on the privileges of the laity The bills for regulating the clergy met with opposition in the House of Lords; and bishop Fisher imputed them to want of faith in the Commons, and to a formed design, proceeding from heretical and Lutheran

CARDINAL WOLSEY.

principles, of robbing the church of her patrimony, and overturning the national religion. The Commons, however, complained to the king by their speaker Sir Thomas Audley, of these reflections thrown out against them; and the bishop was obliged to retract his words.

Though Henry had not the least idea of rejecting any, even of the most absurd Romish superstitions, yet, as the oppressions of the clergy suited very ill with the violence of his own temper, he was pleased with every opportunity of lessening their power. In the parliament of 1531 he showed his design of humbling the clergy in the most effectual manner. An

HENRY VIII. RECEIVING A COPY OF THE ENGLISH BIBLE FROM CRANMER.

obsolete statute was revived, from which it was pretended that it was criminal to submit to the legatine power which had been exercised by cardinal Wolsey. By this stroke the whole body of clergy was declared guilty at once. They were too well acquainted with Henry's disposition, however, to reply, that their ruin would have been the certain consequence of their not submitting to Wolsey's commission, which had been given by royal authority. Instead of making any defence of this kind, they chose to throw themselves on the mercy of their sovereign; which, however, it cost them 118,840*l.* to procure. A confession was likewise extorted from them, that the king was protector and supreme head of the church of England; though some of them had the dexterity to get a clause inserted which invalidated the whole submission, viz., *in so far as permitted by the law of Christ.*

The king having thus begun to reduce the power of

THE REFORMATION.

EDWARD VI.

the clergy, kept no bounds with them afterwards. He did not, indeed, attempt any reformation in religious matters; nay, he persecuted most violently such as did attempt this in the least. Indeed, the most essential article of his creed seems to have been his own supremacy; for whoever denied this was sure to suffer the most severe penalties, whether protestant or papist. Nevertheless, Henry permitted the Scriptures to be translated into the English language, and formally received a copy from Cranmer when the work was completed.

He died in 1547, and was succeeded by his only son Edward VI. This amiable prince, whose early youth was crowned with that wisdom, sagacity, and virtue that would have done honour to advanced years, gave new spirit and vigour to the Protestant cause, and was its brightest ornament, as well as its most effectual support. He encouraged learned and pious men of foreign countries to settle in England, and addressed a particular invitation to Martin Bucer, and

214   THE REFORMATION.

QUEEN MARY.

Paul Fagius, whose moderation added a lustre to their other virtues, that by the ministry and labours of these eminent men in concert with those of the friends of the reformation in England, he might purge his dominions from the sordid fictions of popery, and establish the pure doctrines of Christianity in their place. For this purpose he issued out the wisest orders for the restoration of true religion; but his reign was too short to accomplish fully such a glorious purpose. In the year 1553 he was taken from his loving and afflicted subjects, whose sorrow was inexpressible, and suited to their loss. His sister Mary, (the daughter of Catherine of Arragon, from whom Henry had been separated by the famous divorce,) a furious bigot to the church of Rome, and a princess whose natural character, like the spirit of her religion, was despotic and cruel, succeeded him on the British throne, and imposed anew the arbitrary laws and the tyrannical yoke of Rome upon the people of England. Nor were the methods which she employed in the cause of superstition better than the cause itself, or tempered by any sentiments of equity or compassion. Barbarous tortures, and death in the most shocking forms, awaited those who opposed her will, or made the least stand against the restoration of popery; and, among many other victims, the learned and pious Cranmer, archbishop of Canterbury, who had been one of the most illustrious instruments of the reformation in England, fell a sacrifice to her fury. This odious scene of persecution was happily concluded in the year 1558, by the death of the queen, who left no issue; and as soon as her successor, the lady Elizabeth, ascended the throne, all things assumed a new and pleasing aspect. This illustrious princess, whose sentiments, counsels, and projects, breathed a spirit superior to the natural softness and delicacy of her sex, exerted this vigorous and manly spirit in the defence of oppressed conscience and expiring liberty, broke anew the despotic yoke of papal authority and superstition; and delivering her people from the bondage of Rome, established that form of religious doctrine and ecclesiastical government which still subsists in England. This religious establishment differs in some respects from the plan that had been formed by those whom Edward VI. had employed for promoting the cause of the Reform-

CRANMER.

ation, and approaches nearer to the rites and discipline of former times; though it is widely different, and in the most important points entirely opposite to the principles of the Roman hierarchy.

The cause of the Reformation underwent in *Ireland* the same vicissitudes and revolutions that had attended it in England. When Henry VIII., after the abolition of the papal authority, was declared supreme head upon earth of the church of England, George Brown, a native of England, and a monk of the Augustine order, whom that monarch had created, in the year 1535, archbishop of Dublin, began to act with the utmost vigour in consequence of this change

DEATH OF QUEEN MARY.

in the hierarchy. He purged the churches of his diocese from superstition in all its various forms, pulled down images, destroyed relics, abolished absurd and idolatrous rites; and, by the influence as well as authority he had in Ireland, caused the king's supremacy to be acknowledged in that nation. Henry showed, soon after, that this supremacy was not a vain title; for he banished the monks out of that kingdom, confiscated their revenues, and destroyed their convents. In the reign of Edward VI. still further progress was made in the removal of popish superstitions by the zealous labours of bishop Brown, and the auspicious encouragement he granted to all who exerted themselves in the Reformation. But the death of this excellent prince, and the accession of queen Mary, had like to have changed the face of affairs in Ireland as much as in England; but her designs were disappointed by a very curious adventure, of which the following account has been copied from the papers of Richard, earl of Cork:

"Queen Mary having dealt severely with the Protestants in England, about the latter end of her reign, signed a commission for to take the same course with them in Ireland; and, to execute the same with greater force, she nominates Dr. Cole one of the commissioners. This doctor coming with the commission to Chester on his journey, the mayor of that city hearing that her Majesty was sending a messenger into Ireland, and he being a churchman, waited on the doctor, who in a discourse with the mayor taketh out of a cloke-bag a leather box, saying unto him, *Here is a commission that shall lash the heretics of Ireland*, calling the Protestants by that title. The good woman of the house being well affected to the Protestant religion, and also having a brother named John Edmonds, of the same then a citizen in Dublin, was much troubled at the doctor's words; but watching her convenient time, while the mayor took his leave, and the doctor complimented him down the stairs, she opens the box, takes the commission out, and places in lieu thereof a sheet of paper with a pack of cards wrapt up therein, the knave of clubs being faced uppermost. The doctor coming up to his chamber, suspected nothing of what had been done, and put up the box as formerly. The next day, going to the water-side, wind and weather serving him, he sails towards Ireland, and landed on the 7th of October, 1558, at Dublin. Then coming to the castle, the lord Fitz-Walter, being lord-deputy, sent for him to come before him and the privy council; who coming in, after he had made a speech relating upon what account he came over, he presents the box unto the lord-deputy; who caused it to be opened, that the secretary might read the commission,—there was nothing save a pack of cards with the knave of clubs uppermost: which not only startled the lord-deputy and council, but the doctor, who assured them he had a commission, but knew not how it was gone. Then the lord-deputy made answer, Let us have another commission, and we will shuffle the cards in the mean while. The doctor being troubled in his mind, went away, and returned into England, and coming to the court, obtained another commission; but, staying for a wind on the water-side, news came to him that the queen was dead: and thus God preserved the Protestants of Ireland."

Queen Elizabeth was so delighted with this story, which was related to her by lord Fitz-Walter on his return to England, that she sent for Elizabeth Edmonds, whose husband's name was Mattershad, and gave her a pension of 40*l*. during her life.

In *Scotland*, the seeds of reformation were very early sown by several noblemen who had resided in

THE REFORMATION.

QUEEN ELIZABETH.

Germany during the religious disputes there; but for many years it was suppressed by the power of the pope, seconded by inhuman laws and barbarous executions. The most eminent opposer of the papal jurisdiction was John Knox, a disciple of Calvin, a man of great zeal and invincible fortitude. On all occasions he raised the drooping spirits of the reformers,

JOHN KNOX.

and encouraged them to go on with their work, notwithstanding the opposition and treachery of the queen-regent; till at last, in 1561, by the assistance of an English army sent by Elizabeth, popery was, in a manner, totally extirpated throughout the kingdom. From this period the form of doctrine, worship, and discipline, established by Calvin at Geneva, has had the ascendancy in Scotland.

On the review of this article, what reason have we to admire Infinite Wisdom, in making human events, apparently fortuitous, subservient to the spread of the

Gospel! What reason to adore that Divine Power which was here evidently manifested in opposition to all the powers of the world! What reason to praise that Goodness, which thus caused light and truth to break forth for the happiness and salvation of millions of the human race!

MARTYRDOM OF LATIMER AND RIDLEY.

AMONG the martyrs who perished in the persecution of the Protestants in the reign of queen Mary, Latimer and Ridley were remarkable.— Their conduct at the stake is thus described by a recent writer:—

"Returning to his prison, Latimer remained closely confined till the 16th of October, the day appointed for the execution. Early in the morning of that day, the vice-chancellor of Oxford, with his retinue, repaired to the open space in front of Balliol College, where this melancholy tragedy was to take place; and to prevent any tumultuous interruptions from the people, the ground was kept by an armed force under the command of Lord Williams. Every preparation being completed, Latimer was brought forth by the mayor and bailiffs, together with Ridley. The contrast exhibited in the appearance of the two sufferers was striking, and excited the liveliest sympathy in the spectators. Ridley, in the prime of life and intellect, radiant with holy hope, and rejoicing in being deemed worthy to shed forth his life in this great cause, came forward with an elastic step, arrayed with care and attention in the

HUGH LATIMER.

costly dress of his rank and order. But poor old Latimer—less visibly excited by the greatness of the occasion—came forth with quiet contentment written on his countenance, and arrayed in the same frieze gown, kerchief, and buttoned cap which he had worn at his trial: but in addition to this, he now wore a new long shroud, which came down over his hose to his feet, and marked his preparation for death. Having reached the stake, they affectionately embraced each other, and then kneeled down and prayed; after which they conversed cheerfully together, till Dr. Smith began the appointed sermon. He chose for his text the words—'Although I give my body to be burned, and have not charity, it profiteth me nothing;' and his discourse thereon went to show, that the goodness of the cause, and not the manner of death, made the holiness of the person, which he confirmed by the example of Judas, and of a woman who had lately hanged herself in Oxford; and he alleged that seeing that the persons before him would not save themselves by recanting their heretical opinions, they were in fact their own destroyers. It was an unusually short sermon for that time, not taking more than a quarter of an hour. When it was concluded, Ridley said to Latimer, 'Will you begin to answer the sermon, or shall I?' Latimer said, 'Begin you first, I pray you.' On which Ridley, with his usual ready mastery of his great resources, addressed himself to the task; but the vice-chancellor and the bailiffs ran hastily to him and stopped his mouth with their hands. This drew from Latimer his favourite 'old possy'—'Well! there is nothing shut that shall not be opened.'

"They were then commanded to make ready; and with all meekness they obeyed. Ridley took off the several articles of his dress, and presented them, together with the contents of his pockets, to those who stood near him, who received them with the utmost eagerness. Latimer gave nothing; but very quietly suffered the executioner to disrobe him; and being stripped to his shroud, it was marvellous to behold the change for the better in his appearance; for 'whereas in his clothes he appeared a withered and crooked silly old man, he now stood bolt upright, as comely a father as one might lightly behold.' One chain carried around their bodies, fastened them both to one stake. They accepted thankfully some gunpowder, which Ridley's brother-in-law gave them with the view of shortening their sufferings; and all being ready, a blazing faggot was brought and laid down at Ridley's feet. It was at that moment that Latimer addressed to him the prophetic and memorable words, 'Be of good comfort, Master Ridley, and play the man. We shall this day light such a candle, by God's grace, in England, as I trust shall never be put out.' Then, as the flames arose, he cried, 'O Father of heaven, receive my soul!' and received the flames as if embracing them. He was next observed to stroke his face repeatedly with his hands, and, as it were, bathed them in the fire. His head then dropped, and he expired with little if any suffering. The sufferings of Ridley were protracted and horrible: but at length his body slipped through or fell over the chain to the feet of Latimer, and both were utterly consumed in the fierce heat."

LADY JANE GREY REFUSING THE CROWN.

DEATH OF LADY JANE GREY.

ADY JANE GREY was rather a political than a religious victim. Her religion was protestant, and this may have had some weight in queen Mary's determination to sacrifice her. Lady Jane had declined the crown; but she had afterwards worn it, and it is undeniably true that the sparing of lady Jane's life was hardly consistent with the tranquillity of the kingdom, as plots were constantly in progress to place her on the throne. The last of these was that of Sir Thomas Wyatt.

This insurrection cost the lives of four hundred persons, who were executed in the course of February

LADY JANE GREY.

and March, besides many who were put to death afterwards. The duke of Suffolk was defeated and made prisoner in the midland counties, and Sir Peter Carew, another of the conspirators, was defeated in the west. Carew had the good fortune to escape to France, but the father of lady Jane was captured. During the insurrection Mary and her court were agitated by suspicions, and after the insurrection by revenge. The princess Elizabeth, who was accused of corresponding with Wyatt, was placed under arrest the very day after Wyatt's first rising in Kent, and was subsequently committed to the Tower. Other victims were sent to the same state prison; and Mary being induced to believe that the life of the Lady Jane was incompatible with her own safety and the tranquillity of the country, in three or four days after Wyatt's discomfiture, signed the death-warrant both for Jane and her husband. On the morning of the 12th February, the Lord Guilford Dudley was taken out to Tower-hill, where, after saying his prayers and shedding a few tears, he laid his head on the block and died quietly. The fate of this young and handsome man excited commiseration among the spectators, and as it was calculated that that of his wife would make a still deeper impression, it had been resolved to execute her more privately within the walls of the Tower. Queen Mary showed what she and all Catholics considered a laudable anxiety for the soul of this youthful and gentle sacrifice: during her imprisonment various efforts were made to shake her Protestant faith, and Fecknam or Feckenham, one of queen Mary's chaplains, and a very catholic dean of St. Paul's, assailed her in her last hours with arguments and disputations; but it appears she was steadfast in the doctrines which she had studied under learned teachers. On the dreadful morning she declined a meeting with her husband, saying, that it would rather foment their grief than be a comfort in death, and that they should soon meet in a better place and happier estate. She even saw him conducted towards Tower-hill, and, with the same settled spirit, she beheld his headless trunk when it was returned to be buried in the Tower chapel. The sight was worse than death, but it failed to deprive her of her strength of mind, or of the glorious hope of a happy immortality. By this time her own scaffold upon the green within the Tower was ready; and almost as soon as her husband's body passed towards the chapel the lieutenant led her forth to die. She uttered no moan and shed not a tear, although her two gentlewomen, Elizabeth Tilney and Mistress Helen, "wonderfully wept." She had a book in her hand, wherein she read and prayed until she reached the scaffold. From that platform she addressed a few modest words to the very few spectators who had been admitted to witness her end, stating that she had justly merited her fate for suffering herself to be made the instrument, however unwillingly, of the ambition of others. She then implored God's mercy, caused herself to be disrobed by her gentlewomen, veiled her own eyes with her handkerchief, and stretched her neck across the billet. The executioner was moved, and lingered with his upheld axe. She exhorted him to do his office. At last the axe fell, and her fair head rolled away from the body, drawing tears from the eyes of all present, not excepting those who were most devoted to queen Mary and to the faith she professed.*

The duke of Suffolk, who had never been worthy of the child whom his ambition and imbecility had sa-

* De Thou. Bishop Godwin.

crificed, was publicly beheaded on Tower-hill, on the 23rd of February, eleven days after the execution of his daughter and son-in-law. Sir Thomas Wyatt perished at the same place on the 11th of April; lord Thomas Grey, one of Suffolk's brothers, was executed about a fortnight after, and other executions followed. But the only victim that excited any lasting interest, or that deserved to excite it, was the fair lady Jane. Honest old Fuller, with his usual point, and apparently with little inaccuracy, unless it be in relation to her age, of which some doubts must be entertained, says of her—" She had the innocency of childhood, the beauty of youth, the solidity of middle, the gravity of old age, and all at eighteen; the birth of a princess, the learning of a clerk, the life of a saint, and the death of a malefactor for her parent's offences."

GUSTAVUS ADOLPHUS

CAREER OF GUSTAVUS ADOLPHUS,
KING OF SWEDEN, DEFENDER OF THE PROTESTANT FAITH.

ROM Holland to the Carinthian mountains, and from Prussia to the Alps of Berne, wherever the German tongue was spoken, Luther's and Calvin's doctrines had penetrated, and found a way to the hearts of the people. With the exception of Bavaria and the Tyrol, every district of Germany had at one time or other fought for liberty of conscience; yet there now

remained no vestige of it except in the single city of Magdeburg, whose brave defenders still held out against the assaults of Tilly. In the midst of this melancholy prospect, a new ray of hope broke through the clouds which hovered over Protestant Germany. The throne of Sweden was at this time occupied by Gustavus Adolphus, a zealous and sincere supporter of the Reformation, who had long witnessed with grief the sufferings of his brethren in Germany, but had hitherto been debarred from rendering them any assistance by the wars in which he was engaged with Denmark and Poland. Yet these very wars had given him that unrivalled military knowledge which afterwards produced such glorious results. His Swedes were the best and most formidable soldiers of that day, warlike by nature, hardened by their severe climate, thoroughly disciplined, experienced in the field, full of confidence, and more than all, inspired by a strong religious conviction that the cause for which they drew their swords was favoured by the Almighty. As soon, therefore, as Gustavus had secured an honourable peace with Denmark and Poland, he had both leisure to undertake, and thousands of brave spirits ready to aid him in accomplishing the defence of his brethren in Germany. Besides his zeal for the common cause, the Swedish king had also private injuries to avenge. —Austrians had fought against him in the ranks of the Polish army, and Wallenstein had insulted his ambassador, without his having been able in either case to obtain satisfaction.

On the 20th of May, 1630, Gustavus Adolphus entered the senate-house at Stockholm, to take a solemn farewell of the estates of his kingdom. He had already made the necessary arrangements for the administration of public affairs during his absence, and set his house in order as one who was about to go to death. Taking his young daughter Christina in his arms, he presented her to the estates as his successor, and caused them to swear fidelity to her, in the event of his never returning. He then read a paper, in which his wishes respecting the government of the country during his absence, or in case of his death, during the minority of his daughter, were distinctly explained. The whole assembly melted into tears, and the king himself was so deeply affected, that some minutes elapsed before he could summon sufficient firmness to pronounce his farewell address. "It is not lightly, or without due deliberation," thus he began, "that I involve myself and you in this new and dangerous war. Almighty God is my witness, that I fight not for mine own pleasure. The emperor has offered me, in the person of my ambassador, the grossest insults; he has assisted my enemies, my friends and brethren he persecutes, tramples my religion in the dust, and stretches out his hand to seize my crown. The oppressed people of Germany urgently implore our aid, and, if it please God, they shall not be disappointed. I know the dangers to which my life will be exposed: these I have never shunned, nor do I hope eventually to escape them. It is true that until the present hour the Almighty hath marvellously preserved me: but I shall die at last in defence of my native land. I commend you all to the protection of Heaven. Be upright, be conscientious, walk unblameably: so shall we meet one another again in eternity. To you, my counsellors, I first address myself,—may God enlighten you, and fill you with wisdom, that you may ever advise that which conduces most to the welfare of my kingdom. You, brave nobles, I commend to the protection of God. Go forth, and prove yourselves worthy descendants of those heroic Goths, who laid ancient

Rome in the dust. You, ministers of the church, I exhort to unanimity and concord. Be yourselves ensamples of those virtues which ye preach, and abuse not your dominion over the souls of my people. To you, deputies of the burgher and peasant orders, I wish the blessing of Heaven, a joyful harvest to reward your toils, fulness to your barns, and abundance of all the good things of life. For all, absent as well as present, I offer my prayers to Heaven. I now bid you affectionately farewell—Farewell! perhaps for ever."

On the 24th of June, the hundredth anniversary of the Augsburg Confession, Gustavus Adolphus landed at Usedom in the midst of a violent thunder storm. As soon as he touched the German soil, he fell on his knees, and called God to witness that this campaign was undertaken, not for his own honour, but in the cause of the Gospel. His army at this time consisted of only 16,000 men, among whom were thirty companies of Germans : and so little sensation did his landing produce, that the people of Vienna called him in derision, the " Snow king," who would melt away as he approached the south. The Protestants, on the other hand, looked on him as their deliverer, and named him the "Lion of the north." He was of gigantic height, with an open countenance, large blue eyes, and a mild but majestic bearing; presenting in his whole appearance a remarkable contrast to the gloomy Wallenstein, the ferocious Tilly, and most of the German princes, who affected a mysterious demeanour, to cover their low plans of personal ambition.

Finding himself unsupported by the northern Protestants, Gustavus told the duke of Mecklenburg, it was his intention to march on Magdeburg, and relieve that city : " If none will stand by me," continued he,

TILLY.

"I shall at once retire, make the best peace I can with the emperor, and return to Stockholm. This I shall have little difficulty in effecting; but at the day of judgment you must give an account for having abandoned the cause of God and of his Gospel—yea, even in this world you will have your reward." The electors of Saxony and Brandenburg, who were well aware how valuable their friendship must be to either side, held back for a time, observing an armed neutrality; which Gustavus would not break up by violent means, lest he should at once furnish them with an excuse for joining the emperor. This unfortunate delay decided the fate of Magdeburg; which had received no aid from Gustavus except the sending them one of his officers, colonel Falkenstein, who entered the place in the disguise of a boatman, and took command of the feeble and dispirited garrison.

On the night of the 10th of May, 1631, the imperial party within the walls called loudly for surrender. At four o'clock in the morning Falkenstein hastened to the town-hall, and whilst he was in consultation with the magistrates, Pappenheim, without waiting for orders from Tilly, scaled the walls at a place where the sentinel was unfortunately asleep, and before an alarm could be given, appeared with his men in front of the hall. Falkenstein rushed out, and was instantly shot dead. Still the citizens, in spite of the overwhelming force brought against them, resisted bravely, until their powder failed, when they were obliged to surrender at discretion. Meanwhile the rest of the imperialists had entered at two undefended gates, and a scene ensued too horrible for description. Even a humane general might have found it impossible to restrain such troops in the moment of victory: but this the ferocious old man who commanded the imperialists did not even attempt. Some officers, who implored him to have mercy on the unresisting citizens, were ordered to return in an hour; "I will then," said he, "see what can be done, but the soldier must have something for his labour and danger." In less than half that time, the work of blood was at its height. The furious soldiers spared neither age nor sex. Almost all the men were beheaded, and a great number of the women. Two clergymen were slain as they stood before the altar. On entering the town Pappenheim had ordered some houses to be set on fire: the wind being strong the flames soon spread, and in a short time the whole city, with the exception of a few houses and the cathedral, was a heap of ashes. These scenes continued until the 13th, when Tilly himself entered, and restored discipline.

Four thousand persons, who had taken refuge in the fire-proof cathedral, were admitted to quarter, and for the first time during three days, obtained something to eat. It is said that they owed this favour to the vanity of Tilly, who was flattered at being addressed in a Latin oration by one of their preachers. The terrible commander, in a sort of masquerading dress, which at any other time would have excited laughter,—wearing a short jacket of green satin, and a high-crowned hat with a long red feather which drooped over his ghastly countenance, his whole appearance being, we are told, that of a lunatic mountebank,—rode slowly through the town, gloating on the heaps of dead bodies, with which the streets were covered. In a letter to the emperor, he speaks of this scene of murder and desolation as the greatest victory that had been achieved since the taking of Troy and Jerusalem. "And sincerely," he adds, "do I pity the ladies of your imperial family, that they could not be present as spectators of the same."

Gustavus Adolphus now resolved, come what might, no longer to spare the electors, whose indecision had caused this terrible calamity.

On the 11th of June he appeared before Berlin, and offered George William the choice either of instantly joining him, or seeing his capital laid in ashes. The terrified elector, after a little resistance, signed the treaty of alliance; and Gustavus garrisoned the fortresses of Berlin, Spandau, and Küstrin. Tilly, having been repulsed on the Hessian frontier, had marched to the great plain of Leipzic, in the hope of terrifying the elector of Saxony into an alliance; but that prince now declared himself on the side of the Swedes; and 18,000 Saxons having joined Gustavus Adolphus, the allied army advanced on Leipzic, which was already in the hands of Tilly. The difference between the Swedish and imperial armies, which now met for the first time, was very remarkable. In the camp of Gustavus religious service was regularly performed, sometimes to the army in general, on which occasions the king was always present, sometimes by the chaplain of each regiment to those more immediately intrusted to his charge. The kindness with which the Swedish soldiers treated the unarmed citizens and peasants, the strict morality of their lives, and the gentleness of their manners, rendered them universally objects of respect and love, and presented a striking contrast to the fearful oaths and shouts of licentious revelry with which Tilly's camp resounded day and night, and to the cruelties practised by his soldiers on the defenceless inhabitants.

The Swedish troops had lately been equipped by Gustavus Adolphus with a view to rapid movements: they therefore wore no armour, and were accompanied by only a very light train of field artillery. The imperialists, on the contrary, wore cuirasses, greaves, and helmets, had much less discipline among them than the Swedes, and were encumbered by heavy ordnance. Tilly had intended to await the coming up of two of his generals with reinforcements, before he engaged the enemy; although his own force amounted to 40,000 men, a number equal to that of the united Swedish and Saxon army : but the impetuous Pappenheim having entangled himself in a skirmish with the Swedes, Tilly was obliged to march to his assistance, muttering as he went, "That fellow will ruin me yet in honour and reputation, and the emperor in land and people." Gustavus Adolphus, dressed in a simple grey surtout, with a white hat and grey feather, rode in front of the line, and exhorted his men to fight bravely. The Swedes composed the right wing, the Saxons the left. Tilly's army formed, according to the ancient mode of warfare, one long line, but Gustavus had broken his force into several small masses. The imperial artillery was planted on a ridge of a low hill immediately behind the army.

The battle began on the 7th of September, 1631, with a furious cannonade, which lasted two hours. Then Tilly, abandoning his position on the hills, marched to meet the Swedes; but their fire was so galling, that he was obliged to make a movement to the right, and attack the Saxons, who soon fled in confusion. Meanwhile Pappenheim, at the head of his terrible cuirassiers, had seven times charged the Swedes, and as often been driven back with great loss. Whilst Tilly was engaged with the Saxons the Swedes attacked him in flank, captured his artillery, and turning it against himself, threw both him and Pappenheim into irrecoverable confusion. Four regiments of veterans, who had become grey in the imperial service, resolved to be cut to pieces rather than yield. In detached bodies, they forced their way through the midst of the victorious army, and reached a little wood, where they continued to fight till night came on. The rest of the army fled in disorder, pursued by the Swedes, who cut down hundreds of the fugitives. In all the villages around the tocsin was rung, and the peasants rushed out to wreak vengeance on their oppressors. Meanwhile Tilly, a veteran soldier of seventy-two years of age, who had never before either sustained a defeat or been wounded, stood like a monument of despair, stupified and motionless. Three bullets had already pierced his body; but he refused to surrender himself, and a Swedish officer (called by the soldiers "Long Fritz") was in the act of cutting him down, when he was rescued by duke Rudolph of Lauenburg. The miserable remains of his army took refuge in Haberstadt, where Tilly joined them. During his flight the curses of the peasants rang in his ears, and he was exasperated beyond measure at hearing everywhere the words of a rude song, in which his defeat was celebrated, and the chorus, "Fly, Tilly, fly!" howled by hundreds of voices. After this victory the country people rose in a mass, and joined the standard of Gustavus in such numbers, that in a few days his army was stronger than it had been before the battle.

Leaving his generals Baudis and Banner to follow up his successes in Northern Germany, Gustavus marched to Erfurt, and thence through the Thuringian forest to Wurtzburg, Frankfort, and Mainz. Spiers, Landau, and many other places had already declared for the Swedes; and the banks of the Rhine and the Neckar resounded with shouts of joy, as the army of the liberator advanced. The Swedish soldiers, on their part, delighted with the beauty of the country, and revelling in the unaccustomed luxuries of wine and wheaten bread, were eager to hold out the right-hand of fellowship to men who received them kindly. Ulm sent a deputation to congratulate Gustavus on his successes. The count Palatine Christian of Birkenfeld recruited for his army: Frederick of Bohemia returned to his palatinate: and to crown the satisfaction of the Swedish king, his wife Eleanora joined him at Frankfort.

Meanwhile "that old devil, Tilly," (as Gustavus

always called him,) had begun to rally, and after taking the town of Rotenburg, was entrenching himself in a strong position at Rain on the Lech, in order to cover Bavaria. Maximilian with a considerable force was also encamped in the same neighbourhood. The works on the Lech were nearly completed, when Gustavus advancing to the opposite bank of the river commenced a cannonade, which was kept up during three days without intermission. At the end of that time the imperialists became first aware that the enemy's engineers, under cover of the smoke, had succeeded in constructing a bridge, over which a considerable portion of their army had already crossed the river. In a transport of rage, Tilly rushed forward to meet the Swedes; but his course was arrested by a cannon ball, which shattered his thigh, and produced so ghastly a wound, that he shortly afterwards died in great agony, advising the emperor, with his last breath, at whatever sacrifice of life or treasure, to secure Ratisbon, the key of Austria and Bavaria.

Gustavus now marched to Augsburg, where he caused the Gospel to be proclaimed, and thence to Munich, the gates of which were opened to him on his promising to spare the place. By his side rode Frederick, the deposed king of Bohemia, accompanied by his queen, and a large monkey dressed in the frock and hood of the Capuchin friar. In different parts of the city were found one hundred and forty pieces of cannon, which the Bavarians had buried, after filling them to the muzzle with gold and precious stones. Maximilian would gladly have made peace, but Gustavus Adolphus in no very courtly language told him that he was not to be trusted, adding some coarse remarks, better suited to the manners of that day than to the more refined taste

WALLENSTEIN.

of modern readers. The loss of Tilly now compelled the emperor to enter into negotiation with the only general who was capable of commanding an imperial army at this critical juncture. Since his disgrace, Wallenstein had been living at Prague in more than regal state. His palace stood on the sites of several hundred houses, which had been pulled down to make room for the building: his gardens were full of handsome fountains and aviaries, some of which were so large that tall trees were enclosed within their wires; boys of noble family waited upon him as pages, and many of his former officers were still in his service. His smallest present was a thousand dollars; the lightest punishment which he inflicted was death. During his retirement he had been endeavouring to bring about an alliance between Denmark, Saxony, and the empire, under the auspices, as it was generally supposed, of the emperor himself, although he afterwards thought proper to deny that he had corresponded with the duke of Friedland on that or any other subject during his banishment.

The overtures of Ferdinand were received very coldly by Wallenstein, who refused to listen to any proposals until he was satisfied that the emperor was willing to reinstate him on terms dictated by himself. The conditions, which secured to him an irresponsible command, having been at last conceded, the new dictator commenced recruiting, and in a few months found himself at the head of a considerable army, with which he easily drove the Saxons out of Bohemia.

Gustavus Adolphus had wished to return to Bavaria, and carry the war into the heart of the Romanist states; but intelligence having reached him that Wallenstein had taken Leipzic, he at once determined to march northwards, and on the 27th of October arrived at Erfurt, where he took leave of his wife, with a melancholy foreboding that they were to meet no more on this side of the grave. On the 1st of November he reached Naumberg, whither the inhabitants of the surrounding country flocked in crowds to gaze on the hero. Wherever he appeared shouts of joy and affection welcomed him, thousands flinging themselves on their knees and struggling with one another for the privilege of kissing his feet or the sheath of his sword.

This homage, although only the outpouring of gratitude and admiration, grievously disconcerted Gustavus. "Is it not," he said to his attendants, "as though this people were making a God of me? I pray that the vengeance of the Almighty may not fall on us for this audacious mummery, and show these foolish crowds but too soon that I am only a poor, weak, sinful mortal." "Thus," says Schiller, "did he prove himself doubly worthy of their tears. as the moment drew nigh which was to bid them flow." Having discovered, through an intercepted letter, that Pappenheim had been detached to lay siege to Halle, and that the imperial troops were dispersed in winter quarters, Gustavus abandoned his intention of joining the elector, and advanced at once to attack Wallenstein. Three guns from the castle of Weissenfels gave the signal to the imperialists that the Swedish army was in sight. Wallenstein instantly drew his regiments together, and dispatched messengers to command the immediate return of Pappenheim.

On the 6th of November, Gustavus drew up his forces in nearly the same order which the year before had insured him the victory at Leipzic. The whole army formed two lines, having a canal on their right and in their rear, the high road in front, and the village of Lützen on their left. The infantry under count von Brake, occupied the centre, the cavalry the wings, and the artillery the front of the whole line. Duke Bernard of Saxe Weimar commanded the left wing, and the king himself with his Swedish cavalry took up his position on the right. The order of battle of the second line was the same as that of the first; and behind it was stationed a *corps de reserve* under the command of Henderson, a Scotchman.

DUKE BERNARD OF SAXE WEIMAR.

On the evening before the battle Wallenstein deepened the trenches on each side of the high road which divided the two armies, and placed a strong body of musketeers behind the mounds formed by the earth thrown out of them. In the rear of these was a battery of seven heavy guns; and on an eminence behind Lützen, on which stood a windmill, were planted fourteen lighter pieces, which commanded a great part of the field. The infantry, in five unwieldy divisions, were stationed about three hundred paces in the rear of the high road, their flanks being covered by cavalry. To conceal his weakness, Wallenstein ordered all the horse-boys and camp-servants to mount and form on the left wing, where they were to remain until the arrival of Pappenheim should supply their places with more efficient warriors. All these dispositions were made in the dead of night, and the two armies awaited the dawn of that bloody morning which should prove whether Gustavus was indebted for his previous successes to his own genius, or to the unskilfulness of his opponents. The day at length broke, but an impenetrable fog lay spread over the whole plain, and prevented any movement of the two armies until near mid-day.

In front of the Swedish line Gustavus Adolphus knelt down, and offered up his prayer to the God of battles, whilst the whole army raised Luther's battle-hymn, "A steadfast fortress is our God," the field music of the different regiments playing a solemn accompaniment. The king then mounted his horse, with no defence but a buff coat, the pain of a recent wound rendering the weight and pressure of his armour insupportable; and rode through the ranks, speaking cheerfully to the soldiers, and striving to inspire them with hopes which his own melancholy forebodings prevented him from feeling. "God with us," was the battle-cry of the Swedes; "Jesu Maria," that of the imperialists.

The fog in some measure dispersing about eleven o'clock, the two armies began to be visible to each other, and at the same moment the village of Lützen was discovered to be in flames, having been set on fire by order of the duke of Friedland, lest he should be outflanked on that side. Half an hour later Gustavus gave the signal of attack, and the Swedish infantry rushed forward to carry the trenches, but a murderous fire of artillery and small arms compelled them to retreat. The voice of Gustavus soon rallied them, and they fought with great fury, but without making any impression on the imperialists, until colonel Winkel, with a regiment of cavalry, forced his way across two of the trenches, followed by the Swedish body-guard. The battery was soon carried and the guns turned against the imperialists,—then retaken by Wallenstein,—and again carried by the Swedes, whose right wing was everywhere victorious, but their left, galled by the heavy fire from the windmill battery, was beginning to give way, when Gustavus rode forward for the purpose of rallying them. The swiftness of his horse rendering it impossible for the heavy cavalry to keep pace with their leader, he soon found himself almost alone in the midst of the enemy. Here a subaltern of the imperial army, observing the respect with which the unknown officer was treated by his few followers, naturally concluded that he was a person of importance, and called out to a musketeer, "Shoot that man, for I am sure he is an officer of high rank." The soldier immediately fired, and the king's left arm fell powerless by his side. At this moment a wild cry was raised, "The king bleeds; the king is wounded." "It is nothing," shouted Gustavus; "follow me." But the pain soon brought on faintness, and he desired the duke of Lauenburg, in French, to lead him out of the throng. Whilst the duke was endeavouring to withdraw him without being noticed by the troops, a second shot struck Gustavus, and deprived him of his little remaining strength. "I have enough, brother," he said, in a feeble voice to the duke; "try to save your own life." At the same moment he fell from his horse, and in a short time breathed his last. His horse, bathed in blood, and galloping wildly about the field, gave the first intimation to the Swedish

DEATH OF GUSTAVUS ADOLPHUS.

THE NEW YORK
PUBLIC LIBRARY

ASTOR, LENOX AND
TILDEN FOUNDATIONS
R   L

cavalry that their king had fallen: a furious struggle for the recovery of his remains then took place between them and the Croatians; and the disfigured corpse of Gustavus was soon buried beneath a heap of dead. Meanwhile, the sorrowful tidings had reached the main body, and goaded the Swedes almost to desperation. They fought with a fury which nothing could resist; and the enemy was already retreating, when Pappenheim appeared, and the battle began afresh. Nothing could exceed the fierceness of this second engagement. The Swedish yellow regiment, the flower of their army, lay dead, each man in his rank, without having yielded an inch of ground. Count Piccoluomini, one of the imperial generals, had seven horses shot under him, and received six wounds, but would not quit his post until the battle was decided. Wallenstein rode through the field like one bearing a charmed life: right and left his attendants fell, and his cloak was pierced through and through with bullets; yet he escaped unwounded, to fall at last by the hand of an assassin.

Pappenheim received two shots in his breast and was carried out of the battle. Whilst they were conveying him to the rear a rumour reached him that his great rival was slain. The countenance of the dying man brightened at this intelligence. "Tell the duke of Friedland," he said, "that I lie here without hope of life, but I die in peace, knowing that the enemy of my faith has also fallen." The mists of evening put an end to the fight. So little were the Swedes aware of the advantage which they had gained, that the question of an immediate retreat was seriously discussed between Bernard of Saxe Weimar and General Kniphausen; and great was their surprise when the light of morning made them aware that Wallenstein had withdrawn his troops and left them masters of the field. Had Pappenheim's reinforcement arrived a few hours earlier, the event would probably have been different; and even as it was, something might have been done to save the *materiel* of the army from falling into the enemy's hands; but Pappenheim's fall and the disabled condition of most of his men seemed to have paralysed the hitherto fearless spirit of Wallenstein; for leaving his artillery, his colours, and the greater part of his small arms on the field, he commenced a disorderly retreat towards Leipzic, and the next morning was followed by the miserable remnants of his army. He made, it is true, a feeble attempt to regain the ground, by sending out a body of Croatians to hover round the scene of action; but the sight of the Swedish army, drawn up in good order between Lützen and Weissenfels, soon scared away these irregular skirmishers; and Bernard of Saxe Weimar, who succeeded Gustavus in command of the Swedes, retained undisturbed possession of the field.

But the victory was dearly purchased. More than nine thousand men lay dead on the field of battle: the whole plain, from Lützen to the canal, was strewed with the wounded and the dying; the bodies of knights and nobles were mingled with those of the common soldiers; and even an ecclesiastic, the abbot of Fulda, whose zeal for his faith had brought him to the field as a spectator, paid the penalty of his rashness with his life. But the most melancholy feature of the Swedish triumph was the loss of him who had died to achieve it. For a long time the body of Gustavus Adolphus lay concealed under the heaps of nameless dead, who had fallen later in the day. At length it was discovered near a large stone between Lützen and the canal, covered with the most ghastly wounds, trampled on by horses' hoofs, and stripped of its clothes and ornaments by the hands of those wretches who follow a camp for the sake of plunder. Tears streamed down the cheeks of the rough soldiers as they followed in melancholy procession the remains of him who had so often led them to victory; and when the bereft widow embraced his corpse at Weissenfels, a dismal murmur ran through the ranks, like the wailing of children over the grave of a beloved father. The buff coat of Gustavus, covered with blood, had been torn from his body by the plunderers, and found its way to Vienna, where it was exhibited to the emperor, who, bursting into tears at the sight, exclaimed, " Gladly would I have allowed the unhappy man a longer life, and a joyful return to his country, if his death had not been necessary for the repose of Germany."

Thus fell, in the thirty-eighth year of his age, Gustavus Adolphus, the great protector of Protestantism in Germany.

Pappenheim died of his wounds at Leipzic the day after the battle. He had first distinguished himself at Prague, where, although severely wounded, and supported only by a few soldiers, he had put to flight a whole regiment of the enemy. As a second in command he was excellent, but his wild chivalrous courage rendered him unfit for the chief direction of an army. Tilly always maintained that the battle of Leipzic was lost through his rashness. Like that ferocious leader, he had dyed his hands in blood at Magdeburg; but the habits of his early life were studious and refined, and foreign travel had improved his natural capacity. Unfortunately, however, the fierceness of his temper broke through all restraints on the day of battle.— Superstition maintained that this warlike character was stamped by nature on his brow; and it is certain that whenever violent passion caused the blood to rush into his face, two red lines appeared on his forehead, giving a strangely savage expression to the whole countenance.

A messenger was on the way from Madrid to bring him the order of the golden fleece, when death rendered all worldly distinctions valueless.

The war in which Gustavus Adolphus defended the Protestant cause, known as the Thirty Years' War, was finally terminated by the peace of Westphalia, signed October 24th, 1648, which established the relative claims of the Catholic and Protestant parties on a basis which has remained almost undisturbed to the present day.

CHARLES IX.

MASSACRE OF ST. BARTHOLOMEW.

SAINT Bartholomew's Day, is a feast of the church, celebrated, August 24, in honour of St. Bartholomew. The horrid slaughter of the Huguenots, in France, took place on St. Bartholomew's day, under the reign of Charles IX., in 1572. After the death of Francis II., Catharine of Medicis became regent in the place of her son, Charles IX., then only 10 years old, and was compelled, in spite of the opposition of the Guises, to issue an edict of toleration in

FRANCIS, DUKE OF GUISE.

favour of the Protestants. The party of the Guises now persuaded the nation, that the Catholic religion was in the greatest danger. The Huguenots were treated in the most cruel manner; prince Conde took up arms; the Guises had recourse to the Spaniards, Conde to the English, for assistance. Both parties were guilty of the most atrocious cruelties, but finally concluded peace. The queen-mother caused the king, who had entered his 14th year, to be declared of age, that she might govern more absolutely under his name. Duke Francis de Guise had been assassinated by a Huguenot, at the siege of Orleans; but his spirit continued in his family, which considered the admiral Coligny as the author of his murder. The Huguenots soon found, that the queen-mother still hated them; and Conde and Coligny, therefore, kept

ADMIRAL COLIGNY.

themselves on their guard. The king had been persuaded that the Huguenots had designs on his life, and had conceived an implacable hatred against them. Meanwhile the court endeavoured to gain time, in order to seize the persons of the prince and the admiral by stratagem, but was disappointed, and hostilities were renewed with more violence than ever. In the battle of Jarnac, 1569, Conde was made prisoner, and shot by the captain de Montesquieu. Coligny collected the remains of the routed army; the young prince Henry de Bearn (afterwards Henry IV., king of Navarre and France,) the head of the Protestant party after the death of Conde, was appointed commander-in-chief, and Coligny commanded in the name of the prince Henry de Conde, who swore to revenge the murder of his father. But he was destitute of means, and was unsuccessful. The advantageous offers of

CATHARINE OF MEDICIS.

peace at St. Germain-en-Laye (August 8, 1570,) blinded the chiefs of the Huguenots, particularly the admiral Coligny who was wearied with civil war. The king appeared to have entirely disengaged himself from the influences of the Guises and his mother: he invited the old Coligny, the support of the Huguenots, to his court, and honoured him as a father. The most artful means were employed to increase this delusion. The sister of the king was married to the prince de Bearn (August 18, 1572,) in order to allure the most distinguished Huguenots to Paris. Some of his friends endeavoured to dissuade the admiral from this visit; but he could not be convinced that the king would command an assassination of the Protestants throughout his kingdom. August 22, a shot from a window wounded the admiral. The king hastened to visit him, and swore to punish the author of the vi!

lany; but, on the same day, he was induced, by his mother, to believe that the admiral had designs on his life. "God's death!" he exclaimed; "kill the admiral; and not only him, but all the Huguenots; let none remain to disturb us!" The following night, Catharine held the bloody council, which fixed the execution for the night of St. Bartholomew, August 24, 1572. After the assassination of Coligny, a bell from the tower of the royal palace, at midnight, gave to the assembled companies of burghers the signal for the general massacre of the Huguenots. The prince of Conde and the King of Navarre saved their lives by going to mass, and pretending to embrace the Catholic religion. By the king's orders, the massacre was extended through the whole kingdom; and if, in some provinces, the officers had honour and humanity enough to disobey the orders to butcher their innocent fellow citizens, yet instruments were always found to continue the massacre. This horrible slaughter continued for thirty days, in almost all the provinces: the victims are calculated at 30,000. At Rome the cannons were discharged, the pope ordered a jubilee and a procession to the church of St. Louis, and caused Te Deum to be chanted. Those of the Huguenots who escaped fled into the mountains and to Rochelle. The duke of Anjou laid siege to that city, but, during the siege, received the news that the Poles had elected him their king. He concluded a treaty, July 6, 1573, and the king granted to the Huguenots the exercise of their religion in certain towns. The court gained nothing by the massacre of St. Bartholomew (called, in French ultra papers, in 1824, *une rigueur salutaire*.) The Huguenots were afterwards more on their guard, and armed themselves against new attacks.

Among the more distinguished victims of the massacre of St. Bartholomew, was Pierre Ramus, a learned and celebrated Calvinistic divine. He was residing at Paris when this event took place, pursuing his studies, attended by a young student. During the tumult he concealed himself in an upper room with very small hopes of escape. He was at last discovered by his enemies and severely wounded. He was then thrown into the street, where his body was horribly mangled and dragged about.

Charles IX., who took an active part in the massacre, did not long survive it. He died in horrible torments, and the most vivid terrors of a troubled conscience.

RAMUS EXPECTING THE COMING OF HIS ASSASSINS.

HENRY III.

RELIGIOUS WAR IN FRANCE IN THE REIGN OF HENRY III.

THE members of the Catholic league in the time of Henry III., successor to Charles IX. of France, were bent on the total extirpation of the Protestants. Henry III. was the nominal head of the league; but the massacre of St. Bartholomew was too much for him. He was disgusted and shocked with the horrible cruelty of that proceeding, and he was so moderate in his counsels, that the leaguers hated and despised him. The real leader of the league was Henry, duke of Guise.

Elizabeth, the protestant queen of England, about this time laid an indelible stain upon her glory, by ordering the execution of Mary Stuart, the widow of Francis II., and catholic queen of Scotland; who, flying from her rebellious subjects, had sought an asylum in the dominions of her rival. Elizabeth could not pardon Mary either the superiority of her charms or the title of queen of England, which she had assumed. She kept her in captivity nineteen years; and sent her to the scaffold, at last. The tragical death of this queen, sister-in-law to the king of France, contributed, as much as the defeat of Coutras, to increase the savage zeal of the leaguers, and their contempt for Henry III. That prince had given to his favourite D'Epernon, who was detested by the people, the succession of Joyeuse; and abandoned himself anew, to his frivolous occupations, studying grammar, and learning to decline in the midst of his puppy-dogs, his parrots and his minions. Henri de Guise, however, as prudent as he was brave and ambitious, grew daily in the public estimation, and the league redoubled its audacity. The faction of the Sixteen, in particular, began about this time to render itself formidable. Paris was then governed by a municipal system: the citizens had the guarding of the walls and of the principal posts; and the *echevins** kept the keys of the gates. In each of the sixteen quarters of the city, a sort of council was established, wherein the interests of the holy union were discussed; and whence the chief of the assembly after-

---

* The echevins were magistrates, whose office was analogous to that of an English sheriff.—*Tr.*

IN THE REIGN OF HENRY III. 267

HENRI, DUC DE GUISE.

wards went, to make his report to the council-general of the league. Each of these chiefs being agitated by the same passions, and all having the same interests to support, they were accustomed to assemble together; and thus was formed the celebrated council of Sixteen, of which Bussy le Clerc, formerly a fencing-master, was one of the most violent members. They formed many plots against the liberty of Henry III.; but, constantly betrayed by one of the conspirators, named Nicolas Poulain,—they failed in all their projects. The king, well acquainted with their designs and power, and secretly pressed by Henry of Navarre to form an alliance with him, had serious thoughts of flinging himself into the arms of that party. Then, suddenly assuming a vigorous resolution, he forbade Guise to approach Paris. For want, however, of twenty-five crowns in the treasury, to pay a courier, the king's letter was delivered to the duke by post,—who denied having received it.

Summoned by the leaguers, he entered Paris amid the acclamations of the multitude. His slender escort became swelled, as he passed along, with an idolizing crowd, eager to see him and touch his person or his garments. The people named him the new Gideon—the new Maccabeus. "France," says an historian of the time, "was mad about that man." He alighted at the queen's residence, who conducted him, without guards, to the Louvre, and into the presence of her son. The king deliberated whether he should not cause him to be instantly stabbed:—colonel Alphonso offered his arm for the purpose, but Henry hesitated. —"Why have you come in defiance of my orders?" said he to the duke, as soon as he saw him. Guise pretended that he had not received them; and added, that he was there for the purpose of justifying himself against the calumnies of which he was the object. Then, alarmed at the savage looks of the attendants, he bowed, and retired. On the following day, he came to the Louvre again, but well attended, and more disposed to prescribe the law than to receive it. He demanded that a war of extermination should be waged against the Huguenots, and that the favourites D'Épernon, La Vallette, and all suspected persons, should be driven from the court. The weak monarch yielded, on condition that the duke should assist him to clear Paris of all foreigners, and men without ostensible objects. Guise promised, and the people murmured loudly. The king summoned around him his nobles in arms, and called four thousand Swiss into Paris. They entered, with swords drawn and flags flying. (1588.) The sight of these soldiers rendered the people furious, and excited a general rising. The pavements were soon broken up, and the windows furnished with stones;—chains were drawn across the streets; and, behind these, the multitude threw up a thousand impromptu barricades. The royal troops beheld themselves surrounded, and attacked on all sides, without hope of safety, or chance of retreat. The affrighted king entreated the duc de Guise to put a stop to the confusion and bloodshed. "They are like bulls let loose," coolly replied the duke, "I cannot restrain them." At length, when he considered the time to have come in which he might act, he quitted his hotel, and showed himself to the people, with a wand in his hand. At sight of him, the crowd broke out into frenzied transports, and the barricades fell before him. Guise penetrated to the posts of the unfortunate Swiss, put an end to the combat, opened a way for their escape, and saved their lives. Catherine de Medici hastened to the scene of action, and was carried, over the barricades, to the side of Guise, —with whom she entered into negotiation. He demanded the disinheritance of the Bourbons,—the lieutenancy-general of the kingdom for himself,— hostage-cities,—money,—and war. Catherine prolonged the conference; in the midst of which intelligence was brought to the duke, that the king had fled from Paris. At these unexpected tidings, "Madame," he said, "I am a dead man; the king has departed for my destruction." Henry III., under cover of the tumult, had quitted Paris at full gallop; nor did he deem himself secure until he had reached Chartres,— where he was joined by his troops and his court. This famous day, on which the populace delivered up Paris to the duc de Guise, is known in history as the Day of the Barricades (*la journee des barricades.*)

Guise turned his victory to account, by exercising

the functions of king, ere he assumed the title. He called the people together, created new city officers and additional captains; and then requested the first president, Achille de Harlai, to assemble the parliament, for the purpose of concerting with him such measures as the circumstances required. But that magistrate answered him in these bold and severe words:—" It is a great pity when the valet drives away his master. For me, my soul belongs to God, my heart to the king, and my body is at the disposal of the wicked." Guise still insisting:—" When the majesty of the prince is invaded," intrepidly replied Harlai, "the magistrate has no longer authority." The president Brisson, however, showed himself more pliant, and lent himself to the wishes of Guise. The latter, having failed in his project of getting possession of the king's person, laboured to repel all suspicion of violence from himself. He was unwilling that any should reproach him with having driven away his master before he had it in his power to crush him. He aimed therefore, secretly counselled by Catherine de Medici, at appeasing Henry's anger, and instilled the same desire into the minds of the people. The Parisians, acquainted with the king's taste for processions, conceived the idea of leading one as far as Chartres, and the chiefs of the league encouraged this fancy. Their fiery friends, the monks of all orders, and the most dissolute women, each clad as a penitent, insisted on taking part in this extravagant procession. Henri de Joyeuse, a courtier who had turned monk, walked at their head, under the name of *frere Ange*. Two capuchins were by his side, representing, one the Virgin, and the other, the Magdalen. Frère Ange carried with difficulty an enormous cross of pasteboard; and four powerful attendants scourged him, when he exhibited signs of weakness. Trumpets and kettles announced the march of the train. The frivolous monarch, contrary to general expectation, exhibited only disgust, and saw in this procession of penitents but so many rebels. The negotiations, nevertheless, proceeded, and Henry consented to treat with the duc de Guise. The famous edict of union appeared by which the king seemed to have surrendered himself up into the hands of his enemy. By this edict he bound himself to destroy the heretics to the last man; he disinherited Henri de Bourbon of the crown, named Guise generalissimo, with absolute powers,—and abandoned to him certain fortresses, as pledges, for several years.

These concessions, however, were but a cover to the king's real designs. He had already formed an important resolution; and, in order to its accomplishment, the states-general were convoked anew at Blois. Henri de Guise and the cardinal, his brother, boldly presented themselves there. The greater proportion of deputies were members of the league; and in the opening session, during the monarch's discourse, all eyes were turned upon the duc de Guise as on the true king. His project, which, notwithstanding his great subtlety, he scarcely disguised, was to depose the feeble Henry, and cause himself to be proclaimed in his stead. His pride took delight in listening to his imprudent friends who compared him to Pepin, while they branded the monarch with the name of the idler-king. His sister, the fiery duchesse de Montpensier, transported with rage against Henry III., carried in her girdle a pair of golden scissors, destined, as she said, to shape the monkish crown of the new Chilpéric. These rash speeches were reported to the king, who, without consulting the queen-mother, took at once a violent and decisive part. He partook of the holy sacrament in company with his enemy, and, in sharing the host with him at the sacred table, vowed friendship for the future, and oblivion of the past: at that very moment, he had secretly resolved upon his fellow-communicant's death! A murderer was wanted by Henry; and he cast his eyes upon the forty-five gentlemen of his guard. He sounded, first, the brave Crillon, their chief, who nobly refused. Crillon offered to challenge the duc de Guise to private combat, and to smite him at the peril of his life,—but not as an assassin. Henry commanded him to secrecy. Lognac proposed himself; and the king intrusted the matter to his arm. The hour and place were fixed; but vague rumours got abroad. The partisans of Guise were alarmed, and threatening whispers reached him, in all directions. One day, he found under his napkin, a note, which informed him of the king's designs: without disturbing himself, he wrote, at the bottom—'*he dares not*,' —and flung the note under the table. The next day, (23rd of December,) he presented himself at the council; the door was instantly shut upon him, the guard took arms, and an officer informed him that he was sent for, by the king. He turned in the direction of the royal closet; and was entering, when an assassin plunged a dagger into his throat. Lognac and the guards struck him down; and he fell, pierced with many wounds, before the king's eyes,—who trampled him under foot, as Guise himself had formerly trampled under foot the body of Coligni. His relatives and friends were immediately arrested; and the cardinal, his brother, was assassinated, in his prison.

Such was the bloody catastrophe of the States of Blois. Catherine de' Medici survived the Lorraine princes but a few days. Faithful to her system of seeking for strength wherever she thought it might be found, she had never wholly broken with them; and t is even probable that she, more than once, betrayed

ASSASSINATION OF THE DUKE OF GUISE.

her son, for the purpose of securing the homage and support of the Guises. Their death disturbed her spirit; on being informed of it, she said to the king: —'it is well cut-out my son, but it has to be sewn.' Henry failed to profit by her advice: he remained undecided—omitted to march upon Paris, where the storm was gathering—and swore anew the edict of union, before dissolving the States. He had suffered several prisoners, of great importance, to escape him. His two most formidable enemies, the dukes of Mayenne and Aumale, brothers of the murdered Guises, remained at liberty, although they had been closely pursued, and hastened to stir the people and army to revolt. But the rage of the Parisians had no need of stimulus: the news of the fatal event at Blois provoked the violent explosion of their hatred and fury. Fanatical preachers, at whose head the curé Lincestre distinguished himself, thundered, from the pulpit, against the assassin, and poured forth anathemas on his head. Children, and women, and half-naked men, passed in procession, with tapers in their hands around the cemetery of the Innocents; and there, extinguishing their flambeaux, cried aloud:—'Thus be extinguished the accursed race of Valois!' The duc de Mayenne was proclaimed lieutenant-general of the kingdom; the powers of the Sixteen were confirmed, the half-mad Bussy le Clerc, governor of the Bastille, shut up in that fortress the greater part of those members of the parliament, who were opposed to these disorders; and a new parliament was instituted.

All hope of conciliation with the partisans of the Guises had vanished for Henry III. Sixtus V. redoubled the audacity of the king's enemies, by refusing to absolve him for the murder of the cardinal; and excommunicated him, by the famous bull *In cœna Domini*. On the point of being invested, by Mayenne, in Tousa, one only resource remained to Henry; and he seized it, by allying himself to the king of Navarre, whom he had so recently disinherited. (1589)—'Against the thunders of Rome,' said the Naverrese to him, 'there is but one remedy—victory: after that, you will be instantly absolved, doubt it not. But, if you are vanquished, you will remain excommunicated, branded—aye, doubly branded.' The interview between the two monarchs took place in the Chateau of Plessis-les-Tours. The frankness and honesty of the king of Navarre soon won the confidence, and touched the heart, of Henry III. After a brilliant triumph achieved by La Noue, at Senlis, the two kings advanced together upon Paris. Bourbon fixed his camp at Meudon,—and Henry pitched his on the heights of Saint-Cloud; from whence, contemplating his capital, he gave vent to his anger, in these words: —'Oh Paris, head of the kingdom, but head too huge and capricious, thou hast need of bleeding, for thy cure,—as well as all the rest of France, for the frenzy communicated to it by thee.' But time and power both failed him for the accomplishment of his threat. The monks, Jesuits and curés openly preached the doctrine of regicide, in Paris. A wretched enthusiast, named Jacques Clément, excited to fanaticism by their words, and also by the duchesse de Montpensier, who, in her frantic hatred, is said to have purchased a promise of murder with her favours, made a vow to assassinate the king. The unfortunate man repaired, on the 1st of August, to the camp of Henry III., and asked to speak with him. Being introduced into his tent, he fell on his knees; and, presenting a petition to the monarch, struck him, at the same moment, in the lower part of the belly, with a knife. The king withdrew the weapon from the wound, and smote the assassin with it, in the forehead,—who was instantly

ASSASSINATION OF HENRY III.

IN THE REIGN OF HENRY III. 279

dispatched by the guards. Henry's wound was mortal: he died in the arms of the king of Navarre, whom he named as his successor, advising him to embrace the catholic faith, if he desired to reign over France. The pope, Sixtus V., declared Henry unworthy of Christian burial. In full consistory, he exalted Jacques Clement above Judith and Eleazar; and ordered a magnificent funeral service, for the repose of his soul. With Henry III. the house of Valois became extinct,—after having reigned two hundred and sixty-one years, and given thirteen kings to France.

LOUIS XIII.

HENRY IV.

DECLINE OF THE PROTESTANT POWER IN FRANCE.

ENRY III., before his death, named the king of Navarre his successor; and that prince immediately assumed the title of Henry IV. But the adherents of Henry in the field only numbered six thousand men, and being pursued by the duke of Mayenne with four times that number, he was compelled to retire to Dieppe. But Henry now exerted himself to the utmost; rallied his troops, and brought the enemy to a decisive battle on the plains of Ivry, near Paris. After a close and bloody struggle, the king gained a complete victory. Paris was then besieged, and, being reduced to extremity, the people

HENRY IV. AT IVRY.

THE NEW YORK
PUBLIC LIBRARY

ASTOR, LENOX AND
TILDEN FOUNDATIONS
R   L

opened their gates to the conqueror, who then entered the city in triumph. Henry IV. strove to conciliate the Catholics. Finding that he could not be secure as a Protestant, he publicly renounced that faith, and was then acknowledged king by all. The Protestants, however, obtained an establishment of their privileges by the edict of Nantes. Henry was fortunate in possessing a wise, firm, and fearless minister in the duke of Sully, whose conduct checked the generous imprudence of the king, and secured a vigorous and beneficial administration of the government. In 1600, Henry IV. married Mary of Medicis, who in the next year gave him a son—afterwards Louis XIII. Some disputes in Germany, in which the interests of France were compromised, caused Henry to resolve to take the field in support of the national honour. But, while the army waited for his presence, he was assassinated by one Ravaillac, as he was going to visit the duke of Sully. Thus died a great and good monarch, after a reign which had proved so beneficial as to gain him the title of the father of his country, (A. D. 1610.)

The renunciation of the Protestant religion by Henry IV. was an act in which religious duty was sacrificed to political expediency; and as usual in such cases, the consequences were most disastrous. From the hour of Henry's apostacy the Protestant interest declined. The example of the king served to detach from the cause the powerful nobles who had been its chief supporters. The Protestants however were very numerous among the people, and under the edict of Nantes, they enjoyed a limited toleration until the latter part of the reign of Louis XIV. who under Jesuit dictation repealed the Edict of Nantes and drove nearly all the Protestants out of the kingdom. In the French Revolution of 1789, the people passed at one bound from the bigotry of Romanism to the open and public avowal of Atheism. Napoleon restored the forms of Romanism, and the Jesuits recovered their power under Charles X.

Infidelity however is still predominant among all classes of the men, especially the educated, while numerous earnest devotees to the Catholic religion are found among the women. Michelet, in a recent work, has shown how completely the women of France are subjected to the influence of Catholic priests and confessors. Truly the apostacy of the model king Henry IV. has been followed by disastrous consequences.

CHARLES X.

A PURITAN.

THE PURITANS.

PURITANS, a name given in the primitive church to the Novatians, because they would never admit to communion any one who, from dread of death, had apostatised from the faith; but the word had been chiefly applied to those who were professed favourers of a further degree of reformation and purity in the church before the Act of Uniformity, in 1662. After this period, the term Nonconformists became common, to which succeeds the appellation Dissenter.

"During the reign of queen Elizabeth, in which the royal prerogative was carried to its utmost limits, there were found many daring spirits who questioned the right of the sovereign to prescribe and dictate to her subjects what principles of religion they should profess, and what forms they ought to adhere to. The ornaments and habits worn by the clergy in the preceding reign, when the Romish religion and rites were triumphant, Elizabeth was desirous of preserving in the Protestant service. This was the cause of great discontent among a large body of her subjects; multitudes refused to attend at those churches where the habits and ceremonies were used; the conforming clergy they treated with contumely; and, from the superior purity and simplicity of the modes of worship to which they adhered, they obtained the name of *Puritans*. The queen made many attempts to repress every thing that appeared to her as an innovation in the religion established by her authority, but without success: by her almost unlimited authority she readily checked open and avowed opposition, but she could not extinguish the principles of the Puritans, 'by whom alone,' according to Mr. Hume, 'the precious spark of liberty had been kindled and was preserved, and to whom the English owe the whole freedom of their constitution.' Some secret attempts that had been made by them to establish a separate congregation and discipline, had been carefully repressed by the strict hand which Elizabeth held over all her subjects. The most, therefore, that they could effect was, to assemble in private houses, for the purpose of worshipping God according to the dictates of their own consciences. These practices were at first connived at, but afterwards every means was taken to suppress them, and the most cruel methods were made use of to discover persons who were disobedient to the royal pleasure."

The severe persecutions carried on against the Puritans during the reigns of Elizabeth and the Stuarts, served to lay the foundation of a new empire in the western world. Thither, as into a wilderness, they fled from the face of their persecutors, and, being protected in the free exercise of their religion, continued to increase, till in about a century and a half they became an independent nation. The different principles, however, on which they originally divided from the church establishment at home, operated in a way that might have been expected when they came to the possession of the civil power abroad. Those who formed the colony of Massachusset's Bay, having never relinquished the principles of a national church, and of the power of the civil magistrate in matters of faith and worship, were less tolerant than those who settled at New Plymouth, at Rhode island, and at Providence Plantations. The very men (and they were good men too) who had just escaped the persecutions of the English prelates, now in their turn persecuted others who dissented from them, till at length the liberal system of toleration established in the parent country at the revolution extending to the colonies, in a good measure put an end to these proceedings.

Neither the Puritans before the passing of the Bartholomew act in 1662, nor the Nonconformists after it, appear to have disapproved of the articles of the established church in matters of *doctrine*. The number of them who did so, however, was very small. While the great body of the bishops and clergy had from the days of archbishop Laud abandoned their own articles in favour of Arminianism, they were attached to the principles of the first reformers; and by their labours and suffering the spirit of the Reformation was kept alive in the land. But after the revolution, one part of the Protestant Dissenters, chiefly Presbyterians, first veered towards Arminianism, then revived the Arian controversy, and by degrees many of them settled in Socinianism. At the same time another part of them, chiefly independents and Baptists, earnestly contending for the doctrines of grace, and conceiving, as it would seem, that the danger of erring lay entirely on one side, first veered towards high Calvinism; then forebore the unregenerate to repent, believe, or to do any thing practically good, and by degrees, many of them, it is said, settled in Antinomianism.

Such are the principles which have found place amongst the descendants of the Puritans. At the same time, however, it must be acknowledged that a goodly number of each of the three denominations have adhered to the doctrine and spirit of their forefathers; and have proved the efficacy of their principles by their concern to be holy in all manner of conversation.

OLIVER CROMWELL.

THE PURITANS IN ENGLAND.

THE civil war in England by which a revolution was effected, and king Charles I. dethroned and beheaded, was essentially a religious war. The leaders in it were contending for civil liberty, it is true; but really and avowedly their main object was freedom of conscience, religious liberty, for the enjoyment of which both previous and subsequent events in British history show, that the establishment of civil liberty was essential.

Whatever may be said in disparagement of Cromwell, who became a despot in the sequel, it is certain that his early triumphs were conquests of the Bible truths drawn from the Holy Word. The inspiration of the heroes who dethroned the faithless despot, Charles I. was sacred truth. Most of the great men who commenced the struggle in concert with Cromwell, were sincere, earnest Christians. Nearly all of the most distinguished patriots fell before the war was closed. Sir Henry Vane, the younger, one of the best men that ever lived, opposed the ambitious designs of Cromwell, and was persecuted and imprisoned for his noble opposition to the usurper. He survived, Cromwell, however, and became the most illustrious martyr to the good cause, in the reign of Charles II.

In Vane we recognize the real Christian spirit which directed the grand march of the Revolution; while the political apostacy of Cromwell like the religious apostacy of Henry IV. produced disastrous consequences and retarded the progress of both civil and religious freedom, the spirit that was in Sir Harry Vane still found an abode in many noble bosoms in Old England. This spirit survived the licentious and disgraceful reign of Charles II. defied the tyranny of James II. compelled his abdication and brought forth its legitimate fruits in the second English revolution, called, we think with perfect justice, the glorious revolution of 1688. But for the Puritan spirit, England would long since have shared the fate of France and become half catholic and half infidel. But let us follow the Puritans to America and see what conquests of Bible truths were accomplished by them in our own country.

JAMES I.

THE PURITANS IN AMERICA.

In the year 1610, says a recent historian, a congregation of these people, expelled by royal and ecclesiastical tyranny from their native country, England, had removed to Leyden, where they were permitted to establish themselves in peace under the ministry of their pastor, John Robinson. This excellent person may be justly regarded as the founder of the sect of Independents, or as it is customary to call them in

New England, Congregationalists. The most important feature of their ecclesiastical system is the independence of each church or congregation, and of all bishops, synods, or councils, and its direct dependence on the Head of the Christian church himself. The preaching of such a doctrine could not but offend the government of England. It drew down upon the devoted heads of its disciples the most determined persecution from Elizabeth and James, and exasperated the civil war, which, terminating in the dethronement of Charles I., finally gave the ascendency to the puritans.

It was to avoid the persecution of James I. that the English exiles composing Mr. Robinson's congregation, remained for ten years at Leyden. But, at the end of that period, the same pious views which had originally prompted their departure from England, incited them to undertake a more distant migration. The manners of the Dutch, and especially their neglect of a reverential observance of Sunday, made them apprehensive that the lapse of a single generation would obliterate every trace of the puritan character among their descendants. It was determined, therefore, to seek a new home in some foreign dependency of England. They at first cast their eyes upon Guiana, of which Raleigh had given a glowing description; but subsequently decided to seek an establishment in Virginia. Agents were despatched to England to obtain permission from the king. James, although desirous to promote the increase of the colony which had been planted under his auspices, was unwilling to sanction their religious opinions by taking them under his protection. The utmost he would promise was, to connive at their practices and refrain from molesting them. After accepting this precarious security, they procured from the Plymouth Company a grant of a tract of land, lying, as was supposed, within the limits of its patent; a partnership or joint-stock company was formed, on disadvantageous terms, with certain merchants in London, in order to raise the funds necessary to defray the expenses of emigration and settlement. Two vessels were obtained; the Speedwell of sixty, and the Mayflower of one hundred and eighty tons burthen; in which a hundred and twenty of their number were appointed to embark from an English port for America. These were to act as the pioneers of the whole congregation. They were destined to figure in the new world's history as the celebrated Pilgrims of New England.

They sought retirement—isolation—an opportunity of founding a small community of Puritans, where, apart from all the world, their peculiar doctrines could be transmitted from father to son, without attracting the notice of king or bishop. But they had a higher destiny. They were, in fact, to become the most efficient among the founders of a great empire, in which their own principles should flourish for ages after, and a more liberal system of civil and religious freedom should be learned and taught by their descendants.

All things being prepared for the departure of this detachment of the congregation from Delft haven, where they took leave of their friends, for the English port of embarkation, Robinson and his people devoted their last meeting in Europe to an act of solemn and social worship, intended to implore a blessing from heaven upon the enterprise in which they were about to engage.

The pilgrims sailed from Delft haven on the 22d of July, 1620, for Southampton, whence, after remaining a fortnight, they sailed for America; but they were compelled by the bad condition of the Speedwell and the treachery of its captain, to put back twice before their final departure. The Speedwell was abandoned; a portion of the company, who were dismayed at the evident dangers of the voyage, were dismissed, reducing their number to one hundred and one, including women and children. This company were all crowded into the Mayflower, which set sail from Plymouth on the 6th of September, 1620, bearing the founders of New England across the Atlantic. Never did so frail a bark carry so precious a burden.

The voyage was long and boisterous, and the captain of their vessel, through ignorance or treachery, instead of landing them at Hudson river, whither they were bound, carried them to the north as far as Cape Cod, where they arrived, on the 11th of November. This district was not included in the patent which they had obtained in England; and to supply the want of a more formal title, they composed and signed a written constitution of government, recognising the authority of the English crown, and expressing their own combination into a body politic (November 11th) and their determination to enact all just and necessary laws, and to honour them by due obedience. They then proceeded to elect John Carver for their governor, to serve for one year.

The selection of a spot for their settlement was attended with considerable difficulty and delay. On the 11th of November, some men were sent on shore to obtain wood and make discoveries; but they returned at night, without having met with any person or habitation. On the 15th, Captain Miles Standish, the military leader of the colony, landing for the purpose of exploration with sixteen armed men, observed and followed some Indians without overtaking them; but coming upon a deserted village, they found and examined some graves, but left the arms and imple-

LANDING OF THE PILGRIMS.

THE NEW YORK
PUBLIC LIBRARY

ASTOR, LENOX AND
TILDEN FOUNDATIONS

ments, which they found in them, undisturbed, "because they would not be guilty of violating the repositories of the dead. But when they found a cellar, carefully lined with bark and covered with a heap of sand, in which four bushels of seed corn were well secured, after reasoning on the morality of the action, they took as much of the corn as they could carry, intending, when they should find the owners, to repay them to their satisfaction." This intention was subsequently fulfilled, and to the providential discovery of this seed corn they attributed the ultimate preservation of the colony. During the absence of this exploring party, the wife of William White gave birth to a son, who, from the circumstances of his birth, was named Peregrine. He was the first Anglo-American born in New England.

On the sixth of December, Carver, Bradford, Winslow, and Standish, with some seamen, embarked in a shallop, and sailed round the bay in search of a place for settlement. On landing they were saluted with a flight of Indian arrows; but a discharge of musketry speedily dispersed the assailants. A storm came on. The shallop lost its rudder, and was nearly shipwrecked. Reaching an island on the 9th, they reposed themselves and kept the Christian Sabbath with the usual solemnities. The next day a harbour was found, which they deemed commodious, and the surrounding country was pleasant and well watered. They returned with the agreeable intelligence to their friends, and the ship was brought into this harbour on the 15th. The 18th and 19th were passed in exploring the land; on the 20th, after imploring the Divine guidance and protection, the people landed and commenced the settlement. This day is still celebrated by the descendants of the pilgrims as the anniversary of New England's birth.

DEATH OF CARVER.

They gave the town the name of Plymouth, in remembrance of the hospitalities they had received at the last port in England from which they had sailed. Their first operations consisted in measuring out the land to the different families, laying a platform for their ordnance, and erecting habitations. It was not till the 31st of December, that they were able to celebrate the Sabbath, with its appropriate exercises, in a house on shore.

The hardships undergone by the people in exploring the bay and effecting a landing, sowed the seeds of fatal disease; their provisions were scanty; the winter was severe; and the Indians, remembering the kidnapping exploits of Hunt and others, were hostile. More than half the colonists, including John Carver their governor, died before spring. Those who retained their strength were hardly sufficient to minister to the urgent wants of the sick and dying. In this employ-

THE PURITANS IN AMERICA. 299

TREATY WITH MASSASOIT.

ment, no one distinguished himself more than Carver, the governor. He was a man of fortune, who had spent all in the service of the colony, and readily sacrificed his life in discharging the humblest offices of kindness to the sick. He was succeeded by William Bradford, who was re-elected for many successive years, notwithstanding his remonstrance, that "if this office were an honour, it should be shared by his fellow citizens, and if it were a burden, the weight of it should not always be imposed upon him."

It appears that previous to the arrival of the pilgrims in New England, a sweeping pestilence had carried off whole tribes of natives, in the region where they had now settled. The traces of former habitation were apparent; but no Indians were found residing in their immediate vicinity. The spring, which restored health to the colonists, brought them also an agreeable surprise, in the visit of some Indians whose disposition was friendly. The visit of Samoset, whose previous intercourse with the English fishermen enabled him to salute them with "Welcome, welcome, Englishmen!" was followed by that of Massasoit, the principal sachem of the country, with whom the celebrated treaty was concluded, which was inviolably observed, for more than fifty years, and contributed, during that period, more than any other circumstance, to secure New England from the horrors of Indian warfare.

This treaty with Massasoit was one of the most important events in the history of New England. It averted, in a great measure, from Massachusetts, the horrors of Indian warfare, for half a century.

DEATH OF LADY ARABELLA JOHNSON.

THE NEW YORK
PUBLIC LIBRARY

ASTOR, LENOX AND
TILDEN FOUNDATIONS
R   L

SETTLEMENT OF BOSTON.

THE PURITANS IN AMERICA.

SETTLEMENT OF MASSACHUSETTS.

HE colony of New Plymouth was governed by a company in London. The great mortality which prevailed in the colony at its first settlement and the hardships which the people underwent deterred many of the puritans from emigrating! but the consideration, that the general courts were held, the officers elected, and the laws enacted in London, had still greater influence. It did not comport with the views and feelings

of those who disdained to submit to authority in matters of faith, to consent to remove to the New World, and there be governed by laws which they could have no part in enacting. Representations to this effect were made to the Company, who resolved that the government and patent should be removed to Massachusetts. This wise resolution gave such an encouragement to emigration, that, in 1630, more than 1500 persons came over, and founded Boston and several adjacent towns. Of these persons, all were respectable, and many were from illustrious and noble families. Having been accustomed to a life of ease and enjoyment, their sufferings the first year were great, and proved fatal to many; among others, to the Lady Arabella Johnson, who, to use the words of an early historian of the country, 'came from a paradise of plenty and pleasure in the family of a noble earl, into a wilderness of wants, and, although celebrated for her many virtues, yet, was not able to encounter the adversity she was surrounded with; and in about a month after her arrival, she ended her days at Salem, where she first landed.' Mr. Johnson, her husband, overcome with grief, survived her but a short time.

"Before December, 200 perished. On the 24th of that month, the cold became intense. Such a Christmas-eve they had never before known. Yet the inclemency of the weather continued to increase. They were almost destitute of provisions, and many were obliged to subsist on clams, muscles, and other shellfish, with nuts and acorns instead of bread. Many more died; but, in this extremity, that ardour of conviction which had impelled them to emigrate remained in full force; and they met with a firm, unshaken spirit, the calamities which assailed them."

Of this new colony, who planted themselves at Boston, John Winthrop, Esq., had been chosen go-

SETTLEMENT OF MASSACHUSETTS. 305

GOVERNOR WINTHROP.

vernor in England, and he was re-elected after his arrival. He continued to hold this office for four years and a half. He has left behind an exact journal of the occurrences between the years 1630 and 1649, which affords some curious and interesting illustrations of the manners and condition of these pious emigrants. The houses of the first settlers of Boston were, of course, extremely simple and unadorned. Wooden chimneys were common for many years; and "a wainscot of clap-boards" in the house of the deputy-governor, was regarded as a highly censurable piece of extravagance. The house of the "ladye Moodye" at Salem, a person of high consideration, was nine feet high, having a chimney in the centre. The furniture of the early colonists, was of a somewhat different quality. Much of it was brought from England, and was of considerable value, forming a strange contrast to the humble architecture of the huts or sheds in which it was often deposited. Thus, in an inventory of the effects of governor Winthrop's fourth wife, dated 1647, are mentioned, "silk curtains, brass andirons, *cheny* plates and saucers; and Turkey carpets." The country furnished fish and game in abundance; "and though," says the Governor, (in a letter dated November 29, 1630,) "we have not beef and mutton, yet, God be praised, we want them not; our Indian corn answers for all." Groceries were soon brought over in abundance from England; but tea and coffee were, at that time, luxuries unknown in Europe. Many laws were early made "against tobacco, and immodest fashions, and costly apparel;" and attempts equally misjudged and unavailing were made, to regulate the spirit of gain, as well as to check a disposition to expense. The prices of labour and of commodities were fixed repeatedly by positive laws; but experience soon proved the futility of all such projects. Another feature of their legislative policy has exposed "the pilgrim fathers" of New England to the charge of intolerance. At a general court held in 1631, they ordained, that none but those who had made a profession of religion, and had become members of some church, should be admitted members of the Corporation, or enjoy the privilege of voting. This law, however contrary to just views of political liberty, was in strict accordance with the avowed motives of their emigration. Their object, it has been justly remarked, was, "to plant a church, not an empire; and they were not merely a religious, but a "theological," or rather an ecclesiastical community. The settlers of New England," remarks Dr. Dwight, "fled from persecution. Every government in the Christian world, claimed at that time, the right to control the religious conduct of its subjects. This claim, it is true, finds no warrant in the Scriptures. But its legitimacy never had been questioned, and, therefore, never investigated. All that was then contended for, was, that it should be exercised with justice and moderation. Our ancestors brought with them to America, the very same opinions concerning this subject, which were entertained by their fellow-citizens, and by all other men of all Christian countries. As they came to New England, and underwent all the hardships of colonizing it, for the sake of enjoying their religion unmolested, they naturally were very reluctant that others, who had borne no share of their burdens, should wantonly intrude upon their favourite object, and disturb the peace of themselves and their families. With these views, they began to exercise the claim above mentioned, and, like the people of all other countries, carried the exercise to lengths which nothing can justify. But it ought ever to be remembered, that no other civilized nation can take up the first stone to cast against them."

ROGER WILLIAMS ENTERTAINED BY CANONICUS.

THE PURITANS IN AMERICA.
SETTLEMENT OF RHODE ISLAND

T was not long before a case arose, which put to the test the intolerant nature of their theocratic principles of government. In the year 1634, Roger Williams, the minister of Salem, having occasioned disturbances, by advancing tenets which were considered as not only heretical, but seditious, and being found irreclaimable, was ordered to leave the colony. The cause of his banishment is very dif-

ferently stated. By some writers, he is represented as having been expelled simply for avowing the doctrine, that the civil magistrate is bound to grant equal protection to every denomination of Christians; a doctrine too liberal for the age in which he lived. If Dr. Dwight, however, is correct, this was by no means the fact. "This gentleman," says the learned writer, "came to New England in the year 1631, and was chosen as an assistant in the ministry to Mr. Skelton, at Salem. His peculiar opinions had given offence to the magistrates before his ordination. After he was ordained, he persuaded the church at Salem to send admonitory letters to that of Boston, and to several others, in which they accused the magistrates who were members of them, of gross offences, and denied the character of purity to all the churches but their own. It will naturally be supposed, that these letters were not very favourably received. Soon afterwards, Mr. Williams impeached and denied the purity of even the Salem church, and separated himself from it, because it would not refuse to hold communion with the other churches in New England. In the mean time, he separated from his own wife, and would perform no act of religious worship when she was present, because she attended divine service at the church in Salem. He also influenced Mr. Endicot to cut the cross out of the King's colours, as being a relic of anti-christian superstition; and taught, that it was not lawful for a pious man to commune in family prayer, or in taking an oath, with persons whom he judged to be unregenerate. He would not take, nor, so far as was in his power, suffer others to take, the oath of fidelity, because the magistrates who administered it were, in his view, unrenewed. He also taught, that it is not lawful for an unregenerate man to pray. Mr. Williams, I fully believe to have been an upright man. What was very remarkable, he held the very just as well as liberal opinion, which one could hardly expect to find united with those mentioned above, that 'to punish a man for any matters of his conscience, is persecution.' Efforts were made to reclaim this gentleman; but they were made in vain. He was therefore banished from Massachusetts."

This banishment was not a light matter. He was obliged to leave the settlements in the winter. But he was hospitably received by Canonicus, and found a permanent shelter in Rhode Island.

"In 1638, Mr. William Coddington, one of the original planters of Massachusetts, a respectable merchant in Boston, and one of the first assistants (in council,) disgusted with the proceedings of the government against the Antinomians, and not improbably attached to their doctrines, having sold his estate, quitted the jurisdiction, and, with a number of his associates, settled on the island of Aquidnick (or Aquetnec), in Narrhagansett Bay, and named it Rhode Island."

Such was the commencement of that colony, of which, though Coddington was the first governor, Roger Williams is to be considered as the founder and legislator, as the settlement was made under his advice; and to him is attributed the merit of having first set an example of the equal toleration of all religious sects in the same political community.

BANISHMENT OF ROGER WILLIAMS.

SIR HENRY VANE.

SIR HENRY VANE.

IN 1635, Massachusetts received a fresh accession of emigrants from England, among whom were two individuals who were destined to act conspicuous parts in the subsequent affairs of their native country. One was Hugh Peters, afterwards one of the chaplains of the Protector; the other Mr. (afterwards Sir Henry) Vane. The latter was at this time but five-and-twenty years of age; but, by his grave deportment, his engaging manners, and his ardent professions of attachment to liberty, he so ingratiated himself with the settlers, that, the year after his arrival, he was chosen governor of the colony. His popularity, however, we are told, was transient. "During his administration, the celebrated Mrs. Hutchinson, a woman who was distinguished for her eloquence, and had imbibed the enthusiasm of the age, instituted weekly meetings for persons of her own sex, in which she commented on the sermons of the preceding Sunday, and advanced certain mystical and extravagant doctrines; these spread rapidly among the people, and many became converts. Governor Vane, with Mr. Cotton and Mr. Wheelwright, two distinguished clergymen, embraced them with ardour; but Lieutenant-Governor Winthrop, and a majority of the churches, deemed them heretical and seditious. Great excitement was produced among the people; many conferences were held; public fasts were appointed; a general synod was summoned; and, after much intemperate discussion, her opinions were determined to be erroneous, and she and some of her adherents were banished from the colony.

"Not being again chosen governor, Vane returned in disgust to England; engaged in the civil wars which soon afterwards afflicted the country; sustained high offices in the republican party; and, after the restoration of Charles II., was accused of high treason, convicted, and executed. We copy the account of this atrocious transaction from a British historian.

"The house of commons demanded the trial, or rather the execution, of Lambert and Vane, state prisoners since the Restoration. It is necessary to repeat here, that they were excepted from the act of oblivion, that both houses at the same time petitioned the king for their lives, and that the king promised his compliance. The new parliament disdained the moderation of the convention, and clamoured for their blood. They were accordingly brought to trial in a few days after the prorogation. Neither had sat in judgment upon Charles I.: their crime was their having served the usurpation—under the style and title of the commonwealth. Lambert, a brave soldier, but a weak man, confessed himself guilty, made abject supplication for the royal clemency, and was suffered to reach the end of his natural life in the island of Guernsey, either wholly unthought of, or remembered only to be despised.

"Vane had the reputation of wanting personal firmness. He defended himself on his trial with undaunted resolution, and never gave more shining proof of the elevation of his talents and his principles. The indictment charged him with treason against the person and government of Charles II.; and the overt acts to sustain it were his official acts, as a public servant of the commonwealth. His defence was, first, that he acted under the authority of the parliament, then the supreme, sole, and established governing power of England; next, that the authority of the parliament was legal and supreme, and the cause which it vindicated just and sacred before God and man. The judges decided that Charles II. was King of England *de facto* as well as *de jure*, whilst he lived a wandering exile, repudiated even by foreign courts; and the pretence of this revolting iniquity was, that there was then no person in England assuming the style and title of king. The verdict of guilty against Vane was, under the circumstances, a matter of course. He offered a fruitless bill of exceptions, founded on the king's pledged faith to the late parliament. Charles broke his faith, and thereby left one of the darkest stains upon his personal character.

EXECUTION OF SIR HENRY VANE.

"On the 14th of June, Sir Henry Vane was led on foot to the scaffold at Tower Hill. There are preserved minute particulars of his demeanour and treatment. He was clad in a black suit and mantle, with a scarlet waistcoat showing itself at the breast, his head uncovered, his eye bright, his colour unchanged. It was remarked that he showed the solemn calmness of a mere spectator of the scene. He proceeded to address the people from written notes, but was soon interrupted and reviled by the Lieutenant of the Tower. The sheriff snatched his notes from his hand, whilst the Lieutenant ransacked his pockets for papers, and trumpets were sounded to drown his voice. He appealed from men to Heaven, and submitted to his fate. His last words, as he knelt before the scaffold, were, 'Father, glorify thy servant in the sight of men, that he may glorify thee in the discharge of his duty to thee and to his country.'

"The death of Vane has been ascribed to his having produced the minute of council in evidence against Strafford; and Echard, in his perfidious compilation, ventures to declare the death of Vane on the same spot where Strafford died, a judgment of God. But Charles had not virtue enough to inherit either the remorse or vengeance of his father, for the sacrifice of that famous minister; and his own letter to Clarendon, shows that he broke his faith from fear and hatred of the virtue and intrepidity with which Vane defended his life and vindicated his principles on his trial.

"The king and his chief minister came to the determination of 'putting out of the way' a man in whom the genius of the commonwealth survived. Vane belongs in a peculiar manner to that epoch. It has been remarked, as anomalous and extraordinary, that a diplomatist, an administrator, and statesman, of versatile accomplishments and superior genius, should indulge in the wildest mysticism as a religionist; but the simple and obvious truth is that he was more than ordinarily imbued with the spirit of his age. With the visionary fervour of his religion he combined the first principle to which he would have been led by the light of reason and philosophy—that of religious toleration. In this, however, he but shared a virtue of the Independents. All sects are ready to preach toleration when they are the party oppressed. The Independents alone have passed that sure ordeal of principle, the possession of power. The liberty of conscience, which they asked when they were weak, they gave when they became strong."

ELLIOT INSTRUCTING THE INDIANS.

MISSIONARY LABOURS OF ELLIOT AND MAYHEW.

OR many years previous to the time of King Philip's War, sincere endeavours had been made by Christian missionaries to reclaim the aboriginal inhabitants of New England from the savage state, and to impart to them the blessings of civilization and religion. The most eminent and successful of these missionaries

were John Elliot and Thomas Mayhew. Elliot, one of the ministers of Roxbury, a most humble, pure, and zealous Christian, laboured diligently to overcome the difficulties of the Indian language, and made an Indian grammar, and a translation of the scriptures. Having prevailed upon his converts to adopt the habits of civilized life, he procured from the general court a grant of land for their use in the neighbourhood of Concord, and soon formed a number of flourishing little towns, the residence of "praying Indians." The women in the new settlements learned to spin; the men to dig and till the ground; and the children were instructed in the English language; and taught to read and write. When they had founded their town of *Natick*, on Charles river, they desired Elliot to frame a system of municipal government for them. He directed their attention to the counsel that Jethro gave to Moses; and, in conformity with it they electd for themselves rulers of hundreds, of fifties, and of tens. The provincial government also appointed a court, which, without assuming jurisdiction over them, tendered the assistance of its judicial mediation to all who might be willing to refer to it the adjustment of their more difficult or important controversies. It was not till 1660 that the first Indian church was founded by Elliot, in Massachusetts. There were at that time no fewer than ten settlements within the province, occupied by Indians comparatively civilized.

While Elliot and an increasing body of associates were thus employed in Massachusetts, Mayhew, with a few coadjutors, was diligently prosecuting the same design in Martha's Vineyard, Nantucket, and Elizabeth Isles, and the territory comprehended in the Plymouth patent.

When Mayhew was subsequently lost in a voyage undertaken in order to enlist the sympathies of the mother country in the cause of the Indians, his aged father supplied his place. The benevolent and disinterested labours of these pious men were blessed with complete success, so far as they extended. Those within the sphere of Mayhew's influence preserved their friendship for the whites inviolate. Although when isolated from the other tribes, they were necessarily destined gradually to dwindle away, a remnant still remains to inherit the blessings dispensed by their early friend. The settlements of Elliot, being situated in the theatre of King Philip's war, were destined to a far different fate.

In that disastrous time, the Indian converts of Elliot though unwilling to engage in hostilities, were drawn into the quarrel; and as a necessary consequence, nearly all their smiling happy Christianized villagers were utterly destroyed. After the war was over, Elliot gathered the remnant of his converts together and resumed his work, which he continued to the close of his life, under every species of discouragement.

GENERAL VIEW OF MISSIONS.

A MISSION is an establishment of people zealous for the glory of God and the salvation of souls, who go and preach the Gospel in remote countries, and among infidels. No man possessed of the least degree of feeling or compassion for the human race can deny the necessity and utility of Christian missions. Whoever considers that the major part of the world is enveloped in the grossest darkness, bound with the chains of savage barbarity, and immersed in the awful chaos of brutal ignorance, must, if he be not destitute of every principle of religion and humanity, concur with the design and applaud the principles of those who engage in so benevolent a work. We shall not, however, in this place, enter into a defence of missions, but shall present the reader with a short view of those that have been established.

In the sixteenth century, the *Romish church* particularly exerted herself for the propagation of their religion. The Portuguese and Spaniards pretend to have done mighty exploits in the spread of the Christian faith in Asia, Africa, and America: but when we consider the superstitions they imposed on some, and the dreadful cruelties they afflicted on others, it more than counterbalances any good that was done.

For a time, the Dominicans, Franciscans, and other religious orders, were very zealous in the conversion of the heathen; but the Jesuits outdid them in all their attempts in the conversion of African, Asian, and American infidels. Xavier spread some hints of the Romish religion through the Portuguese settlements in the East Indies, through most of the Indian continent, and of Ceylon. In 1549 he sailed to Japan, and laid the foundation of a church there, which at one time was said to have consisted of about 600,000. After him, others penetrated into China, and founded a church, which continued about 170 years. About 1580, others penetrated into Chili and Peru in South America, and converted the natives. Others bestirred themselves to convert the Greeks, Nestorians, Monophysites, Abyssinians, the Egyptian Copts. "It is, however," as one observes, "a matter of doubt whether the disciples of a Xavier, or the converts of a Loyola and Dominic, with their partisans of the Romish church, should be admitted among the number of Christians, or their labours be thought to have contributed to the promotion or to the hindrance of the religion of Christ. Certain it is, that the methods these men pursued tended much more to make disciples to themselves and the pontiffs of Rome, than to form the mind to the reception of evangelical truth. With ardent zeal, however, and unwearied industry, these apostles laboured in this work. In 1662 we find the pope established a congregation of cardinals, *de propaganda fide*, and endowed it with ample revenues, and every thing which could forward the missions was liberally supplied. In 1627, also, Urban added the college *for the propagation of the faith;* in which missionaries were taught the language, of the countries to which they were to be sent. France copied the example of Rome, and formed an establish-

MISSION HOUSE AT ST. CROIX, WEST INDIES.

THE NEW YORK
PUBLIC LIBRARY

ASTOR, LENOX AND
TILDEN FOUNDATIONS

ment for the same purposes. The Jesuits claimed the first rank, as due to their zeal, learning, and devotedness to the holy see. The Dominicans, Franciscans, and others, disputed the palm with them. The new world and the Asiatic regions were the chief field of their labours. They penetrated into the uncultivated recesses of America. They visited the untried regions of Siam, Tonquin, and Cochin-China. They entered the vast empire of China itself, and numbered millions among their converts. They dared affront the dangers of the tyrannical government of Japan. In India they assumed the garb and austerities of the Brahmins, and boasted on the coasts of Malabar of a thousand converts baptized in one year by a single missionary. Their sufferings, however, were very great, and in China and Japan they were exposed to the most dreadful persecutions, and many thousands were cut off, with, at last, a final expulsion from the empire. In Africa the Capuchins were chiefly employed, though it does not appear that they had any considerable success. And in America their laborious exertions have had but little influence, we fear, to promote the real conversion of the natives to the truth.

In the year 1621, the *Dutch* opened a church in the city of Batavia, and from hence ministers were sent to Amboyna. At Leyden, ministers and assistants were educated for the purpose of missions under the famous Walæus, and sent into the East, where thousands embraced the Christian religion at Formosa, Columba, Java, Malabar, &c.; and though the work declined in some places, yet there are still churches in Ceylon, Sumatra, Amboyna, &c.

About 1705, Frederic IV., of Denmark, applied to the university of Halle, in Germany, for missionaries to preach the Gospel on the coast of Malabar, in the East Indies; and Messrs. Ziegenbalg and Plutscho were the first employed on this important mission; to them others were soon added, who laboured with considerable success. It is said that upwards of eighteen thousand Gentoos have been brought to the profession of Christianity.

A great work has been carried on among the Indian nations in *North America*. One of its first and most eminent instruments was as we have already seen Mr. Elliot, commonly called the Indian apostle, who, from the time of his going to New England, in 1631, to his death, in 1690, devoted himself to this great work by his lips and pen; translating the Bible and other books into the *natic* dialect. Some years after this, Thomas Mayhew, Esq., governor and patentee of the islands of Martha's Vineyard, and some neighbouring islands, greatly exerted himself in the attempt to convert the Indians in that part of America. His son John gathered and founded an Indian church, which, after his death, not being able to pay a minister, the old gentleman himself, at seventy years of age, became their instructor for more than twenty years, and his grandson, and great-grandson, both succeeded him in the same work. Mr. D. Brainerd was also a truly pious and successful missionary among the Susquehanna and Delaware Indians. His journal contains instances of very extraordinary conversions.

But the *Moravians* have exceeded all in their missionary exertions. They have various missions: and, by their persevering zeal, it is said upwards of 23,000, of the most destitute of mankind, in different regions of the earth, have been brought to the knowledge of the truth. Vast numbers in the Danish islands of St. Thomas, St. Jau and St. Croix, and the English islands of Jamaica, Antigua, Nevis, Barbadoes, St. Kitts, and Tobago, have, by their ministry, been called to worship God in spirit and in truth. In the inhospitable climes of Greenland and Labrador they have met with wonderful success, after undergoing the most astonishing dangers and difficulties. The Arrowack Indians, and the negroes of Surinam and Berbice, have been collected into bodies of faithful people by them. Canada and the United States of North America, have, by their instrumentality, afforded happy evidences of the power of the Gospel. Even those esteemed the last of human beings, for brutishness and ignorance, the Hottentots, have been formed into their societies; and upwards of seven hundred are said to be worshipping God at Bavians Cloof, near the Cape of Good Hope. We might also mention their efforts to illumine the distant East, the coast of Coromandel, and the Nicobar islands; their attempts to penetrate into Abyssinia, to carry the Gospel to Persia and Egypt, and to ascend the mountains of Caucasus. In fact, where shall we find the men who have laboured as these have? Their invincible patience, their well-regulated zeal, their self-denial, their constant prudence, deserve the meed of highest approbation. Nor are they wearied in so honourable a service; for they have numerous missionaries still employed in different parts of the world.

Good has been also done by the *Wesleyan Methodists*, who are certainly not the least in missionary work. They have several missionaries in the British dominions in America and in the West Indies. They have some thousands of members in their societies in those parts.

In 1791, a society was instituted among the *Baptists*, called, 'The Particular Baptist society for propagating the Gospel among the Heathen;" under the auspices of which missionaries were sent to India, and favourable accounts of their success have been received. We learn, with pleasure, that through their indefatigable industry, the New Testament, and part of the Bible, have been translated and printed in the Bengalee; and that parts of the Scriptures have been translated into ten of the languages spoken in the East.

In the year 1795, *The London Missionary Society* was formed. This is not confined to one body of people, but consists of Episcopalians, Presbyterians, Seceders, Methodists, and Independents, who hold an annual meeting in London in May. As the state of this society is before the public, it would be unnecessary here to enlarge; suffice it to say, that it is now on the most permanent and respectable footing. "It has assumed consistency and order; it combines integrity of character, fortitude of mind, and fixedness of resolution, with continual progression of effort for the exalted purpose of presenting the doctrines of the blessed Gospel to the acceptance of the perishing heathen, and of exhibiting an uncorrupt example of their tendencies and effects in their own characters and conduct."

Besides the above-mentioned societies, others have been formed of less note. In 1699, a society was instituted in England for *promoting Christian Knowledge*. In 1701, another was formed for the propagation of the Gospel in foreign parts. In Scotland, about the year 1700, a society was instituted for the *Propagation of Christian Knowledge*. Recently, some clergymen of the established church have formed one among themselves. Societies for spreading the Gospel also have been instituted in various other places.

In the United States, the Christians of all denominations have not been wanting in efforts to disseminate the truths of the Bible. Missionary societies exist in almost all of the large cities; great sums of money are annually collected and expended in the cause. A large number of the missionaries have distinguished themselves by their courage, persevering energy, fortitude and sacrifice. Among the laborers in the work of religious enlightenment, are many of the gentler sex, who have clearly proved that when animated by a strength of faith and a love of humanity they are equal to as trying exertions as their sterner co-operators. There is no part of the heathen world they dare not visit, to teach the joys of peace and love.

From the whole, it seems evident that the light and knowledge of the glorious Gospel will be more diffused than ever throughout the earth. And who is there that has any concern for the souls of men, any love for truth and religion, but what must rejoice at the formation, number, and success of those institutions, which have not the mere temporal concerns of men, but their everlasting welfare, as their object? My heart overflows with joy, and mine eyes with tears, when I consider the happy and extensive effects which are likely to take place. The untutored mind will receive the peaceful principles of religion and virtue; the savage barbarian will rejoice in the copious blessings, and feel the benign effects of civilization; the ignorant idolater will be directed to offer up his prayers and praises to the true God, and learn the way of salvation through Jesus Christ. The habitations of cruelty will become the abodes of peace and security, while ignorance and superstition shall give way to the celestial blessings of intelligence, purity, and joy. Happy men, who are employed as instruments in this cause! who forego your personal comforts, relinquish your native country, and voluntarily devote yourselves to the most noble and honourable of services! Peace and prosperity be with you!

SEIZURE OF GUY FAWKES.

THE GUNPOWDER PLOT.

AMES I., had not been more than a year on the throne when a horrible plot was formed by some desperate and fanatic Roman catholics, to blow up the parliament house with gunpowder, when the king, the royal family, and all the peers of England should be assembled. Of this atrocious plot, named the Gunpowder Plot, the following are some of the leading circumstances.

The idea was first conceived by Robert Catesby, a

gentleman of good birth and property, which last, however, he had squandered in riot and dissipation. He communicated it to two of his friends, John Wright and Thomas Winter, which last went over to the Netherlands, and there engaged in the plot one Guy Fawkes, a gentleman of good family in Yorkshire, who having run through his small patrimony, had entered the Spanish service. When Winter and Fawkes came to London the plan was communicated to Thomas Percy, a kinsman of the earl of Northumberland, to whom he acted as steward, and a house adjoining the parliament house was taken in his name, and Fawkes, as his servant, was put in charge of it. Another house was taken at Lambeth, in which the powder, timber and other things requisite for their purpose, might be kept.

These preparations were made in the spring of the year, and as parliament was not to meet till the February of the following year, the conspirators did not commence operations till the beginning of December. Catesby and his associates then entered the house in Westminster, well supplied with tools and with hard eggs and baked meats for their support, and began to run a mine thence under the parliament house, Fawkes standing sentinel while they wrought. They never stirred out, or even went up stairs, lest they should be seen, and every night they spread over the garden the matter which they had extracted during the day. They thus wrought till Christmas-eve, when learning that the meeting of parliament was put off till the following October, they separated for the holydays.

Their number was increased when they renewed their labours in the month of February. The new associates were Wright's brother Christopher, Winter's brother Robert, and John Grant of Norwood, near

Warwick. And we may here observe, that, with the exception of Catesby's two servants, Keyes and Bates, all engaged in this diabolical conspiracy were gentlemen, and all but Percy and Catesby men of unexceptionable moral character and of independent fortune. We may hence learn how baneful are the effects of false religion on the mind and heart when it could engage such men in such an undertaking.

We need hardly observe that the conspirators were superstitious men. Accordingly, we are told, that as they were urging on their mine they one day distinctly heard the tolling of a bell under the parliament house. Fawkes, when called down, heard it also; but when they had sprinkled the place with holy water the sound ceased, and the same remedy always proved efficacious whenever it was renewed. Some time after they were startled by a rushing noise over their heads; they thought at first that they were discovered, but on inquiry they found that it was caused by a man named Bright, who was selling off his coals from a cellar under the house of lords. They now saw that by taking that cellar they might terminate their labours, and it was accordingly taken in Percy's name, and twenty barrels of gunpowder were conveyed to it from the house in Lambeth, and covered over with billets and faggots of wood, and lumber and empty bottles were scattered over the ground to deceive those who might happen to enter the cellar.

During the summer the plot was communicated to three gentlemen of good birth and large fortune, namely, sir Everard Digby, Ambrose Rookwood, and Francis Tresham. As parliament was certainly to meet on the 5th of November, the conspirators made their final arrangements. Fawkes was to fire the mine by means of a slow match, and as soon as he had lighted it he was to hasten on board a small vessel which would be lying ready in the river, and carry the news over to their friends in Flanders. Digby was on the same day to assemble a number of the catholic gentry under pretence of a hunting party at Dunchurch, in Warwickshire, and seize the king's only daughter, the princess Elizabeth, who was in that neighbourhood, and proclaim her queen.

On the 26th of October, as lord Monteagle, a catholic peer, was sitting at supper at his house at Hoxton, near London, an anonymous letter was handed to him by a page, who said he had received it from a strange man in the street. It desired him to make some excuse for not attending parliament, "for God and man," it is said, "had concurred to punish the wickedness of this time," with other mysterious hints. Lord Monteagle went that very evening to Whitehall, and showed the letter to Lord Salisbury and other lords of the council, and next day, when the king, who had been out hunting, returned to town, a council was held on the subject of the letter. James himself was the person to discover its meaning, but it was determined not to search the cellar to the last moment. Accordingly, on the eve of the meeting of parliament the lord chamberlain and some others entered the cellar. They saw Fawkes there, but made no remark; in the night a magistrate was sent, who arrested him as he was coming out, and six and thirty barrels of powder were found in the cellar when it was searched. Fawkes, when taken before the council, avowed and gloried in his design, but refused to name his accomplices.

Such of the conspirators as were in London fled as soon as they heard of the apprehension of Fawkes. When they came to Dunchurch their dejected looks told their story, and all who were there dispersed to provide for their security. As they went along the catholic gentry drove them from their doors with reproaches. At length they reached Holbeach, the house of Stephen Littleton, one of their friends. There, as they were drying some of their powder which had been wetted, a burning coal fell into it, and Catesby and some others were much injured by the explosion. Next day the sheriff of the county appeared and summoned them to surrender. On their refusal he ordered an assault on the house. Rookwood, Thomas Winter and the two Wrights were wounded. Catesby and Percy, who had placed themselves back to back, were shot through the bodies by two balls from one musket, and both of them died of their wounds. The whole party were then made prisoners. Digby and others who were not there were captured in different places, and all were conveyed to London. They all, like Fawkes, confessed their crime, and all were executed as traitors. They died glorying in the deed for which they had suffered.

From the confessions of some of the conspirators it appeared that Father Garnet, the superior of the Jesuits in England, was acquainted with the plot. A warrant was issued for his apprehension, and as it was suspected that he was concealed at Hendlip Hall, the seat of Mr. Abington, near Worcester, the sheriff of the county surrounded and searched the house. So well, however, were the places of concealment contrived, that it was not till the eighth day that Garnet was discovered. He was brought up to London, and being tried and found guilty, he was hanged on a gallows in St. Paul's churchyard.

Though there can hardly be a doubt of Garnet's guilt, the church of Rome has made him one of her saints, and therefore an object of worship to pious catholics. As miracles are required to prove sainthood, we are told that a new kind of grass sprang up

THE GUNPOWDER PLOT. 325

on the spot where he last stood in Hendlip lawn of the form of an imperial crown, and that the cattle never touched it. A spring of oil, too, burst out of the earth at the place where he suffered martyrdom. But the miracle that made most noise at the time was that of Father Garnet's Straw. This was an ear of the straw used at his execution, which a young catholic picked up, and on which appeared the face of the martyr. The privy council found it necessary to institute an inquiry into the matter, and it of course proved to have been a pious fraud.

SANDWICH ISLANDS.

AMONG the more recent conquests of the Bible, the wonderful success attending the self-denying labours of American missionaries in the Sandwich Islands is worthy of special commemoration. The islands of Hawaii, Maui, Molokai, Ohau, Lanai, Nihau, &c., in the North Pacific Ocean, were inhabited, before the arrival of these missionaries, by a race of uncivilized and savage people, addicted to the most absurd superstitions and the most revolting idolatry. Those isles of the sea are now the home of a sober, industrious people, advancing in intelligence and in the arts of civilization. The Bible has been printed in their language, and the natives have been taught to read it. When the first missionaries arrived from America, they were obliged not only to learn the language of this barbarous tribe, but, in order to render their work efficient, it was necessary to reduce the crude elements of an uncouth tongue into a system. An alphabet was formed, and the language was reduced to writing. Schools were opened in every district,—school-books were printed and brought into extensive use,—religious tracts were published and circulated,—the New Testament and portions of the Old were translated, and finally the whole Bible was placed within the reach of the natives. The effects of this beneficial system of instruction were soon apparent. These islands underwent a moral revolution. The power of the simple yet sublime truths of the Scripture was manifest in the change effected in the life of the nation. The poor, half-clothed, often naked savages, rude, ignorant, degraded by superstition and idolatrous rites, became a civilized people; and now the project has been discussed, if not entertained, of admitting them into the Union of the great North American Republic. The Sandwich Islands have taken their place in the rank of nations: their independence has been acknowledged by the great maritime powers of the world. These facts are among the wonders of the age. They fill some of the brightest pages in the history of the nineteenth century. There are, it is true, some darker shades in these annals, which will stand upon the record as an indelible reproach to the missionaries of the order of Ignatius Loyola. The policy of the Jesuits of late years has been to follow in the wake of Protestant missions, and pursue a system of perverse proselytism, with a view to turn the labours of others to their own account. The attempt of the French government, under Louis Phillippe, to force French brandy and Popery upon the poor natives at the cannon's mouth, is one of the most nefarious acts on record. The partial success of the first efforts of the papal emissaries has gradually waned, and the light of Christianity has triumphed over the darkness of papal imposture. The land has been filled with schools and churches, and with pleasant dwellings and fruitful fields. Missionaries of the gospel have given to this people the Bible, with the ability to read it. Probably no community has, in the same short space of time, been so completely emancipated from a state of barbarism and brought out into the light of the gospel as the Sandwich Islands. When the first missionaries arrived in 1820, scarcely thirty-five years ago, they found a besotted race, degraded in every respect; but that generation has passed away, and the large proportion of the population, in respect to their habitations, dress, mode of living, manners and pursuits, thought, taste, intelligence, &c., now bear the aspect of enlightened civilization. This language is, of course, to be understood relatively. A nation sunk in indolence, ignorance, and mental imbecility, and besotted in sin, cannot be elevated to enterprise, intelligence, and moral greatness in a day. Britain did not rise from her barbarous origin to the summit of her glory in many centuries; but we must remember, also, that social reformation advances, under the stimulus of the great moral appliances now in operation, with far greater rapidity than in any former age; and though the work of training up a nation just emerging from barbarism, and teaching it refinement, is not like the putting up of a shepherd's tent; though it may require years and generations to establish habits of physical, intellectual, and moral energy of the highest standard,—yet the fruits already produced are a precious earnest of the ripe results which will accrue, when this progressive training shall be more matured. The history of the mission in the Sandwich Islands is remarkable on account of the signal manifestations of Divine power attending the preaching of the gospel. A deep and widely-extended religious influence seemed at once to pervade the minds of the people, and converts to the Christian faith were gathered in like the multitudes at the day of Pentecost under the first preaching of the apostles. In an almost incredibly short space of time, more than twenty thousand converts were found professing the Christian faith; and though many of these were unfaithful, very many also gave abundant evidence of their sincerity and steadfastness, and proved to be genuine converts to the power and faith of the gospel. One of the missionaries, Mr. Coan, makes the following judicious remark respecting the native converts:

"To say that these thousands have all entered by 'the door,' or that they are all 'sheep,' would be more than we can say of any church. Should but one-half, or one-fourth of them reach heaven, the sight will be glorious. Should one-half fall away within one year, my soul shall not feel discouraged. The way of life and the way of death are before them, and, by the help of God, I am resolved, without ceasing, to warn every man, and to teach every man, night and day, with tears."

The fruits of the influence of Bible truth are apparent, not only in the improved moral and religious character of a people, but they are seen in all the departments of social life. This connection between pure morality, religion, and industrial pursuits, is always most intimate. Habits of sobriety and diligence, combined with strict integrity, are themselves sources of social prosperity. These the Bible inculcates and enforces, and all true Christians practise them; so that the diffusion of the Scriptures, and the discipline which they exercise, when honestly received, upon the affections and the habits of a people, are always elevating in their effect upon the masses. Without attempting to offer a sketch of the mission to the Sandwich Islands, we have merely referred to a few of the leading facts in the narrative, as an apt illustration of the power which accompanies the Bible, when its sacred truths are brought to bear upon the conscience and heart, even of the most ignorant and degraded of the great family of man. The conversion of the many thousands who have professed the Christian faith in the isles of the North Pacific Ocean, and their wonderful elevation in the scale of civilization, may well be recorded among the later conquests of the Bible, as worthy of grateful commemoration.

POPERY AND THE BIBLE IN IRELAND.

WITHIN the last years, a most astonishing change has been effected in some of the Roman Catholic districts of Ireland. The southern portions of that island have, until recently, been under the predominance of a most bigoted and arrogant priesthood. Probably no part of Europe has ever been afflicted with a more undisguised exhibition of Romanism at ease, than the districts to which we have already adverted. Strong in the numbers and in the ignorance, and consequent superstition and devotion of their parishioners, the priests ruled that section of the province with despotic authority, and the people were, in consequence, sunk into a state of barbarism almost without a parallel in the annals of civilization. The most grotesque superstitions were incorporated into the popular faith as a matter of course; but the priests were not at pains to disguise, or in the least conceal, the most revolting features of their system. Popery was literally rampant in the south of Ireland. The policy of the Romish priesthood was to exclude every influence that could by any means, direct or indirect, tend to render the people dissatisfied with their condition, or in the least suspicious of the natural connection between their religion and the physical degradation, wretchedness, and poverty of the peasantry under their control. By exciting the most absurd and wicked prejudices, they had succeeded in rendering their deluded devotees proof against the efforts of their Protestant neighbours to lift them from the slough in which they were voluntarily, though still ignorantly, content to wallow. Especial pains were taken to warn the poor papists

POPERY AND THE BIBLE IN IRELAND.   341

FAMINE IN IRELAND.

against the insidious wiles of the "Bible readers." They were threatened with all the terrors of excommunication by bell, book, and candle. Under no circumstances were they to tolerate in their houses the hateful presence of these "heretical emissaries," who went about from house to house, and from hovel to hovel, seeking permission to read the Bible to the inmates. The most violent among their partisans were incited by the flatteries and suggestions of the priesthood to acts of violence, in order to deter the Bible readers from the prosecution of their missionary work. They were constrained either to abandon it, or to go literally with their life in their hand, in peril of violence and death. A mission among the Thugs could scarcely have been more adventurous or hazardous. In the face of the greatest difficulties, these offices of Christian benevolence were continued. The uniform kindness of the "Readers" produced its legitimate fruits. The poor peasant who was nursed in sickness and comforted by gifts of mercy, when his priest deserted him, or paid him visitations of extortion and reprimand, began, despite of his prejudices, to suspect that the heretics were not so bad as they had been represented. He gradually became willing to listen to the reading of the Scriptures. He found in them lessons of wisdom and love, and words of soberness and truth to which he had all his life been a stranger. For the life of him, he could not understand why his priest should so strenuously forbid him to read the Bible, or have it read to him by another, and yet at the same time declare that it was the revelation of God's holy will, and that the foundation of the Roman Catholic Church was laid by apostles, Jesus Christ himself being the chief corner-stone. "Surely this is a strange thing!" he would naturally say to himself. "If the Protestant Bible is a bad book, why do not the priests let us have the Douay Bible, which they say is the true one? They may let us have it, too, but then what good will it do us, if we cannot read a single letter in the book? Why do they not teach us to read? And if they will not give us, who are older, the opportunity of learning, why do they keep our children in ignorance? Surely, if they loved Christ, they would not only keep his commandments themselves, but they would teach us to do the same; and one of his commands is, 'Search the Scriptures!' But the priest says, 'No, you shall not search them!' Whom shall we obey? The parish priest, or the Saviour? Jesus Christ, or the pope of Rome?" By this simple process of homely and quiet reasoning, some of the most inveterate enemies of the Bible readers had been brought to question the soundness of the Romish tenets, and gradually, as the dawning light kindled into the brightness of conviction, they stood forth and boldly testified their conversion to the Protestant faith. This avowal excited the rage of the priesthood, and the vindictive spirit of their superstitious followers was excited by inflammatory appeals to the basest and wildest passions. The terrors of excommunication were paraded. The anathema of the church was hurled at these converts to Protestantism. The faithful were commanded, under pain of damnation, to shun all fellowship with the apostates. They were taught that by holding any kind of communion with them, they were putting their own salvation in the utmost jeopardy. The only safety for the convert to the faith of the Bible lay in removal from the district. Some, however, boldly stood their ground. They preached Christ more eloquently by patient suffering than by the most systematic presentations of theological truth. The ready wit of the genuine Irish character was a source of annoyance to the priesthood; for if they encountered the Bible readers, or their converts, at any popular gathering, as they frequently did, "their reverences" were sure to get the worst of it; and at times, despite of their prejudices, the people would laugh at the predicaments in which their priests were placed. The popular sympathies, in every such contest, are naturally with the champions of their own class or social rank; and the homely, quaint, and sometimes keenly-pointed repartee would be applauded in the excitement of the controversy, when, under other circumstances, the offender would have been visited with the discipline of the shillelagh. This was the state of the parties when Ireland was visited, a few years ago, in the mysterious providence of God, by the terrible famine, and its usual concomitant, the still more dreadful famine fever, before which the starving thousands of Ireland quailed, and a wail of agony, a cry of the famishing for bread, startled every Christian sympathy of surrounding nations. The Roman Catholic portion of the population felt the horrors of this desolation most keenly. It fell chiefly upon the lower order of the tenants and peasantry, and these constitute the large proportion of the Roman Catholics of Ireland. The appalling calamity afforded the very opportunity which was most needed and best calculated to display the relative tempers of the opposite systems of Protestantism and Popery. The poor papists found that their only reliable friends were the very Bible-reading heretics whom they had been taught to persecute and to hate. They discovered that while the priest passed by on the other side, the Samaritan, whose fellowship they had shunned, was always ready to minister to their relief. They found out who were their "neighbours;" and an Irishman, if he seldom forgets an enemy, never forgets a friend. The evidence was so palpable, the fruits of the two systems stood out in contrast so marked, and the utter rottenness of Popery was so glaringly betrayed, its hollow professions of charity and mercy were so covered with contempt, that the population of the stronghold of Popery in Ireland seemed swayed by a common impulse, and the fetters of Popery dropped, as though stricken by an unseen hand, from the limbs of hundreds and thousands, who openly bore witness to the power of gospel grace and truth, and became the willing and zealous advocates of the Bible. The revolution threatened at one time to carry every thing before it by storm; but the process is none the less sure because it has become less impetuous. A steady, healthful change is in progress, and the beneficial effects are visible in the improved appearance of the people, and of their homes, and in the remarkable reformation in their morals. Idleness, drunkenness, Sabbath-breaking, and profanity are the peculiar fruits which invariably mark the prevalence of Popery. This fact is abundantly illustrated both in the Old and the New World, but it is most strikingly exemplified in contiguous countries, professing on the one side the Romish, on the other the Protestant faith. In Ireland, it has been a common subject of remark. The genius of the two religions seems to indicate its presence so soon as the dividing line has been crossed. You pass through the Protestant districts, and on every side you are greeted with tidy homesteads, well-tilled fields, a thrifty and intelligent yeomanry. The rights of property are respected, the laws are reverently obeyed, and the very land smiles in the broad sunshine of heaven. But you cross the boundary between this region and a district occupied by a Roman Catholic population, and, as if on purpose to furnish you with as marked a contrast as the world can give, you find the whole land wearing the garb of mourning and distress. The sky is as genial and the soil is as generous as ever, but the habitations are filthy, and the inmates are dirty; and instead of the air of neatness and comfort to which you had been accustomed, you find yourself assailed by scenes of slovenly unthrift, encountering continually, as you proceed, a lazy, vicious, swearing, drunken generation, and by their fruits you do know them to be the subjects of that "Man of Sin." The same indications are visible on the continent of Europe. In crossing from the Protestant cantons of Switzerland to the Roman districts, you seem to pass from a garden smiling with the blessing of God to a field cursed with the blight of heaven. The land seems to mourn. The same sad contrast strikes you in the morals of the people. The monuments of idolatry are venerated only by those whose morals have been debauched, and who love darkness rather than light, because their deeds are evil. We confess we regard the conflict which is at present waging in Ireland, between the friends and foes of the Bible, as, in many respects, invested with peculiar interest. If the Pope is, as we believe, always and everywhere, a usurper, he is emphatically such in the Emerald Isle. The primitive church in Ireland was purely Protestant and Christian. The man who is lauded as the tutelary saint of Ireland was a thorough Protestant. St. Patrick's writings, which are still extant, confirm this statement. He condemns the doctrine of purgatory as an innovation upon the faith of Christians, and maintained the leading doctrines of the gospel in opposition to the falsehoods and errors of Rome. Popery is an exotic in Ireland. Todd, in his history of the primitive church in Ireland, shows that the Christian religion was embraced far sooner in the south than in the north, and yet the south of Ireland has, for many years, been the hot-bed of Romish superstition and intolerance. It is in evidence, that before the close of the fifth century, Christianity was the religion of that whole country, and its establishment in the north was later than in any other part of the island. Ireland, too, in former ages, has contributed largely to aid the conquests of the Bible in other lands. Among its worthies, the name of Columba will always be held in highest veneration. His mission to the Western Isles of Scotland was attended with incalculable blessings. Moore has, in his allusion to Iona, which he calls "the temple of the living God," finely portrayed the powerful influence exerted by it upon the religious character of Europe and the world:

> "Thou wert the temple of the living God,
> And taughtest earth's millions at his shrine to bow.
> From thee ran
> That fire which lit creation in her youth,
> That turned the wandering savage into man
> And showed him the omnipotence of truth."

The monastery of Iona was, for centuries, the first seminary of learning in Europe. Irish missionaries carried the gospel to France, and among them were men of holy devotion and zeal unsurpassed by any preachers of righteousness since the days of the apostles. There is scarcely a country in the south and west of Europe, where Irish missionaries did not preach the gospel and erect schools of learning. It is asserted by Dr. Lanigan, that prior to the time of John Scotus, the Irish had extended their missions even to Iceland, which they called Thule, or Tyla. The primitive church of Ireland did more to extend the conquest of the Bible than any other contemporaneous branch of the Christian household. Hallam, in his "Middle Ages," confirms this fact. He mentions that "the establishment of public schools in France is due to Charlemagne. He was compelled to invite strangers from countries where learning was not so completely extinguished. Alcuin of England, Clemens of Ireland, Theodolph of Germany, were the three paladins who repaired to his court. With the help of these, he revived a few sparks of diligence, and established schools in different cities of his empire." John Scotus was a native of Ireland, who flourished in the ninth century. He surpassed most of the men of his age in his knowledge of the Greek language, and the historian already quoted, Hallam, pays a merited tribute to his genius. "I am not aware," says he, "that there appeared more than two really considerable men in the republic of letters from the sixth to the middle of the eleventh century—John, surnamed Scotus, or Erigena, a native of Ireland; and Gerbert, who became pope, by the name of Sylvester II.; the first, endowed with a bold and metaphysical genius; the second, excellent, for the time in which he lived, in mathematical science and mechanical inventions." These facts, and we might mention many more, did space permit, are sufficient to show that Popery is a plant of foreign growth in Ireland—a weed which has infested its fertile soil and overrun the land, which was first sowed with good seed that brought an abundant harvest. We look upon the process which is now developing, by which the tares are destined to be plucked up, with peculiar interest, and we trust the day is not distant when the south of Ireland shall again erect its trophies to the power of the Bible, and once more be numbered among its conquests.

THE BIBLE IN FRANCE.

WITHIN the last year, a remarkable revival of the doctrines of the Reformation has taken place in France. The history of the Reformation in that country, with its details of the sufferings endured by the dauntless Huguenots, is familiar to every intelligent reader. No country in the world has furnished the names of a larger number of martyrs and confessors to the Protestant faith. The massacre of St. Bartholemew in 1571, begun in Paris, and prosecuted in Lyons and in other of the most important cities of France, alone occasioned the murder of a host of unsuspecting and unarmed Christians, including women and children, who were ruthlessly put to death in cold blood. The number of these victims is variously estimated at from forty to one hundred thousand. The streets literally were red with Protestant blood, and the channel of the Seine, in some points, was choked with the bodies of the slain; and it should never be forgotten, that the papal authorities of Rome, so far from condemning those atrocities, celebrated the monstrous outrage upon humanity by a solemn jubilee of thanksgiving, the Pope heading a procession of dignitaries, which repaired to the Cathedral of St. Peter's and offered a Te Deum, or thanksgiving to God, for the slaughter of the heretics. A medal was struck, bearing on one side, the effigy of the reigning pontiff, and on the other, an angel with a drawn sword, while the dead bodies of the hated heretics are strewn upon the ground, and this picture is surrounded with the inscription, "Hugonotorum strages"—the massacre of the Huguenots! After the revocation of the Edict of Nantes, by which toleration, formerly secured to the Huguenots, was perfidiously withdrawn, the brutal king of France, Louis XIV., instituted what he called *dragonnades*, or visitations of armed dragoons to the districts inhabited by the Huguenots who had survived the cruelties of his predecessors; and multitudes were put to death, sent to the galleys, or banished, until, at last, Protestantism was almost extinct in France. But the blood of the martyrs is the seed of the church. It is the seal which consecrates the land as eventually pertaining by right of peaceful conquest to the precious Bible. The recent revival of Protestantism in France, is, therefore, vested with deep interest. It is due, primarily, to the circulation of the Scriptures in that country by means of colporteurs, who travel from village to village, and distribute copies of the Bible to all who are willing to receive them. Whole communities, including hundreds at a time, have been shaken by the power of the truth, and with simultaneous enthusiasm the bonds of Popery have been rent asunder, and the people have come out into the liberty of the gospel of divine grace. This is a glorious triumph. It is the beginning of the ovation of the Prince of Peace in that country. The same or similar results are perceptible in Belgium, which may perhaps deserve the bad eminence of being regarded as the stronghold of Popery in Europe. The Scriptures have silently been enshrined in the homes and hearts of a multitude who are feeling their way into the light, and swelling the ranks of them who glory in the power of the Bible.

PROTESTANTISM AND THE REVOLUTION OF 1848.

IN viewing the religious aspect of the old monarchies of Europe, we are forcibly impressed with the singular fact, that while Protestantism, or the religion of the Bible, is invading the dominions of Romanism, and in some instances, intrenching itself in the former strongholds of its enemy, those countries which have heretofore been most decidedly Protestant are suffering most severely from the aggressions of Rome. This is probably due, in the latter case, to the unnatural and constrained union of church and state. The spirit of Protestantism is a free spirit. It pines away in any atmosphere except that of liberty. Its first demand is the freedom of conscience, and it flourishes only where it is untramelled by religious privileges which are to be enjoyed only at the expense of its neighbours. Wherever any form of religion is established by laws of a partial, and therefore unjust, character, the strength of Protestantism is impaired. Our own country is best adapted by the nature of its institutions for the vigorous growth of Bible religion, because those very institutions are, in fact, modelled upon the basis of revealed religion. Freedom to worship God according to the dictates of conscience is itself a principle which can be found in no other than the code of the Scriptures, and this must be conceded before Protestantism can find a soil adapted to its successful cultivation. The glorious maxim, that *God alone is Lord of the conscience*, is essential to its health, if not to its very life. The religion of the Bible teaches men to regard, as an inalienable right, that which some governments concede only as a gracious privilege. Protestantism is not content with toleration, for that implies the right of the power which tolerates to adopt an opposite policy, should circumstances render it expedient for despotic authority to claim it; therefore, the religion of Protestantism teaches them to demand from others what it concedes to all—*equality*. It claims superiority over none who differ from its creed, and it recognises no authority in the court of conscience, except that of its Judge in heaven. Every departure from these great principles is a violation of the law of its organization. The countries of Europe in which an effete Protestant form of religion maintains a lingering life, are all examples in point. The nations must learn to prize religion unshackled by the encumbrance of civil encroachments upon the domain of conscience, before the great problems of social happiness and prosperity can be solved to the satisfaction of all.

The Bible is, of all books, the most aggressive. It wages an uncompromising war against every form of despotism and wrong. Its maxims are the purest expressions of genuine philanthropy. Its morality is summed up in the exercise of true charity. It teaches "what things soever ye would that men should do to you, do ye even so to them." This is a doctrine hateful only to tyrants and oppressors, but sweet and comforting to the oppressed, because it teaches them that the sympathies of Heaven are with them. Doubtless, this is the grand reason of Rome's implacable hostility to the Scriptures. The Bible is identified with the cause of humanity. It is emphatically the people's book. Priestcraft and tyranny, imposition and imposture of every kind and degree, are its natural enemies. It ·kes them all. Hence, so soon as the real na-

THE FRENCH ENTERING ROME.

ture and tendencies of Bible religion are discerned by the masses under all despotic governments, they are charmed with its free spirit. They see in it the emanations of the most exalted love. They pant for the enjoyment of the freedom which it alone confers upon a nation. There can be no doubt, that the revolutions which convulsed Europe in the years 1848-9 were, to a certain extent, attributable to the influence of Protestantism. Unfortunately, it was embarrassed by allies of doubtful, or rather bad, reputation. The "friends of light" in Germany, France, and Italy, and indeed throughout the continent, were radical infidels of the most malignant type. In all Roman Catholic countries, the usual primary result of disgust with the established form of religion is the repudiation of all religious obligation. The first transition from Popery is to infidelity. It is unjust to confound the various forms of unbelief with Protestantism. They have really nothing in common. Their opposition to Romanism proceeds from principles which are totally discrepant. Infidelity is a negative of all religion, whether good or bad. Protestantism is the affirmation of Bible religion, and the negation of all falsehood, superstition, and error. It is not surprising that revolutions, originating in the absence of religious principle, and in erroneous conceptions of the nature of civil liberty, should end precisely as the political crises of 1848-9 terminated. They had no stamina. The wild offshoots of enthusiasm, they blazed like the rocket in mid air, and fell to the earth when the momentum which impelled them was exhausted. Doubtless, men of better principles participated in the movement, and gave character and tone to the revolutionists in some countries, but we cannot deny that the predominant influence was a spirit of hostility, not only to despotism, but to law. Liberty, in the acceptation of the "friends of light," was only another word for licentiousness. They ignored all constitutional authority, and claimed for every man the right not only to think, but to do as he pleased. In Italy, the power of this movement was felt with terrible force. The papal authorities were overwhelmed by the waves of popular indignation. The pope sought safety in ignominious flight. The republic was proclaimed. The Roman revolution partook more largely of a Protestant character than any other among the simultaneous insurrections of that period. There were expressions of regard for the pure gospel, as well as of horror for the festering corruptions of Popery. The dark habitations of cruelty were thrown open to the light of day. The victims of papal malice were brought forth from their dungeons. The halls of the Inquisition were exposed to public view. The implements of torture were on exhibition, and the few months of freedom under the sway of the Italian patriots did more to convince the subjects of the pope of the iniquity of the papal system, than all the chicanery of Rome can undo in the next generation. The preaching of the impassioned Gavazzi carried conviction to the hearts of thousands of Italians, who thronged to hear the wondrous orator; and his clear expositions of Jesuitical intrigue, the blazing contrasts which he could so eloquently portray, between the faith of the gospel and the falsehoods of Rome, burned in the very souls of his hearers with the glow of truth, and fired them with detestation of the hateful despotism whose yoke they had broken. The brief period during which the patriots of Italy held the reins of government, was characterized by a comparative moderation, which was certainly admirable, in view of all the incentives to violence which offered temptations on every hand. Much of this was due to the conservative and restraining power of the religion of the Bible. The eventful days of the revolution constitute an epoch in the history of Rome, the moral effects of which can never be wholly obliterated. Though the people were finally subdued by French and Austrian bayonets and cannon, the very means employed by the pope to regain his throne produced a deep-seated hostility to the papal dynasty, which cannot easily be eradicated. When Rome was bombarded by the French, the cannon-balls of the enemy were paraded in solemn procession about the city, with the significant motto, "Confetti di Pio Nono mandate a suoi figli!" *The sweetmeats sent by Pius IX. to his children!* The bombs of the French excited hatred against the Romish religion, and as most of them fell in the suburbs, ruining the houses and maiming the families of the poor people, the very portion of the Roman people formerly most devoted to their religion learned to curse the pope and his clergy, in whose name these horrors were committed. The following extract of a letter from Padre Bonaventura, to a friend, expresses the views which a Roman Catholic priest was constrained to adopt in view of the horrors of that period:

"I find these sentiments have become more common than is generally supposed. They have penetrated even the hearts of the women. Thus, twenty years of apostolic labour which I have endured, to attach the Roman people to the church, are sacrificed in a few days! Behold, what I have seen and predicted in all my letters comes to pass! Protestantism is, in fact, now planted among a portion of this good and religious Roman people; and, horrible to tell! this has been brought about by the priests themselves, by the miserable politics into which they have led the pope. Ah! my dear friend, the idea of a bishop who rains grape-shot upon his dioceses—of a shepherd who cuts the throats of his sheep—of a father who devotes his children to death—of a pope who means to reign, to impose himself upon 3,000,000 of Christians by force—who means to establish his throne upon ruins, corpses, and blood! this idea, I say, is so strange, so contrary to the letter and spirit of the gospel, that there is no conscience that does not revolt at it—no faith which can bear up against it—no heart which does not groan at it—no tongue which is not moved by it, to cursing, aye, even to blasphemy! Ah! better, a thousand times better, have lost the temporal power, the whole world, if necessary, than to have given such a scandal to his people!"

This is the language of an Italian priest, who regards Christianity as identified with the religion of Rome, and who is, therefore, disposed by all the force of national predilection and religious preference, to put the most favourable construction upon the most doubtful appearances; and yet all these preposessions give way before the overwhelming force of the evidence of papal corruption and cruelty. There are facts connected with this part of our subject, which ought to be spread out before the American people in such a form as to compel the attention of every candid mind. Dr. Achilli, an Italian priest, whose renunciation of Romanism has drawn upon him a series of relentless persecutions, designed manifestly to destroy the force of his testimony, but who is certainly quite as worthy of credit when standing before the world as a Protestant, as he possibly could have been when exercising the functions of a Romish priest, makes the following statements respecting the Inquisition at Rome:

INQUISITORIAL CHAMBER.

THE INQUISITION AT ROME IN 1848.

At a meeting in the Rotunda, Dublin, recently, in connection with the Italian Evangelical Society, Mr. Philip Dixon Hardy stated that he was anxious to put a question to Dr. Achilli. It had been denied that some of the things which were alleged to have taken place had ever occurred. The question he wanted to put was this: "Was it a fact that, at the time Pio Nono left Rome, the Inquisition was in Rome, and is now in Rome?" This had been denied, and he wished his friend to give an answer.

Dr. Achilli thereupon rose, and said: "Pius IX., on leaving Rome with his cardinals, left there the Inquisition, and he left it, hoping that by means of its work he would be the better able to return to Rome; and it is the fact that the Inquisition is still in Rome, and was at work in Rome after the departure of Pius IX. Pius IX. left Rome in the month of November, 1848, and I was in Rome in the month of February, 1849, and in the same month of February, 1849, the Roman republic was proclaimed; and eight days after the proclamation of the republic, the *Te Deum* was chanted in the cathedral of St. Peter's; and I believe I stated here before, that on that occasion, I, with ten or twelve of my companions, visited together the prison of the Inquisition. That is to say, we went to examine whether the palace of the Inquisition was attended by any one or not, and this was what we found: We found, in this palace of the Inquisition, the commissary-general of the Inquisition, together with his two companions, his secretaries and his chancellors, and, in addition to that, we found the jailers of the Inquisition; and I myself asked one of the jailers whether there were any prisoners in the cells, because, I said, if there are jailers, we naturally may suppose there are also prisoners.

"But the jailer, according to the laws of his order and of the Inquisition, was not at liberty to give me an honest answer, and was satisfied with merely shrugging up his shoulders; but for me the answer was sufficient, and I understood by the shrug of his shoulders he meant to say there were plenty of them. And it was in consequence of this automatic answer that my companions, among whom were some French officers, were very much inclined to cause an uproar in the Inquisition. They wanted, right or wrong, to examine the cells and dungeons, and to compel the jailers to open the gates; but I begged my friends to desist from such a thing, and I advised them rather to make known this state of matters to the government. And that was done, and the government sent officers to verify whether the Inquisition was still in operation, and they found matters as I have described them. In addition to that, the government found three prisoners in the dungeons of the Inquisition, and one of these prisoners was a bishop that had been there in his cell for twenty-five years.

"I will not wait to tell you the reason why this unfortunate man was twenty-five years confined in a dungeon. I only state the fact that he had been, and was there; and this bishop, together with another prisoner, were almost carried in triumph through the streets of Rome; and every child in Rome knows that Bishop Cashiur, from Cairo, was carried about in triumph after having been delivered from the prison of the Inquisition. But I will also tell you another case. There was another of the prisoners of the Inquisition, although he was not immured in the dungeon of the Inquisition itself, he was imprisoned in one of the convents of Rome; and whoever has been at Rome will know the convent of Franciscan friars, called the Convent of Aracoeli. This prisoner was a wretched monk, of about sixty years of age, and this unfortunate creature had been for twelve years immured in a most horrible hole. This unfortunate man was not a Roman, he was not an Italian; you will be surprised to hear that he was an American; not an inhabitant of the United States, but a man from the republics of the South. This wretched monk, when he heard that the Republic was proclaimed in Rome, and that the Inquisition was thrown open, contrived, by some means or other, to let it be known that he was there, and the messenger brought the news to the National Assembly that this poor man was a prisoner in the Convent of Aracoeli.

"A deputation was at once sent to the superior of the convent, in order to ascertain the truth of the matter, but the father abbot strenuously denied it. However, they compelled him by threatening him, and at last he condescended to open the door of the cell. The monk was drawn out; and the wretched man, after twelve years' immurement there, was almost reduced to blindness, and he was scarcely able to stand on his legs; and they had to support him to enable him to go along. In this state he was brought before the National Assembly, and I was there myself. I have seen him with my own eyes; and if any would deny it, I appeal to Rome, to every one in Rome, to confirm the truth of what I have stated. On arriving at the National Assembly, the monk was an object of natural curiosity, and every one hastened around to examine him, and every one was anxious to hear something from him, and he had but one answer for all: "I have not the most remote idea why I was for twelve years kept in that dungeon; and I had always settled in my mind, and was at peace with myself, never having the slightest hope of seeing the daylight again." And he turned round and thanked them one after another, for he said it was to them he owed his life.

"He then asked for some assistance to enable him to return to his own country, and on that same evening a collection was made among us, and we gave him a small sum to enable him to return to America, and I believe at this moment the monk is in South America, thankful for his deliverance. Therefore, there is no doubt the Inquisition existed in Rome up to the first days of the Roman Republic; and that the Inquisition was restored with the return of papal government, I am myself a living proof; and when you will consider that the papal government itself has not the hardihood to deny that I was in the Inquisition—when the government has confessed and acknowledged it—you will scarcely find any one else to deny it. Therefore, you may well conclude from this that the Inquisition is still in existence at this present moment in Rome; and if I were rash enough to go to Rome now, I still would tell you what would happen, though you may well guess it, I don't think I would ever see the face of the sun again!"

A still more direct and circumstantial statement is furnished by an Italian, Giovanni Tomaso Baldasare, whose account of the opening of the Inquisition of Rome was published in the New York Presbyterian, February 1st, 1850:

"I was an eye-witness of the opening of the Inquisition of Rome in May last, and ask the attention of all Americans to what I have to say. O people! in this country, which you inhabit, there are Roman Catholic churches. Listen to me with attention, lend me the feelings of your hearts. I shall endeavour to destroy, as far as in me lies, any false impression which you may entertain respecting them, that you may be no more deceived by the false preachers of the holy gospel of Christ, by the hypocrite and anti-Christian Roman Church. I have something to reveal to the civilized people of North America, and particularly to worthy republican citizens of New York, in this happy place where I enjoy the liberty which I hold most dear. You may derive profit from what I have to communicate.

"In the year 1849, while I was in Rome, at the time when the Republic was in existence, the representatives of the people, partly in order to enlighten the minds of that nation, long debased by oppression, determined to set at liberty the persons languishing in dungeons, the unhappy victims suffering every kind of cruelty in that mansion of death. False accusations, unjust suspicions, or the cruel caprice of him who claims the title of the Vicar of Christ, had condemned many an unfortunate brother to end his life in that abode of sorrow.

"In the month of May, 1849, the great edifice of the so-called *Holy Office and Tribunal of the Sacred Inquisition*, was opened, at the command of the Constituent Assembly and the Triumvirate which then governed Rome. An immense concourse assembled, and a great crowd entered. A great multitude of people passed through and examined it. I was among them. Let the reader accompany me, in imagination, while I guide him through that vast building.

"We approach the magnificent portal. Here is a splendid staircase, which, in contempt of humanity, stands to claim our admiration. Having mounted these steps, we enter the grand hall of the *Tribunal* of the Holy Office. You may be struck with the architectural elegance of its execution. Of the three doors, two, on the right and left, lead to the apartments over the Tribunal, the cells for prisoners. There are other staircases near the same doors, which lead to the cortili, or little courts.

"Let us first enter this middle door. What a spacious and immense hall! Observe how nobly it is adorned. Cast your eyes at the pavement, and remark the fineness of the carpet, on which have proudly walked the cruel lords of this mansion, the priests and cardinals, whom we must hereafter forever name the executioners, the murderers of poor humanity. In this superb hall are two doors, in the opposite walls; and over that on the right hand is written:

"'*Chi entra senza permesso è scomunicato.*'
["'*Whoever enters without permission is excommunicated.*'"]

"By the door which opens on the left, you enter a large chamber, at the extremity of which is the Tribune, where the Cardinals seated themselves in judgment over their poor fellow-men. The footstools are all carved and gilded; and the thrones are covered with rich and ornamental scarlet drapery. In front of these superb seats is the bar of judgment, formed with a bench, on which sat the accused. These were guarded by keepers, who, after the sentence, are to lead them to their fate. In this hall of justice, we observe four doors in the opposite walls. In the middle of the floor, under each, with a refinement in the art of cruelty, are placed boards, so balanced on pivots, that whoever steps upon one of them, instantly drops into a deep pit, which seems to descend into the bowels of the earth!

"What thoughts does the sight bring up to the imagination! We see the poor, accused, innocent prisoners, first trembling and weeping before the Tribunal, then hear the sentence pronounced of many years of imprisonment; then one is led across the hall, ignorant of the unseen danger. A man, a woman, or perhaps a young girl, approaches one of these doors; treads without suspicion upon the small revolving plank. Instantly it turns—the victim falls into a deep chasm, apparently bottomless, and I believe near a hundred feet deep! He is dashed upon the floor of a subterranean cell, scarcely five feet by eight in size, with bones broken, if not killed. There he lies, half dead, alone, in darkness. Not a ray of light, not a pillow, a covering, or even a wisp of straw is to be found, to lean upon, or to guard from the dampness and cold.

"After the first terrible act of this tragedy had been performed, not till the following day, was any thing like compassion shown to the sufferer. A basket was then let down by a cord containing a light, and a little bread and water. If, after a little time, the prisoner took any portion of the food or drink, it served as a sign that he was not dead. Then, three days afterwards, the experiment was repeated; but this was the last time, whether he was dead or alive.

"Let us proceed in our examination of the building. The two doors, which, as I said before, lead beyond the Tribunal, bring us to numerous chambers, used as prisons. There were confined persons accused of not attending mass, of not confessing within a certain time, of murmuring against the court of Rome, &c. We ascend from it, by the staircases near the same two doors, into the cortili, or little court-yards, the walls of which are injured, and apparently smoked. They are dingy with words written with charcoal; and every sentence we can read has something to fill the heart with pity or horror. Here is one of the court-yards surrounded by cells for prisoners, placed in three ranges, one above another. They are made very strong, with grated windows. They are not protected from the cold by glass, but open to the air; and the doors are so made as to admit the wind. The floors are made of bare earth. The walls are black, and laid without plaster. A sack of straw and a ragged coverlet are the only bed; and even during the coldest weather no fire is allowed. The food, for six days of the week, is boiled beans, without oil or butter, with a little bread and water. On Sundays they had four ounces of flour pasta, for soup, and three ounces of meat.

"We pass that court by a door, and enter a giardinetto, or little garden, with three sides, and three terraces, and surrounded with cells much worse than the former; and here we find two chambers, quite remarkable, and well fitted to excite attention, as they contain a new kind of torture. In one we may enter, and find only an oven. What can have been its use in a place where they made no bread? It was heated for the purpose of forcing the wretched prisoners to confess, even when they had nothing that they could confess. If they communicated nothing, they were burned to death. The second chamber contains a second oven, like the first.

DUNGEON OF THE INQUISITION.

"In this little garden are two gates, by which is the descent to the subterranean apartments; and through these lies the way to the pits under the trap-doors, opening at the entrances of the hall of justice. Here we find a large cavern. Let us pass down to see the catacombs, and see the dear bones of our poor brethren, who have fallen martyrs under the empire of tyrants. You will shrink back and turn pale. The air is damp, chilly, oppressive, and deadly; and the feelings are excited by the thoughts which fill the mind.

"There we found a cave, a catacomb; and now a hole, at the bottom of which are bones and hair. It is a deep hole, extending above, up to the hall of justice. These are the remains of the bodies of our martyred brethren, who were left here to die. You will cover your eyes with your hands, and tell me you have seen enough. And indeed it is enough to tell to our other brethren, and to publish to distant nations. It will show what tyrants are capable of, and how they can oppress mankind.

"Let us depart from this abominable place, and publish to all the world, that Roman priests are rapacious wolves, dressed in sheep's clothing. They are whited sepulchres, hypocrites. They pretend simplicity, but show themselves the oppressors and persecutors of the human race. Look at Italy, where the gospel should introduce civilization, peace, and love. By their means it is filled with ignorance, error, slavery, tyranny, murder, war, poverty, superstition, idolatry, and death.

"O inhabitants of New York, and of the United States! in concluding this brief description which I have given of the Holy Office, or Tribunal of the Inquisition, I wish to put a question to you: Have you, in your country, places so terrible, punishments so severe and cruel, tortures so excruciating, or impiety so detestable, under the influence of your ministers, such as we have had to endure under the priests of Rome?

"I conclude by saying, Be careful and vigilant, and do not suffer yourselves to be deceived by the Pharisaic priests of the Romish church. Do you observe, O citizens of New York, what they do in this very city? First, they fill the heads of their credulous believers with a thousand superstitions and idolatries, and make them live in ignorance. Next, like bloodsuckers, they fix themselves upon them, until they have drawn the last drop of their blood, and after all they pretend to send them to the infernal regions. Do we not see that they carry on a lucrative traffic in their churches? They sell an Agnus Dei for two shillings; a baptism cost three or four dollars; a little water, one or two dollars. The contributions made in the churches every Sabbath, amounting to ten, a hundred, or sometimes, perhaps, a hundred and fifty dollars, do not satisfy them. Confession must come in to finish all. They say that, in order to be saved, they must perform pious works, that is, give masses for their souls, the souls of their deceased friends, and also the souls in purgatory. I ask you, O Americans! whether this is theft or not? Whether they are robbers or not? They sell the blood of Christ in the market.

"I have only to add, that, wherever Romish priests have set their foot, have been brought in terror, despotism, tyranny, aristocracy, and, little by little, superstition, idolatry, ignorance, misery, slavery, wars, and murders. Love, then, the gospel of Christ; be faithful followers of his doctrines.

"And let us pray the Father of lights, the Giver of every good thing, the Comforter of every heart, our Lord Jesus, that all minds may be enlightened, and all hearts may be inflamed with the knowledge of our duties toward Christ; that grace may be given us to learn his holy gospel, and all the human race may know it, and may obey it in such a manner, that by the help of God, we may come into the unity of the faith, *unus ovile*, that is, one only body in Christ Jesus.

"May God bless us and comfort us! Amen.

"Giovanni Tomaso Baldasare,
"*An Italian Evangelical Christian.*

"*New York, Feb. 1st, 1855.*"

We have given this somewhat large space to a notice of the aspect of the great conflict between truth and falsehood in the heart of Rome, because it is but common justice to form our estimate of the real character of a system by the influence which it exerts at home. If it be true, that the best idea of a man's character or disposition may be gained by observing his conduct when acting in the unrestrained freedom of his domestic habits, then by this test, Rome must stand convicted before the world of all the perfidy and cruelty which history has recorded against her.

THE MADIAI.

E may notice in this connection, as eminently worthy of record among the conquests of the Bible, the interesting facts touching the imprisoned Madiai. Francesco and Rosa Madiai were natives of Tuscany. Francesco was the son of a yeoman, or small landed proprietor, in the neighbourhood of Florence. He acted as courier to many families, and gained the confidence of his employers. The harsh treatment of his confessor had, in early life, somewhat shaken his faith in the established religion of the country. Having confessed that he had eaten meat during Lent, in compliance with the advice of his physician, the father confessor, with a burst of furious invective, told him that for this offence "he was damned in body and soul!" Francesco was sent away without absolution; and he declares that for some time afterward, "he scarcely knew of what religion he was; that he still attended the service of the Romish Church, but felt as if he was not satisfactorily performing his Christian duties." While on a visit to his brother, who had married an American lady in Boston, he had opportunities of becoming acquainted with the habits of a free people, and made some proficiency in reading the English Bible, but he was still, to use his own words, "in much darkness as to scriptural truth." Shortly after his return to Florence, he was engaged in the service of an English family as a courier. Here his acquaintance commenced with Rosina Pulini, who afterward became his wife. As she understood English, he persuaded her to read to him, every evening, a chapter in the Bible, and to explain it to him in Italian, as he was unable at that time to procure a copy of the Scriptures in Italian, simply because no Italian Bibles were in circulation. The instruction received in this humble way was of great advantage to his spiritual comfort. After his marriage, Francesco and his wife kept furnished apartments in Florence, which were frequently occupied by English families. At this time, they were still members of the Roman Catholic Church, but, to adopt the language of the Misses Senhouse, in the volume entitled, "Letters of the Madiai and visits to their prisons," "They became so disgusted by the careless and scandalous manner of performing religious worship, by the open and shameless profligacy of the priests, and by the blind superstitions of the people, that they began prayerfully and earnestly to read and search the Scriptures, in order to examine into these matters of faith for themselves; their eyes were thus gradually opened, and they saw the glaring errors and delusions of the Romish religion, which they finally abjured. They attended divine service at the Swiss church so long as they were able; when all places of Protestant worship were closed to them, they assembled with their brethren in the faith, 'in an upper room,' there to read and study the Scriptures, to pray to God and to praise him. Their lives and conversation were so blameless, that even their accusers were unable to establish any charge against their moral and social conduct. They were remarkably true and just in their dealings, generous and charitable to the poor, ready to forgive, grateful for kindness, loyal to their earthly sovereign, and devoted and faithful subjects to the King of kings. Thus were they bright examples to all around them; but their good and attractive qualities did not touch the hearts or influence the judgment of their enemies. The sole crime of apostasy from the faith of Rome overweighed all other considerations; indeed, their unimpeachable character rather increased the bitter malice of their accusers, as it made more evident their unjustifiable treatment of them, and so cast an additional odium on their persecuting church."

The progress of Protestantism in Tuscany excited the wrath of the Romish authorities. They complained of it as an encroachment upon the divine rights of the true church. The first overt act of intolerance was the expulsion, from Tuscany, of Captain Packenham, a British officer of great intelligence and piety, on the charge of Protestant propagandism. The next step was a government veto, prohibiting the Florentines from attending the Swiss Protestant church, under penalty of fine and imprisonment! All this illiberal policy had the very opposite effect from that which was desired by the Romish authorities. The people were stimulated with a zeal to look into these forbidden things; they were all the more intent upon hearing these " dangerous" and *heretical* preachers. Religious reunions for the purpose of reading the Scriptures and prayer, were held in secret, and converts to the faith of the Bible increased daily. The vigilance of the police was called into requisition, and on one occasion, Mons. Geymonat, a young Waldensian pastor, was discovered in the act of reading the Scriptures to a few Italians. For this *heinous crime* he was thrown into prison, and after some time his zealous persecutors sent him out of the country, manacled like a felon, and lodged in one foul dungeon after another, until he reached the frontier. Another minister of the Waldensian church, Mons. Malan, was in a summary manner expelled from Tuscany, on suspicion of having been guilty of a similar offence. The event which occasioned the greatest excitement at this time was the severity exercised toward a distinguished Tuscan nobleman. Among the few "noble of this world" who were found in the ranks of the converts to the Protestant faith in Tuscany, was Count Pietro Guicciardini, one of the Florentines who had been commanded to abstain from all further visits to the Swiss Protestant chapel. Finding that liberty to worship God in accordance with conscientious conviction was denied him in his own country, he resolved to leave it. Some days before the time fixed upon for his departure, he met a few Christian friends, who had, like himself, renounced the faith of Rome, and who had gone without previous concert or arrangement to the house of a mutual friend, and while engaged with them in reading the Bible, the police entered the room, arrested them all, and escorted them to the Bargello, where they were imprisoned ten days, and then condemned to a six months' detention in one of the prisons in the Maremma, an unhealthy district on the coast. This sentence was commuted to banishment for the same length of time. For the sole offence of reading the Bible to his countrymen, Count Guicciardini was treated like a felon and a traitor. Not a word was alleged against his character as a citizen or a loyal subject. His persecutors admitted that his life had been outwardly unexceptionable, and that they had no ground of accusation upon which to base their justification of this severity, except that he had become a Protestant. We hear much said about the light of the nineteenth century, but this fact stands on the page as an occurrence of the winter of 1850-51! The injustice practised toward Count Guicciardini was the beginning of fiercer measures of discipline. The *church* was bent upon putting a summary stop to the proceedings of the Bible readers in Tuscany. All who were even suspected of Protestantism, as well as the more decidedly heretical who were known to be readers of the Bible, were arrested and set to prison on the charge of apostasy, or *Empietà*. Francesco and Rosa Madiai were among the victims of this cruel and foolish intolerance. Of Rosa, we have already spoken as an ardent and devoted Protestant Christian. Her conversion was the more remarkable, as she had been for many years noted on account of the singular zeal she had displayed in professing the Romish faith. The Misses Senhouse mention that they were informed by a member of a family with whom Rosa resided for seventeen years, "that during that period her attachment to her ancient faith was openly avowed, and so well known to them that they were all convinced, had any reproach ever been cast upon her religion, or had any attempt been made to undermine her opinions, great as was her attachment to the family, she would instantly have resigned her situation, and have left them." This fact is interesting as a trait of the sincerity of her conversion, and it becomes important, in view of the defamatory attempts which were made to impugn the genuineness of the conversion of the Madiai, by charging them with mercenary motives. Rosa Madiai, at the time of her trial, refuted this charge by stating with genuine and characteristic simplicity: "Had we been influenced to change our religion by interested reasons, we should have done so when we were residing for so many years in a Protestant country and in Protestant families." A more conclusive refutation could not have been given. As to the "interested" motives imputed to them, these could hardly influence the subjects of the Tuscan government, which rewarded conversion to the Protestant faith, with imprisonment in the filthiest dungeons and with all manner of contempt and obloquy! So far as things temporal were concerned, the change involved the loss of every possession which the mercenary spirit takes into account. The profession of faith in Christ, and of preference of his word over all the silly traditions of Romanism, was made by these converts with the full consciousness of the perils which it included. They counted the cost; they knew the penalty; they were prepared to suffer it, and they gloried in their tribulation. They knew it was encountered for the sake of the gospel. They had a source of enjoyment which their oppressors could not destroy, for the peace of God which flows from faith in his promises is far beyond the reach of a persecuting hierarchy. The world cannot give it, neither can the world take it away. Not that the sacrifices which they made were the less painful or real. It is something to exchange a happy home for the dungeon of solitary imprisonment, to bid adieu to the loved companionship of congenial spirits, and endure the society of blaspheming jailers; to be shut out from the cheerful sunlight and the refreshing air, and locked up in the foul atmosphere of a gloomy prison. It is a great privation to be denied the enjoyment of the fellowship of Christian worship, and instead of the music of prayer and praise, to be stunned with the discordant groans and outcries of despairing criminals; but it is a great privilege, also, to be enabled to suffer all these things, not only without a murmur against Providence, but even with joyful acquiescence in the dispensation which had counted them worthy to suffer reproach for the glorious gospel of the Son of God. For ten weary months they endured imprisonment before they were brought to trial. During all this time the Madiai were permitted to see one another only once, for a few minutes, in the presence of the jailer, and this favour was granted at the request of the English chargè d'affaires, Mr. Scarlet. Their books were taken from them. The Misses Senhouse, in company with two friends, Miss Grant and the Rev. G. Hamilton, with great difficulty obtained a government order authorizing them to see the prisoners once a week, in the presence of their respective jailers. The account which they give of their visits of mercy is full of deep interest, and is a most affecting narrative, but our limits will not admit the circumstantial details, for which we refer the reader to the narrative published by the Presbyterian Board, 265 Chestnut street. Suffice it to say, that at their first interview, Rosa entered the office of the governor, or director of the prison, attended by a male and female jailer, the latter as repulsive as filth and ugly ferocity could well make her. She is represented as "the very personification of all cruelty and all vileness." These Christian friends embraced Rosa tenderly, and the governor ordered the virago, who eyed them with disgusting suspicion, to leave the room. The prisoner appeared composed, and conversed freely on religious subjects. The interview lasted an hour. Francesco, whom they saw on the following day, was cheerful. "He declared himself happy at the honour put on him to suffer for righteousness' sake, and professed the most absolute resignation to the will of God, whatever that might be, whether to suffer torture or death." The severities of their imprisonment brought on sickness which had well-nigh proved fatal. Francesco was transferred from the Bargello to the Murate, a new prison. On one occasion, his Christian friends, having brought some of his favourite psalms, which they had copied for him, handed the MS. to the director for inspection. At their next visit it was returned with the remark, that "profane writings were inadmissible!" "Portions of the Roman Catholic Bible with notes, and a few religious books, were at this time permitted, but after their sentence, all save the Roman

Catholic Bible were withdrawn." When, at the expiration of ten months, the trial came on, the Madiai, prejudged and foredoomed, were condemned—Francesco to FIFTY-SIX MONTHS' HARD LABOUR in the prison at Volterra, and Rosa to FORTY-FIVE MONTHS' imprisonment in the Ergastolo at Lucca! When the Madiai attempted to defend themselves, or their religion, from false imputations, the presiding judge shouted "Silence; it is not permitted you to speak of your religion before a Roman Catholic audience!" With wonderful patience and composure, they heard their sentence, embraced each other in silence, and were led away by their guards, separately, to undergo their doom. What shall we say to these things? The facts speak for themselves. In our own country an attempt was made to deny and pervert them, but the publication of the official documents silenced this attempt to divert public attention from them. The church of Rome was arraigned at the bar of the public opinion of the civilized world. The charge of remorseless, persecuting cruelty was clearly made out; and from every land in Europe, and from the free Republic of North America, the cry of shame! was raised, until even Rome was startled by the hiss of infamy which was poured in scorn upon the ferocious monsters who had perpetrated this outrage upon humanity and upon the age. Every Protestant government in Europe remonstrated against the injustice. At first, their protests were received with contemptuous indifference, but they were repeated with greater earnestness, and at last the Tuscan government found itself overwhelmed with disgrace, and the Madiai were suddenly thrust out of their prisons and hurried out of the country! Their liberation was literally one of the "conquests of the Bible." It was a triumph. Before the world, the history of that dark transaction—dark in the infamy which its shadow casts upon an unjust government and a tyrannical priesthood, but bright in the heroism and constancy of these humble, yet noble confessors of the truth—stands forth a double monument of Romish ferocity and impotence, and a trophy of the moral power of the Bible in nerving its witnesses with fortitude in the face of torture and death; and, also, in controlling the public opinion of the civilized world, and rousing the indignant remonstrances of enlightened governments against the renewal of outrages which in past ages have rendered Rome a byword of reproach, a hissing and contempt among the nations! After a cruel imprisonment of nineteen months, the liberated Madiai met on board the ship which conveyed them in safety from the land which was not worthy of them. Let it not be said that too much stress is laid upon the story of the Madiai, and that their sufferings, however cruel and enormous, are not a sufficient warrant for the interest they have excited. Every Protestant in the whole world, every friend of human rights, owes them a debt of gratitude. Admit that they were poor, obscure, and humble in their origin and station—they have proved themselves noble and honourable in the highest sense of the word. They have earned for themselves so much the more renown by their unflinching defence of the truth which alone can make the nations free. They have torn the mask from the face of Popery; they have, by their patient endurance of outrage and wrong for conscience' sake, presented an unanswerable refutation of the smooth falsehoods with which the unprincipled advocates of Romish superstition seek to pervert and blind the popular mind in Protestant countries. They have proved before the world that Rome has not changed her character, and that her nature is as untamed as the tiger's, which still thirsts for blood, though the bars of its cage are happily between it and those whom it would fain rend and devour. In the language of M. D. Hill, Esq., in a recent pamphlet on this subject, we may conclude this notice of the Madiai: "On this memorable prosecution, posterity will look back as giving the date of another expansion of the Protestant influence; and even to the sufferers the consolation may be vouchsafed, of knowing that the afflictions which they have borne has been the appointed means of rescuing multitudes from a worse than Egyptian bondage. Even so, O Lord! Amen!"

As documentary evidence, from which there is no appeal, we append the official form of the sentence pronounced against the Madia:

THE SENTENCE.

"*Sentence against Francesco, son of the late Vicenzio Madiai, and Rosa, his wife, accused of impiety.*

"The decree of this court, of 25th November, 1851, having been examined, and likewise the act of accusation of the same year, the witnesses having been heard, in a public discussion, the Public Minister having summed up, and Odvardo Maggiorani, counsel for the Madiai, with the accused themselves, having been last heard, the results of the discussion seem to be the following:

"That Francesco and Rosa Madiai, born and brought up in Catholicism, separated from it four or five years back, to embrace the religion called by them Evangelical, or religion of the pure gospel; that they lent their house for reunions, and when the teacher who generally presided at these was banished from Tuscany, and by means of the police this sect was broken up, and the number of those who assembled at the house of the Madiai much diminished, the meetings, nevertheless, still continued, and one was held on the 17th

August, 1851, when the public force surprised three individuals there, who, together with a child of fifteen, whom the Madiai had lodged in their house for a short time, were occupied in reading the Bible, translated by Diodati, each one having a copy under his eye;

"That in the house of the said Madiai were not only many copies of the said Bible, and others in the English language, and books of prayers for the use of the heterodox, but besides various works of the same nature, and even many copies of each;

"That, also, with others, Francesco held language insinuating that the so-called 'Evangelical' religion merited preference to the Catholic belief;

"That, with two women who served the Madiai, and a third who lived with them about eight months, from December, 1850, they displayed the intention of leading them to abjure Catholicism and embrace the pure gospel, holding withal readings and discourses tending to throw discredit on the clergy and the doctrines taught by them, particulary on purgatory, denying its existence; upon the holy sacrifice of the mass, declaring it an invention of the priests, and impugning the real presence in the consecrated host; upon the intercession of the Blessed Virgin Mary and the saints, declaring it impossible and dishonouring to God; upon the authority of the High Pontiff, denying his power; upon the observance of other festivals than Sunday; and upon the mortification consisting in abstaining from certain kinds of food, declaring it an invention of sinful men; upon the sacrament of communion and upon sacramental confession, declaring the first misunderstood and wrongly administered, because it is not true the changing of the bread and wine, and because the wine ought not to be denied to the laity; and reproving the second, because made to man and not to God;

"That with one of these women, older than the others,

who generally maintained the discussion upon such matters, their attempts were of no effect; That with the young, needy, and very ignorant, aided with pecuniary assistance, and by continued instruction, they succeeded in making her abandon the true religion, to adopt that professed by her master; That the Madiai also gave themselves the trouble of teaching her to read, that she might be able to understand the books which they afterward supplied, namely, the Bible, translated by Diodati; and another, entitled 'Book of Common Prayer,' printed in London, in 1848, by the 'Society for the Promotion of Christian Knowledge,' in which are found those maxims and doctrines condemned by the Catholic Church, which the Madiai had verbally taught, particularly that the existence of purgatory and the worship of images are foolish inventions; that in the sacrament of the eucharist there is not any transubstantiation, and other similar atrocious heretical depravities abovementioned;

"That the same young woman admitted to the reading of the Bible, which they did together, (commenting on it in the way already mentioned,) abandoned the practice of the Catholic worship; and, to obey the injunction of Madame Madiai, (who accused her of idolatry,) she left off using the rosaries which she possessed; partook twice (being conducted to the place by Madame Madiai) of the communion made by them, in commemoration of the Last supper, and did not awake from her error until reconducted to her paternal home for a few days, and carrying with her the Italian Bible; this being found, caused the discovery of her wanderings;

"That the Madiai, denying that sectarian meetings were held at their house, acknowledge that a few friends there met together, to attend to the practices of the newly-embraced religion, and declare the apostasy of the young woman in their service to have been made spontaneously by her, and not in consequence of their insinuations;

"That, notwithstanding this, neither their opposition, nor the witnesses brought forward, have succeeded in destroying the facts objected against them in the accusation;

"That Francesco has suffered imprisonment for the present procedure from the 17th of August, 1851, and Rosa Madiai from the 27th of the same month and year;

"Whereas, with regard to the Madiai, accused of impiety, committed by means of proselytism, it appeared foreign to the question all that referred to liberty of conscience and religious toleration, because the first is not offended when the citizens are commanded to render an account merely of external acts, and the latter is guarded, not trampled upon, when it seeks to hinder others from being seduced to abandon the religion they profess;

"Whereas, precisely for this, the penal laws, agreeably with the declarations of the clearest writers, recognise in proselytism a crime civilly imputable;

"Whereas, resulting from the preceding facts, it is undeniable that the Madiai laboured, on many different occasions, and even with success, to make proselytes to the religion newly embraced by them, it only remained to be considered, whether in such a fact existed the extremes required by the sixtieth article of the law of 30th November, 1786, for the application of its penal ratification;

"Whereas, the extreme of guilty intention in such a crime occurs whenever the intention of the agent is directed to increase the ranks of dissenting sects, to the prejudice of the religion of the state, and that of evil done according to the facts, now established in our jurisprudence, it is certified that these acts, though not committed in public places, have been done in the presence of many persons, and are extensively propagated, and engendered a grave scandal:

"It is declared evident that impiety was committed by Francesco and Rosa Madiai, by means of proselytism to the so-called Evangelical Confession, or Religion of the Pure Gospel, to the prejudice of the Catholic religion, predominant in the Grand Duchy, in the time and way above mentioned.

"And whereas, the crime of impiety, by means of proselytism, is manifestly contemplated by the sixtieth article of the law of the land of 30th November, 1786, and is repressed never with less than exemplary punishment: of which all the circumstances of the case being considered, it appears that the second degree is proportioned to the delinquency, represented in virtue of successive laws, by the nature and amount of penalty, afterwards mentioned;

"Whereas, the deductions of the defence have all been replied to by the previous proposition of facts and consideration of right—

"The following articles having been examined—the sixtieth of the law of 30th November, 1786; 1, 4, 9, 14, of the decree of 4th March, 1849, confirmed by the other of 5th May following, and 34 and 35 of the police regulations of 22d November, 1849, and 55 of the above-mentioned law of 30th November, 1786, &c.—

"Francesco, son of the late Vicenzio Madiai, and Rosa his wife, are condemned,—the former to the punishment of fifty-six months' seclusion in the prison of hard labour at Volterra, and the latter to forty-five months of Ergastolo, (the female galleys,) calculated in the one case from the 26th of November, 1851, and in the other, from the 27th of the same month and year: they are likewise condemned to pay the expenses of the trial, and made subject to the *surveillance* of the police for three years after the completion of their imprisonment."*

THE BIBLE IN MADEIRA.

FROM Tuscany, and this record of the barbarism, which, by her own showing, disgraces the statute-book of the Grand Duchy, we would call the attention of the reader to a brief review of facts in Madeira, illustrative of still mightier conquests of the Bible, and still more violent hostility to the liberty which the Bible confers. The island of Madeira lies in the Atlantic Ocean, nearly opposite Morocco, on the coast of Africa, in about 30° deg. north latitude. It derives its name, *Madeira*, or timber, from the abundance of its forests. Since 1419, (when it was discovered,) it has been a part of the dominions of Portugal, and subject to its laws. The Roman Catholic religion is established by law, and, of course, the Bible is a proscribed book. In 1838, Dr. Kalley, a Scotch physician and a missionary of the Free Church of Scotland, came to Madeira, with the design of residing on the island. He was ignorant of the language, and, in order to acquire it, opened a school for the instruction of the

---

* Authentic statements represent the number of converts from Romanism in Tuscany at from twenty-four to twenty-six thousand.

Portuguese in English. He endeavoured to establish schools for the promotion of education in the island. These schools were maintained at his own expense. They became very popular. In a short time, eight hundred adults were instructed in these institutions, besides children. Not only were the common people delighted with the benevolent zeal of Dr. Kalley, but the municipal authorities of the city of Funchal, the capital, voluntarily passed a vote of thanks to Dr. Kalley, for what they termed "his disinterested acts of benevolence and philanthropy,—such as the establishment of schools, in different parts of the island, at his own expense, furnishing the people with medical attendance and medicines gratuitously, &c."

The first book in which they were taught to read English was the Bible. Dr. Kalley had brought a supply of Portuguese Bibles, also, from Scotland. The people were in a state of most deplorable ignorance. They had no knowledge of the Bible whatever, and it was a rare case to find any one *who knew there was a book containing a history of Jesus Christ!* In a short time, hundreds of these hitherto ignorant people became intelligent readers of the Scriptures. The usual results followed. In the course of their readings, they met with many things inconsistent with the religious tenets which they had hitherto held. Some applied to the priests for a solution of their difficulties. The answers were not satisfactory. The priests were annoyed at inquiries displaying an intelligence which they could not successfully combat, and ere long both the schools and the Bible were denounced. The bishops and priests, indignant at the growing interest of the people in the Scriptures, declared that "the Bible was a book from hell," and the sentence of excommunication was denounced against all who should read it. In five years' time, Dr. Kalley had circulated so many copies of the Bible, that the remotest corners of the island were supplied with it. Many of the inhabitants had quietly renounced Romanism and embraced the Christian faith. In 1843, the storm which had long been gathering, began to break. Dr. Kalley was warned to flee. He refused. Several of the converts were sent to prison. The houses of the people were ransacked. Copies of the Bible were taken away and destroyed. The priests threatened to burn all they could find. The registrar of each parish was furnished with a copy of the following

ORDER.

"*Sir:*—On the receipt of this, you will summon to your presence the teachers, male and female, of all the schools established and supported by Dr. Kalley, existing in your parish; and in the presence of two witnesses, charge them henceforth not to teach any living being. If, after being duly notified, any of them should continue to teach, you can immediately send them to this administration in charge of two officers of police. You will cause this order to be faithfully executed, and report the result by Monday next, giving the names of all who have been notified, &c. God save you!

"J. C. TERREIRA UZEL,
"*Administrator.*"

The Bible readers were reported by the priests to the government, and were summarily arrested and sent to prison. One poor peasant was excommunicated. For about a year he eluded the search of his persecutors; but having been convinced by the pleading of the public prosecutor in an analogous case, that the ancient cruelties of Popery were not sanctioned by the existing charter, he ventured to teach an evening school in the Lombo das Fayas, in the parish of St. Antonio de Serra. One night a party of men, led by the church beadle, came to the school with a fictitious warrant, and attempted to apprehend him. He refused to submit. His pupils took part with him, and the beadle went his way with his *posse*, without, however, having been subjected to the slightest violence. "This conduct of the schools," says Capt. Tate, of the British navy, who was an eye-witness of the atrocities he describes, " was represented as '*Sedition and resistance of justice,*' and the public prosecutor denounced them as Miguelites led on by Dr. Kalley! On that day week the judge and public prosecutor, with a notary and about sixty soldiers, proceeded at night to the Lombo das Fayas. The houses of the scholars, chiefly Bible readers, were broken open—thirty men and women were taken prisoners—most of them were bound—many of them were beaten, and some of them very severely—and their houses were given up to be sacked by the soldiers, who committed the most horrible atrocities. With scarcely any clothes on (for they had been roused from their beds by the soldiers) twenty-two of them were conveyed to Funchal, in a Portuguese frigate, which, to complete the melancholy farce, had been sent to support the operations of the soldiers, (!!!) and there committed to prison." There they remained for *upward of twenty months,* supported by English generosity. At the end of this period they were brought to trial, and were honourably acquitted of every charge, but *they were remanded to prison till they should fully pay the jail fees.* The acquittal of these poor men exasperated their bigoted enemies. The priests stirred up the worst passions of their devotees. The most atrocious outrages and personal violence were perpetrated. The poor Christians were waylaid, beaten, and sometimes left for dead, maimed and bleeding, at the roadside. One of the public newspapers, the Imparcial, edited at that time by the brother-in-law of the governor, openly recommended the cudgel " as the best means of convincing the country people" of the errors of the new religionists, " because they were not accustomed to arguments, but would understand the power of a stick." This same print at another time recommended the gallows and the stake as the only remaining cure for heresy! Dr. Kalley was the special object of the vengeance of the government and priesthood, but the trouble was to know how to assail him. The treaty between England and Portugal guaranteed to the subjects of the respective governments *liberty* to enjoy their religion without molestation in Madeira. The ingenuity of Romish priests is not easily thwarted. In the code of laws enacted by the Inquisition in Portugal, in 1603, they found the very article they so much desired. Dr. Kalley was arrested and detained in prison five months. The reader will be interested in hearing Dr. Kalley's own statement, and we give it in the form of an address delivered by him, on the 6th of November, 1846. At a meeting of the Protestant Association in London, held on the evening of the day already specified, Dr. Kalley proposed the following resolution:

"That the proceedings at Madeira, whether as regards the treatment of native Portuguese or of British subjects, manifests a determination, on the part of Popery, to crush all examination of, or secession from, her erroneous system."

"Mr. Chairman, I have no power to 'stir men's blood,' like a reverend gentleman here, nor would I seek to do so. I come merely as a witness in a court of justice, to tell truly and dispassionately what I have seen—to give testimony on the great question,— Is Popery changed, or is she not?

"I beg to refer to a document issued by the highest ecclesiastical authority in Madeira, dated three and a half years ago, and published from all the pulpits in Madeira. It was issued by Sebastian Casimero Medina e Vasconcellas, Vicar-General of the bishopric of Funchal, in the name of the Bishop Don Januario Vicente Camacho. It was addressed to 'all vicars, and curates, public prosecutors, and officers of justice, to all persons, civil and ecclesiastical, of every rank and degree,' and 'required, and commanded them not to touch, or hold communication with Francisco Pires Soars and Nicolau Tolentino Vieyra,' who had dared to leave the communion of Rome, and join the Presbyterian communion at Madeira. These two men were declared to be 'excommunicated by the curse of Almighty God, and of the blessed St. Peter and St. Paul, with those of Gomorrah and Sodom, and with Korah, Dathan, and Abiram, whom the earth swallowed alive for their disobedience.' This document goes on to say,—'Let no one give them fire, water, bread, or any other thing that may be necessary for their support. Let no one pay them their debts. Let no one support them in any case which they may bring before a court of justice. Let all put them aside as rotten and excommunicated members, separated from the bosom and union of the Holy Mother Catholic Church, and as rebels and contumacious.' It further excommunicated, *ipso facto*, all who do not comply with these commands,—every debtor who should pay these men their just debts, every judge who should dare, in a court of law to do them justice, every charitable person who should give them water, fire, or any thing necessary to existence; and the excommunication against those who should assist them or do them justice, implies the very same penalty as was imposed upon them.

"There is so strong a disinclination in this country to believe any evil of Popery, that no doubt we shall be told that that excommunication was a mere form, and meant nothing. Let it be remembered, however, that from every parish pulpit in Madeira it was announced, that no man should pay these persons their just debts; and not only were they authorized not to pay them, but were actually threatened with excommunication if they did. Does this mean nothing?

"Let it be known, that the persons who were so excommunicated were obliged to hide themselves from the light of the sun for months; that they were at last compelled to tear themselves from the bosom of their families, and leave their father-land; and that they are at the present day wanderers in a strange land, one being in the East, and the other in the West Indies.* After this let every impartial man judge whether that excommunication was a mere form, and meant nothing.

"To show that the priest's interference with the law, and malediction against every judge who should do justice to an excommunicated person, is not an unmeaning form, I beg to relate a case which occurred in a court of justice this present year: Two men were partners as sawyers of wood; one was the owner of two-thirds of the property, and the other of one-third. The former had learned to read, and had received the precious truth, that Christ died for our sins, and that his blood cleanseth from all sin, and had renounced the worship of the host, virgin, images, and pictures; the other still adhered to these forms. The owner of the two-thirds wished to dissolve partnership, and proposed to pay the other his one-third of the property, and retain it all, or that the owner of the one-third

---

* He is now in the office of the American Protestant Society.

should pay him his two-thirds, and retain it. These propositions being refused, he then proposed that the whole of the property should be sold, and the proceeds divided between them; this also being refused, he brought the case before the judge. The owner of the one-third had nothing to advance but that the other had not been at mass or confession for two years, and of this he brought a certificate from the priest of the parish. The judge considered the whole case, especially the priest's certificate, and then passed sentence, that as the owner of two-thirds had not been at mass or confession for two years, he was virtually excommunicated; and being excommunicated he was incompetent to appear in any court of justice! He, therefore, gave the verdict in favour of the owner of the one-third, leaving him with the property, and sentenced the other to pay all the expenses of the process! and from that sentence there was no appeal. It was published in the Madeira newspapers in the end of July, 1846.

"I cannot, at this late hour, enlarge on the proceedings of Popery in Madeira; I would merely glance, for a few moments, at one or two of her atrocities.

"On the 31st of May, 1845, a man was tried for having had a meeting of his relations in his own house for reading the Scriptures and prayer, and for having refused to pay homage to a piece of cloth fixed upon a stick, and called the Holy Ghost. For these crimes he was sentenced to six months' imprisonment in the jail at Funchal. When I was in jail, in 1843, there was no mass said there, nor had there been for years; but in 1844 there were from twenty to thirty prisoners in the jail, who being convinced that there is a God, and but one, felt assured that a bit of bread is not that God, and whose hearts revolted against paying divine homage to any created thing. When the priests found they had in their power victims whom they hoped to compel to offend their God, it was required that mass should be said in the jail every Sunday and holiday, and that all the prisoners should be obliged to attend. The man who was condemned for having had the meeting in his house, and for not worshipping that which they blasphemously called the Holy Ghost, was ordered to mass with the rest on the first of June. He refused to go. The jailers attempted to force him, but in vain. Soldiers were called. He grasped the iron bars of the jail window, in order to prevent himself from being dragged to mass. He was struck with the butt-ends of their muskets. His grasp was overcome by violence, and at the point of the bayonet he was driven to what he regarded as idolatry. He went, but did not kneel there; he could not. After mass he felt that he had done wrong, even though compelled; he felt that it would have been better that his blood should have been shed there, than that he should have offended his God, and he resolved, that on the ensuing Sabbath no power on earth should compel him to attend. During that week he conversed with many of his fellow-prisoners, and having received more instruction than they, he reasoned with them from the Scriptures. On the 8th of June, twenty prisoners refused to go to mass, and no power could force them; blows and bayonets failed. What was the result? There is, in the jail at Funchal, a place called the Bomba. Respecting that place, I may mention that the day after my release from prison, I sent a friend to distribute bread to the prisoners, and on coming out of the Bomba he gave unequivocal manifestations of his being sick, and nearly fainted—it is a most abominably disgusting den of filth. In that place there were, on the 7th of June, fifteen persons confined for various offences; and on the 8th, when the prisoners refused to go to mass, there were five more added. I wished to go and take the dimensions of it, but could not get admission, and asked a friend to take them for me. He did so; and the paper he brought to me stated that the Bomba is twelve feet square, by eleven feet high; and in that loathsome room twenty men were confined night and day. For what? For refusing to pay that homage to a bit of bread, which man owes to his God!

"We are told, Christian friends, that Popery is changed, that she persecutes no more, that there is not a country on earth where Popery now persecutes, and that she is so changed that she would never wish to persecute. We answer, Popery does not drag out her victims and burn them at the stake in open day: no, for as yet she dare not. But she does what she dares; those who will not obey her despotic commands she throws into the Bomba, that there they may endure a death far more lingering, and far more horrid than at the stake. Let men look into the Bomba, in Funchal jail, and answer whether Popery does not now persecute.

"Reference has been made to the Scriptures, and to the desire of Romanists and others, to exclude the Bible from the schools; Popery has been long known as the enemy of knowledge, but especially of Biblical knowledge. In England she wishes to persuade men that she is not the enemy of the Bible itself, but only of spurious and adulterated editions, and she made a similar profession in Madeira. In 1840, the bishop expressed a wish to see a copy of the Bible that was being put into the hands of his people. One was gladly sent to him. On the 21st of May he placed it in the hands of three canons of the cathedral of Funchal, and appointed them, as a commission, to examine it, and to report to him, as to its correctness or incorrectness. Two years and four months afterward he published a pastoral, wherein he stated that that commission had reported 'that there was scarcely a verse of any chapter either of the Old or New Testament which was not more or less notably adulterated;' and he added, that he 'excommunicated, *ipso facto*, all who should read those Bibles.' We have already seen what excommunication implies; and we now find the bishop coming forward with all his authority, and excommunicating, *ipso facto*, all who read those Bibles But they were declared to be of a spurious and adulterated edition. On reading his pastoral, I was confounded; I did not believe that the British and Foreign Bible Society had issued an unfaithful reprint of Pereira's Bible, and could not suppose it possible that three canons should risk their character by stating a bare-faced falsehood. What was my surprise, in finding, upon getting a copy of the Lisbon edition of the Bible, and comparing it with that of the Bible Society, that in the Gospel of St. Matthew there was not an alteration in any verse of that book. I immediately published an answer to the pastoral, advising that his excellency the bishop should suspend his curse on the word of God till it could be seen whether the other books were as correct as St. Matthew's Gospel. In consequence of the pastoral, the judge came to the jail with the public prosecutor, and other judiciary officers, and ordered all the boxes of the prisoners to be searched for Bibles; and he took away every copy of the Scriptures that he found there! The chief police magistrate went to a school, supported by English charity, and took away thirty Bibles, and all the Testaments that he could find! During the course of the ensuing week, the commission published an answer to my observations. In it, they reasserted what they had said, 'that there was scarcely a verse of any chapter, either of the New or Old Testament, which was not adulterated.' The comparison of the two editions went on; upwards of 5000 verses were examined; and the result was a complete refutation of the commissioners' report. Within two months after the bishop's curse on these books of God, there came from Lisbon an order from the Portuguese government, in which Her Majesty the Queen approved of these very Bibles, and stated that they were approved of by the archibishop also. But, notwithstanding this, the bishop's curse still rests upon the book of God; the priests, from the pulpit, declare that it is a book from hell, and should be burned with the hands that handle it: and when my house was attacked, on the 9th of August, 1846, every copy of the sacred Scriptures which was found was actually thrown into a fire, on the public street, by the mob, when they ascertained that their expected human victims had escaped their outrage. Suppose that in the present distressed state of Ireland a man should go through one of her most famishing villages, selling bread at a reduced price to those that could pay for it, and giving it gratis to those who could not, and that some, whose pecuniary interests were interfered with by the gratuitous distribution, should seek to persuade the people that the bread was poisoned, and should endeavour to incite them to trample it under foot and murder their benefactor, who would not call such conduct atrocious? But suppose, further, some of the famishing creatures to have tasted the bread, and found that it not only did them no harm, but that it actually restored their drooping limbs, and gave them new life; if, then, these selfish and cruel tyrants were to snatch it from their hands and cast it into the fire, and then beat, imprison, and excommunicate them merely for feeding upon it and giving it to their dying children, what words could we find powerful enough to characterize their guilt? Their guilt, however, would be as nothing, compared with the guilt of those who snatch the bread of life from men who are eagerly seeking to feed upon it, that their souls may live forever."

In order, as we proceed, to furnish the proper vouchers, we introduce a copy of the sentence of excommunication pronounced against the two converts, part of which Dr. Kalley quotes in the foregoing address:

"Sebastio Cazemiro Medinna Vasconcellas, Leader of the Choir in the Cathedral, Synedic Examiner, Vicar-General of the bishopric of Funchal, in the island of Madeira, for the Most Excellent and Reverend Don Januaro Vicente Comacho of Her Majesty's Council, Dean of the Cathedral of Funchal, Commander of the Order of Christ, Bishop Elect of Castle Branco, Temporal Governor and Vicar-General of the Bishop of Funchal, Porto Santo, and Arguinot—

"To all the reverend vicars and curates, assistants and chaplains, as well as to all judges and justices of peace, to the delegates of the attorney-general, to the administrators of councils, and all officers of justice, and to all ecclesiastical and secular persons of every degree and condition in all the bishopric and out of it, whom this my letter may reach, who may hear it, or get notice of it in any way, health and peace forever in Jesus Christ our Lord, who is the true remedy and salvation of all. I make known to you, that, having proceeded to an examination of witnesses, as competent to my office, it was proved by them, and confirmed by my sentence, that Francisco Pires Soares, married, and Nicolau Tolentino Vieyra, bachelor, both of this bishopric, residing in the parish of Santa Luzia, near the parish church, apostatized from the union and bosom of the Holy Mother Roman Catholic Church, and became sectaries of the Presbyterian communion, incurring by this ecclesiastical censure and canonical punishment of the greater excommunication. The censures requiring to be aggravated, I ordered this present letter to be written, by which I require and command, under pain of the greater excommunication, all ecclesiastics, ministers and officers of justice, and others above mentioned, as soon as they shall have notice of it, not to touch or hold communication with those who are excommunicated by the curse of Almighty God, and of the blessed St. Peter and St. Paul, with those of Gomorrah and of Sodom, Dathan and Abiram, whom the earth swallowed alive for their great sins and disobedience. Let none give them fire, water, bread, or any other thing that may be necessary to them for their support. Let none pay them their debts. Let none support them in any case which they may bring judicially. Let all put them aside as rotten and excommunicated members, separated from the bosom and union of the Holy Mother Catholic Church, and as rebels and contumacious; for if any do the contrary, (which God forbid!) I lay, and consider as laid, upon their persons, the penalty of the greater excommunication. Therefore were their names and surnames expressly declared; and that all may know this, I order the reverend parish priests to publish this at the meeting on the first Sabbath or holy day, and to affix it on the door of the church, from which let no man take or tear it under pain of excommunication, until, by making satisfaction for all, they merit the benefit for absolution.

"Given in Funchal, under the seal of the Vicar-General and my signature, on the 27th of April, 1843. Jacinto Monteiro Cabrão, Writer to the Ecclesiastical Council, wrote this.

"SEBASTIO CAZEMIRO MEDINA E VAS."

All these means, however, proved ineffectual. The power of the pure word of God was mightier than all the wrath of its enemies. The Bible continued to make its conquests. Converts still made their way to the standard of the gospel, and rallied around it. The Bible was torn in pieces and burned in the fire, but its truths could not be torn from the hearts of those who loved it. The persecuted Christians, immured in the same prisons with the most abandoned felons, calmly committed their cause to God, and endured bonds and imprisonment, rejoicing that "the word of God was not bound." Among the many sufferers for conscience' sake, there was one whose case excited profound sympathy, and, in the later stages of its development, intense sensation, throughout the Protestant world. Mrs. Maria J. Alves was one of the many godly women who had given the most unquestionable evidence of devotion to the truth and faith of the gospel. She was selected as a fit subject of Romish discipline, and the enemies of vital piety resolved to make an example of her, in order to inspire others with terror. On the 31st of January, 1843, she was taken from her family of seven children, the youngest an infant, and committed to prison. In a filthy dungeon, in Funchal, she spent month after month. Her sufferings were protracted, in the vain hope of procuring, by these means, a renunciation of her faith. Her firmness enraged the priests and government officers. On the 2d of May, 1844, she was brought to trial before Judge Negrao, president of the court. The indictment contained three charges: apostasy, hersesy, and blasphemy. She was, however, tried on only one charge, viz., blasphemy. The accusation was, *that she had refused to confess that the consecrated host, or wafer, in the hands of the priest, is the real body and the real blood of Jesus*

Christ, and had also refused to adore it! This was the blasphemy laid to her charge. When asked by the judge, "Do you believe that the consecrated host is the real body and real blood of Jesus Christ?" Mrs. Alves replied, with clear and emphatic utterance, "*I do not believe it!*" It can scarcely seem credible, but it is, nevertheless, the fact, that immediately after this frank avowal, the Judge arose, and passed upon her, in the following words,

THE DEATH SENTENCE.

"In view of the answers of the jury, and the discussions of the cause, &c., it is proved that the accused, MARIA JOAQUINA, perhaps forgetful of the principles of the holy religion she received in her first years, and to which she still belongs, has maintained conversations and arguments condemned by the church: maintaining that veneration should not be given to images; denying the real existence of Christ in the sacred host; the mystery of the most holy Trinity; blaspheming against the most holy Virgin, the mother of God; and advancing other expressions against the doctrines received and followed by the Roman Catholic Apostolic Church; expounding these condemned doctrines to different persons: thus committing the crimes of heresy, blasphemy, &c.—I condemn the accused Maria Joaquina *to suffer* DEATH, as provided in the law, the costs of the process, &c. to be paid out of her goods.

"JOSE PERREIRA LEITO PITTA ORTEGUEIRA NEGRAO,
"*Judge, &c.*

"FUNCHAL ORIENTAL, *in Public Court, May* 2*d*, 1844."

We ask, in amazement, is it possible that a sentence so monstrous could be passed by a court claiming to be controlled by regard to the purity of the benign gospel? The answer is, Rome is prepared for any extremity when her power is defied by those whom she can punish. Millions have paid the penalty to which Mrs. Alves was doomed. The sentence ought not to excite the least surprise. It is only a confirmation of the boasted immutability of the Romish Church. She always has persecuted, and she always will persecute, rebels against her authority—ay, and follow them to the death, when she has the power, and dare exercise it. The sentence of Mrs. Alves produced intense sensation. The Christian world stood aghast with horror. The British subjects on the island determined to leave no means untried to save her life. They drew up a petition to the Queen of Portugal, praying for a reverse of the sentence. An appeal was taken by her counsel, and carried to the higher court of Relacao, at Lisbon. The decision of this court reached Lisbon in April, 1845, nearly a year after sentence had been passed. During this period, Mrs. Alves was held in imprisonment. The decree was of a singular character. In the first place, "The court confirmed the sentence from which the appeal had been taken, that is, the sentence of death for apostacy, heresy, and blasphemy. But as the defendant had been tried only on the charge of blasphemy, she could not competently be condemned for *heresy* and *apostacy*, and, *therefore*, the sentence was commuted;" thus plainly implying, at least, that if she had been found guilty on the other grounds also, she would have been put to death! She was spared, therefore, on the ground of a legal technicality—not because she was not adjudged worthy of death by the Supreme Court at Lisbon. In consideration of the length of time she had already spent in prison, the court sentenced her to imprisonment for three months from the date of the sentence, with a fine of six dollars. At the expiration of this time, she was detained to pay the expenses of prosecution, &c., so that, in fact, she was incarcerated in that gloomy prison between two and a half and three years. Finally, she was released, and repaired with her husband and sister to Trinidad, intending to seek a home in the United States.

Dr. Kalley, in speaking of this outrage, says: "Maria Joaquina, wife of Manuel Alves, who had been in prison a year or more, was *condemned to death.* Yes! condemned to death in 1844, for denying the absurd dogma of transubstantiation, refusing to participate in the idolatry of worshipping the wafer-idol, and, in the words of the accusation, blaspheming against the images of Christ and the mother of God—in plain language, refusing to give that worship to senseless blocks of wood and stone which is due only to God!"

For a short season the storm seemed to abate, but the lull was only temporary. The converts were prosecuted with renewed vigour. A new governor, notorious for his violent hatred of Dr. Kalley, was inducted into office. He was pledged to drive Dr. Kalley out of the island, and suppress this Protestant *rebellion.* The means which were adopted, and which proved at last successful, so far, at least, as to secure Dr. Kalley's expulsion, are among the most disgraceful that ignorance, bigotry, and cruelty could invent. Mobs were headed by the priests. The houses of British Protestants were assailed. The Misses Rutherford, inoffensive and pious ladies, were assailed in their own homes, because they were known to be Protestants and friends of the Bible; and, after a series of outrages which we cannot detail, Dr. Kalley's house was forced open by the mob. His valuable library was seized, together with all his manuscripts and papers, and, amid fiendish yells of exultation, the books were thrown into the road in front of the house, thrashed with clubs, and afterward burned to ashes. The copies of the sacred Scriptures were the objects of especial fury, and were consigned with shouts of derision to the flames. Dr. Kalley escaped in disguise, and took refuge on board a British vessel. It may be asked where, who, or what was the British consul? This man was a Mr. Stoddart. His sympathies were with the mob, and he failed utterly to afford the least protection to his countrymen, or to do any thing to vindicate the insulted flag of his country. The English ambassador at Lisbon was a man of different stamp. His spirited representation and demands for redress compelled the Queen of Portugal to send a royal commission to investigate the affairs at Madeira. The administration was compelled to resign, but the trial of the savages who had been most active in this work of persecution was a judicial farce. Not one of them was punished. Even those who were arrested *in the very act of murdering the Bible readers*, were acquitted! Such is Popery in the nineteenth century! After the expulsion of the British Protestants, the native converts were literally hunted like wild beasts on the mountains. Houses were ransacked for Bibles, and wherever found, the precious volumes were at once committed to the flames. More than two hundred of the converts were received on board the British ship William at one time, and made their way to the island of Trinidad. Despoiled of their property, driven from their homes, they joyfully endured the loss of all things for the sake of Christ. The persecutions which they suffered with exemplary meekness, touched the hearts of many of their enemies. A strong tide of sympathy set in their favour, but the civil authorities and the priests urged on the work of ridding the island of the "Calvinists," as the converts were called, and spared no pains to destroy all the Bibles that could be found. Ingenuity and piety devised means to elude the search, and some hundreds of copies were preserved from the destroyer, and are still on the island. The "seed of the kingdom" is not yet extirpated in Madeira. A thousand converts fled to the West India islands. Many of these were brought over to the United States, and through the agency of the American and Foreign Christian Union, found an asylum in the far West. For the details, of which the foregoing is a more outline, we refer the reader to a little volume published by the American and Foreign Christian Union, entitled *Facts in Madeira*, from the pen of the late excellent and lamented Rev. Herman Norton, a man who will be held in lasting veneration by those who knew him best, and who being dead, yet speaks in the fruits of his labours which still follow him. These facts are undeniable. No ingenuity of Romish sophistry can blot them from the annals of this century. The official documents under the hand and seal of the dignitaries of the Romish Church and state are enough to convict them in the face of their most impudent denials. An extract from the PASTORAL letter of the bishop who left Madeira for Lisbon in the beginning of 1846, saying that he would not return until Dr. Kalley was driven away, and who came back in October of the same year, contains some choice *morceaus* of Romish piety. The bishop speaks of the "proud and satanic philosophy of the inimical man" (Dr. Kalley) "spreading and burning the pious field of the church." He assures the faithful that among other calamities, the *potato disease* was owing "to the presence of that *heretic*" on the island! Perhaps, then, the continuance of the *rot* might, on the same principle, be traced to his lordship's return. This devout pastor says to his flock, "The Lord compassionating your troubled situation, condescended to excite and direct by way of MODERATION and CHARITY, your PURIFIED RELIGIOUS ZEAL and *natural energy,* and by an extraordinary mode, and perhaps strange in the eyes of the world, to snatch from the midst of this flock, already almost torn to pieces, THAT WOLF from Scotland. Blessed be the God of mercies, and Father of all consolation, who thus condescended to SUCCOUR us and CONSOLE us!!" Then he orders that a solemn Te Deum shall be sung in all the churches, as an act of praise to God for their deliverance from the presence of the heretics, whom their "*moderation,*" and "*charity,*" and "*purified religious zeal,*" and "*natural energy,*" had removed from the island of Madeira. What is this but an imitation of the mockery and insult offered to high heaven in 1572, at Rome, in honour of the massacre of St. Bartholomew? If Popery is the same in all ages, Christianity is also the same. The Bible is the same, and its religion is the same. Its conquests are the same. It is always mighty, through God, to the pulling down of the strongholds of Satan, and the hundreds who were rescued from the bondage of Popery in Madeira, proclaim that the power and wisdom of God, displayed in his word, are mightier than all the craft and cruelty of the enemy.

CONTRAST BETWEEN JESUIT AND PROTESTANT MISSIONS.

THE relative power of Protestantism and Jesuitism derives some interesting illustrations from the history of Christian missions. The conquests of the Bible within the present century are such as to cheer every pious heart. Protestant England has opened the way for the free and unrestrained circulation of the Scriptures among the one hundred and fifty millions of India, and a pure Christianity is winning new conquests every day, through the power of this sacred instrumentality. In Ceylon, where Jesuit missionaries planted the cross of Rome, two centuries ago, and gathered congregations of what they termed converts, scarcely a vestige of the results of their labour remains, and at this very hour the buildings erected by the emissaries of the Pope are occupied by the missionaries of the American Board! What has been their success in Japan? The government of Japan, in consequence of the intrigues and interference of the Jesuits, not only banished them from the country, but has ever since closed its ports against commerce with Christian nations,* and every year, the expulsion of the followers of Loyola is celebrated by the public ceremony of trampling on the cross, which has been the emblem of their falsehood and craft all the world over.

How have they fared in China? Similar interfe-

---

* This has been somewhat modified by the success of the late American expedition under Commodore Perry.

rence in the affairs of government occasioned the suppression of the order and its banishment from the empire, and left the prejudice of jealousy, which still remains, though generations have passed away since the Jesuit yoke was broken and spurned with indignant contempt, even by the Chinese. Their operations, still carried on in China, are all secret, and the result of three hundred years of toil amounts to this sum total—that Jesuitism in that vast empire is proscribed and despised.

What has been the result, on the other hand, of Protestant missions in that country? Within the last thirty or forty years, since the establishment of the first *Christian* missionary station in China, the Bible has been given to the Chinese in their printed language, and thus the sacred Oracles have been made accessible to the four hundred millions, nearly one half the population of the earth, who dwell in that hitherto benighted empire: for it must be remembered that amid all the diversity of dialects spoken in China, the written language is the same throughout.

Be it remembered, also, that the missionaries connected with the American Board of Commissioners for Foreign Missions alone, have reduced *fifteen* oral languages to writing, and given not only the Bible, but a Christian literature also, to nations that until recently were in the lowest condition of savage life.

Let it be recorded, also, that Protestant ministers have already given the Bible to the nations of the earth in TWO HUNDRED AND FIFTY LANGUAGES AND DIALECTS, and are now circulating the Scriptures by millions of copies annually.

And now take one fact more as an illustration of the relative power of vitality of Jesuitism and Protestantism. Roman missionaries, sons of Loyola, have been operating for *one hundred and fifty years* on the

Pacific coast, upheld by the Mexican government, and yet it is a sober truth, that natives of that region are actually sending their children to the Protestant mission schools in the Sandwich islands, in order to secure a liberal education, though the Protestant mission has been established there only within the last thirty years! These are startling and significant facts. The success of the Jesuits, though at times wonderfully rapid, resembles the storied apparition of the Indian juggler's tree, which sprouts before you and presently shoots up a stem and branches, on which the leaf buds, and blossoms expand, covering the shrub with foliage and flowers, and anon, offering fruit in various stages of maturity; but as suddenly vanishing when you attempt to pluck and eat. These are the men who proclaim the downfall of Protestantism, and speaks vauntingly of its "*decline!*"* Protestantism has, it is true, sometimes declined in Roman Catholic countries, in a very natural way. The exhibitions of "moderation," and "charity," and "purified religious zeal," and "natural energy," such as those displayed in Madeira, and which the bishop lauds so piously, have at times proved successful, and Protestantism has declined after the Jesuits have succeeded in putting many Protestants to death and driving the remnant out of the country. But we have one precious comfort. The blood of Christian martyrs consecrated the soil to Christ, and the earth which drinks it in, is sealed as the heritage of the God of the Bible. In due time it will be claimed and taken into possession by *Him* whose right it is to reign. The foregoing facts establish a twofold truth. They teach that no instrumentality is so potent in its moral influence upon a

---

* See the Author's Lecture on Jesuitism, Vol. VIII. Prot. Quart Review, p. 100.

people, and so certain to elevate our race in all that is truly excellent, as the Bible; and on the other hand, they prove that Rome's hostility to the Bible is as unrelenting as it ever was, and that she regards it as the deadly enemy which batters down and overthrows her strongholds wherever it has free course. Hence, we need not be surprised that in our own happy country, the efforts of papal emissaries are directed with such earnestness to the destruction of the influence which, of all others, they most dread, THE BIBLE IN THE PUBLIC SCHOOLS. This hostility has been displayed in the miserable attempt to exclude the Bible from the Common Schools. The plea that the Roman Catholic Church is by this means deprived of its share of privilege, is an absurdity. The Bible is not a sectarian book. It is the volume of Christian revelation. Its tenets furnish the only basis of a pure morality. The demand for the exclusion of the Bible from the public schools, or for a division of the school fund as the alternative, is an insult to the American people. It is tantamount to a claim of papal recognition. The priests might as well ask us to acknowledge the power of the pope as supreme. The question is simply, Bible or no Bible, and a most momentous issue depends upon the answer. Retain the Bible, and you maintain the free institutions which are the glory of this nation and the hope of the world. Keep it in the places which it now occupies, and let the education of the youth of our country be moulded by its free spirit, and you train the coming generation in the principles of genuine liberty; but banish it from the public schools, and Rome gains an advantage. The great obstacle in the way of her progress is removed. This concession is an entering wedge. It will be followed by increased demands, and the arrogance of Rome, gaining fresh strength from every indulgence, will insist upon still larger tribute. The only safe policy is to resist at the outset. This is a Protestant country, and such it will remain, if Protestants are true to themselves and to their God. Because it is a Protestant country, it permits no union of church and state. For the very purpose of forever excluding such union, the maintenance of its free Christian character is essential. Roman Catholics ought to know that their religious privileges are secured to them most effectually by the very Book which of all others they are taught to suspect, if not to despise. So long as the Bible retains its hold upon American sympathies, the rights of conscience will be respected. Every assault made upon the Bible, every attempt to impede its free circulation, can have no other effect but to rivet the chains of despotism. No book is so surely and consistently the poor man's friend as this; and no greater injury can be done to the race, than to blot out the pure light which beams from its pages, to solace the mourner in the night of sorrow, and guide the bewildered traveller through darkest shades into the glorious sunlight of heaven.

The attempt made in the year 1844, to banish the Bible from the common schools of this city, was defeated, and that most signally. The little children sang the Pope's army into confusion, and "We won't give up the Bible!" became as popular an ode as any national hymn:

> "We won't give up the Bible,
>   God's holy book of truth;
> The blessed staff of hoary age,
>   The guide of early youth;
> The sun that sheds a glorious light
>   O'er every dreary road;
> The voice that speaks a Saviour's love,
>   And calls us home to God!
>
> "We won't give up the Bible
>   For pleasure, or for pain;
> We'll buy the truth, and sell it not,
>   For all that we might gain;

BURNING THE BIBLE.

Though man should try to take our prize
    By guile, or cruel might,
We'll suffer all that man can do,—
    And God defend the right!

" We won't give up the Bible,
    But spread it far and wide,
Until its saving voice be heard
    Beyond the rolling tide;
Till all shall know its gracious power,
    And with one voice and heart
Resolve that from God's sacred word
    They'll never, never part!"

THE IMMACULATE CONCEPTION OF THE VIRGIN MARY.

THE recent decision of the council held at Rome, respecting the Immaculate Conception of the Virgin Mary, has taken that portion of the Protestant Church by surprise whose attention had not been specially attracted by the notes of preparation which had heralded the probable result of the deliberations, even before the startling conclusion had been reached. It is evidently a foregone conclusion. The matter had been previously determined upon by those whose influence is paramount at Rome, and all that was expected from the Council was simply to clothe the figment with the proper vesture of authority. This has been done according to the requirements of the canon law, and all that remains for the faithful is the prompt acquiescence of an obedient mind. Had the decision been of an opposite character, it is easy to see that Rome would not have been true to the law of her peculiar progress. Her superstitions have always been of a culminating character. The massive proportions of her system have been built up with marvellous symmetry, and it was necessary that this top-stone should be brought forth with shoutings, though we cannot unite in the acclamations of "grace, grace unto it!" The proverb, *Rome was not built in a day*, is as true in its symbolic as it is in its literal import. It is a system of accretions. One perversion of the pure doctrines of revelation has followed in regular, logical order upon another. There is a wonderful congruity in the falsehoods of Romanism. They are dovetailed into each other with rare artistic skill. They follow in the order of necessity. Rome has been forced to adopt the stupendous errors of which her system is an aggregate, in order to be consistent with her antecedents. Thus one falsehood has not only paved the way for a second, but rendered its succession a logical necessity. It would be easy, if our limits allowed, to illustrate this truth in detail, and to show the connection between the progressive errors of Rome; but this topic, however interesting in its bearings upon the philosophy of papal imposture, would require an extent of discussion inconsistent with our present design. The general fact of the accretive nature of the Romish system will be sufficiently established by a reference to the history of the leading dogmas of Rome. The reader will, it is true, be frequently puzzled to determine what are the real doctrines of the papal system, if he searches for them in the decrees of councils. He will find among the very popes some of the sturdiest patrons of opinions and doctrines which other popes condemn as rankest heresies. He will find some councils asserting in dogmatic form the very article which others incontinently denounce. He will be bewildered in following the chain of "Catholic Unity" in doctrine, by discovering that a theory which has at one period been lauded as sacred and imperishable truth, is most fiercely cursed in another period as an infernal and diabolical falsehood. The power of a principle which Rome dignifies with the name of faith, but which in her case may more appropriately be termed credulity, will be taxed to the utmost tension of its tough resistance, before the candid mind can rest content with the papal claim to infallibility. Thus, it was not till the fifth century that Rome could categorically decree that the title, "Mother of God," was justly applied to the Virgin

Mary. This *honour* belongs to the Council of Ephesus, A. D. 431. Before that time, many doctors and churches regarded this title as unwarrantable and blasphemous, and protested against its use as a profanation. So too in regard to the use of images and pictures as helps to devotion. One of the Nicene councils, in the fourth century, authorized their use in churches, and yet a general council, held A. D. 754, in which 388 bishops were present, solemnly condemned their use in churches. Now the obedient follower of Rome's behests is placed, at the outset, in a most perplexing quandary. The modern creed of Pope Pius IV. requires him to declare that he "*receives and professes all things that are declared by the sacred canons and general councils.*" How is he to find out what these things are, *all* of which he professes to receive? It would require a lifetime to find out *all* that the sacred canons and general councils have enshrined in the mystic enclosure of "Catholic" faith. Close on the heels of this difficulty comes another. Who can tell how many general councils possess proper authority? If he looks into this matter, he will find divers rival factions, all claiming the assent of his faith to their jarring opinions. One party reckons eighteen general councils. Another party allows the same number, but selects some on the list of its candidates for acceptance, and substitutes others in the place of those which are rejected. Thus, one party recognises the councils of Lyons, Florence, Lateran, and Trent, and another repudiates them, and adopts in their room those of Pisa, Constance, Basil, and the second of Pisa. Then again, he will be perplexed in receiving "ALL things that are declared by the sacred canons and general councils," by the awkward discovery, that the authority of councils is entirely too fluctuating to afford a foundation for faith;

because authority which is deemed absolute in one age is utterly rejected in another. The church has not yet decided, in such form as to reduce these discordant elements to the right proportions of faith, which of the councils presenting claims for œcumenical honours and endorsement, ought to be regarded as challenging the homage of the willing and obedient faithful. The perplexed neophyte is compelled at last to accept a unity destitute of union, and as the safest course, he dutifully refers all these matters to the decision of his spiritual superiors. The claims of Rome are, in all soberness, the most preposterous that ever challenged the assent of the human mind. She has gone forward in the march of superstition, encumbering her creed with progressive denials of the sacred doctrines of divine revelation, until scarcely a truth of the gospel has remained intact or inviolate. The doctrine of the Trinity is practically annulled by the honours which are paid to Mary and the saints. The mediatorial offices of Christ are nullified by the same superstition. The atonement of the Saviour is despoiled of its efficacy by the works of satisfaction and penance enjoined as essential to salvation. Justification is rendered nugatory by confounding it with sanctification. The grace of God is made of none effect by stupid traditions of men respecting human merit. The work of the Holy Ghost, in renewing a fallen nature, is superseded by the pretended efficacy of sacraments, and these again are made engines of priestly power by the doctrine of intention, according to which, the efficacy of the sacrament is made dependent on the will of the administrator; so that, for instance, a subject is not baptized, although all the formulæ of the external rite have been observed, unless the person officiating *intends* to administer the ordinance in good faith. Not a sacrament which Christ instituted is left in the form which the Master ordained; and instead of accepting two, Rome has fabricated seven sacraments. She has not only perverted the doctrines of the Scripture, but she has made additions of her own, teaching for doctrines the commandments of men. She has thus incurred the twofold curse denounced in the book of God, at the solemn closing of the canon, against those who add to and who take from the words of God's book, and has forfeited her share in the blessings of eternal life, and drawn upon her own head the fearful plagues which God denounces upon them who commit this twofold sacrilege. Her measure is well-nigh filled. The doctrine of the Immaculate Conception destroys the scriptural basis of Christ's incarnation. Christ assumed our nature with all its infirmities, but without its sins. The Apostle Paul declares, "When the fulness of the times was come, God sent forth his Son, made of a woman, made under the law, to redeem them that were under the law, that we might receive the adoption of sons." But if the conception of Mary was immaculate, she was not made under the law, and thus the whole analogy of faith is destroyed. *Christ* then was not made under the law; he did not, in this case, assume true human nature, and the fitness of his subjection to infirmity is no longer apparent. Whence should this infirmity proceed? Not from the Holy Ghost, of whom he was conceived, for there is no infirmity in the Holy Ghost. Not of the Virgin Mary, of whom he was born, because if her conception was immaculate, he could derive no infirmity from her. Hence, we have no longer a High-priest who can be touched by a feeling of our infirmities, seeing he was in all points tempted like as we are, yet without sin. Thus the whole sympathy between Christ and members of his mystical body is destroyed. Rome, by this mad imposture, utterly sunders the last shred that could bind the person of a believer to the person of Christ, and in this fell decision renders herself utterly apostate from Christian faith and hope.

Such is the tendency and the last result of this crowning act of Rome's folly. We propose now to trace the outlines of her doctrine respecting the character and worship of the Virgin. And here let us say, in the sadness of honest sincerity, that this decision of the papal power has done more to strengthen the hands of infidelity in Roman Catholic countries, than any other offence against God and humanity perpetrated in Rome's name, for the last century. In lands illumined by the light of Protestant Christianity, this result can hardly follow, because there, unbelievers know that Rome is not the type of Christianity. We deny that her religion is the religion of Christ in any sense. The system in its whole development is no more entitled to such designation than Buddhism. Bread compounded of flour and arsenic is no longer bread. It is poison. If men will eat it, they will learn that death is in the pot. It was there before; it has been there for centuries, but Rome has poured the very essence of death into the cauldron, from which she deals out the wine of her fornication to deluded millions, who drink and die. She has intensified the venom by which she destroys souls by this last violation of the truth of God.

The very discussion of the doctrine of Rome respecting the Virgin Mary is embarrassing. We hold that the Church of Rome, in all the honours with which superstition has crowned the mother of Christ, has really, though not designedly, done injury to her memory. Rome has made a goddess of the meek mother of Jesus. We honour her memory. We would give to her all the meed of reverence which the Scriptures allow. We say, with the mother of the

Baptist, "Blessed art thou among women!" We would remember that Gabriel saluted her, "Hail, much favoured, the Lord is with thee: blessed art thou among women!" She was highly honoured, in that she was chosen to be the mother of Christ as to his humanity; but we protest against the blasphemy which would make her the mother of God. In all that we say, therefore, let not a thought be suggested, as though we would in any manner detract from the honour which God himself has put upon her who was blessed among women. The primitive church had no idea of Rome's superstition. In vain will the Scriptures be searched for any warrant for the fabulous stories which Rome has incorporated into her teachings respecting her. The period of her death is not recorded, and is not known. Rome has discovered that, and the time of her resurrection and assumption into heaven also. Not a single instance can be cited in which the apostles of our Lord even consulted her, to say nothing of the honours of worship which Rome ascribes to her. The Scriptures, after the history of the resurrection and ascension of the Saviour, mention Mary but once, (Acts i. 14,) and in that passage she is spoken of in connection with other women: "These all" (the apostles) "continued with one accord in prayer and supplication with the women, and Mary the mother of Jesus, and with his brethren." This is the only positive and well-defined allusion to her after the ascension of Christ. The Apostle Paul, in Romans xvi. 6, says, "Greet Mary, who bestowed much labour on us," but what Mary this was, deponent sayeth not. As if, therefore, on purpose to show the utter absence of all foundation for Rome's grotesque superstition, the oracles of God are silent respecting the closing history of Mary's life. The apostles loved her as the mother of Jesus. They loved her for her own and for her Master's sake; but they never honoured her as the mother of God; they never bestowed any such title upon her, or treated her in any other respect than as an heir with themselves of the righteousness of God by faith. Had they done so, the fact would have been stated. A doctrine so important, so essential to the whole system of Christianity, if Romanism be Christianity, could not have been thus excluded from the sacred canon without a fatal and most culpable neglect. It is, indeed, impossible that it should have formed a part of the revealed Scriptures, because from its nature the whole doctrine of Rome respecting Mary is utterly contrary to the plainest truths of the gospel. It was not until the corruptions of the predicted apostasy were becoming rampant, that the title of *Mother of God* was allowed by authority of council. This was done, as already stated, at the Council of Ephesus, A. D. 431. This blasphemy was pregnant with a brood of idolatrous superstitions. It was the cockatrice egg, which broke out into a generation of vipers. In close union with this was the invocation of the saints, a practice which grew out of the veneration in which the martyrs of the Christian faith were held. Most of the apostles, and very many of the pastors whom they appointed over churches, and many who succeeded these pastors, were martyrs. Their constancy was held in veneration by surviving Christians. So far, this may have been without offence. The memory of the just is blessed; but there was, perhaps, too much stress laid upon the suffering of a violent death, and too little regard paid to the testimony of a godly life. Christians met for prayer and praise at the graves of these martyrs. They wished to emulate their zeal, their self-denial, their fidelity. Gradually, they looked to the martyrs instead of looking to Jesus. They began to invoke them; first, in the form of bold apostrophe, and then as joint intercessors with Christ. They wronged the priestly office of the Saviour, and they became idolaters! When Mary had been installed as an object of invocation, her worship soon overtopped all other. In the early part of the sixth century, the notion began to prevail that *the holy name of the Virgin should be invoked in every prayer.* Peter Fullo, a Eutychian heretic, has the bad distinction of promulging this maxim, and from this period forward, mariolatry has grown, until the whole system of Rome has become a grand scheme for the adoration of the Virgin, and the prerogatives which rightcously belong to God only have been transferred to her. She soon took precedence of all the apostles in the honours which were paid to her. In the seventh century, Pope Martin ordained, "Whoever does not honour and adore the blessed Virgin, the mother of God, let him be accursed." Ere long, it became common to address her as *the queen of heaven,* the *window of heaven,* the *gate of paradise,* and the like. History is filled to overflowing with the blasphemous absurdities and lying legends which are recorded respecting her. PELBART, a Romish author, who lived in the latter part of the fifteenth century, and whose book is dedicated to Pope Sixtus IV., has preserved a vast number of the silly legends which have been handed down as verities worthy of all belief. He tells us that the Virgin lived, according to some accounts, until she was fifty-eight years old; according to others, till she was just sixty-three; and, according to others, till she was still older. At last, in answer to her prayers that she might be taken out of this world, an angel was sent from heaven with the promise that in three days her desire should be granted. This angel brought her also a palm-branch from paradise, with a strict injunction that it should be carried before her bier at her funeral; and presented her, also, with a suit of mourning which her son had sent to her. The Virgin, among other requests, demanded that she might be buried by all the apostles, and that in her departure she might meet with no malignant spirits. Her wish was promptly acceded to. Upon this, she communicated to the saints and virgins the good news. St. John was then preaching at Ephesus, and lo! in the midst of his sermon comes a clap of thunder, and he was borne through the air on a white cloud, and set down comfortably at the door of the Virgin's house. She welcomed him, and commended to him the care of her funeral. St. John was in great trouble, according to the legend, and broke out into passionate lamentations and complaints against the providence which was about to remove "the holy mistress of our religion, the mirror of sanctity, and our only consolation." The sight of the palm and the mourning suit reconciled the good man to the dispensation. St. John, with all his heart, desired that all the apostles might be present at the solemnity, when, marvellous to tell, they came from the four corners of the earth, through the air, on white clouds, and were set down safely before the house, and, entering, were marvellously astonished to find St. John there, as well they might be. After reciting their Ave Maria, however, they became more composed. Then the story runs that Christ came with the nine orders of angels, and after the celestial choir had sung a number of admirable hymns, the Virgin rendered up her soul, with these words of the fortieth psalm, "So Jesus, in the volume of thy book, it is written of me, I delight to do thy will, O my God!" The funeral took place according to the arrangement. The wicked Jews deeming this a favourable opportunity to get rid of all the apostles at once, made an attack on the funeral procession, with the high-priest at their head; but the unhappy man, on reaching forth his hands to lay hold of the bier, found both his arms missing, they having broken off at the elbows, at which he made a lamentable howling; and no wonder that he should. Peter told him, with characteristic frankness, that there was no help for him, except to kiss the bier and profess the Christian faith, which he forthwith did, and then, oh, wonder! his arms were immediately fastened on again. The body of the Virgin was then consigned to the tomb, but after three days, angels came and took it up to heaven. This is Pelbart's story. It beats Munchausen. Whatever may be said by Romanists respecting its credibility, or their faith in it, and the priests will tell you you may either believe it or let it alone, as it is not binding on the faithful, the latter part of the fable, for it is all of one piece, is obligatory. The church of Rome annually celebrates the festival of Mary's assumption into heaven, and we have a "Church of the Assumption" in Spring Garden street, in our own city. The story of the Holy House of Loretto, in which Mary is said to have been born, and which was miraculously transported from Nazareth in Judea to Loretto in Italy, not by the ordinary mode by land and sea, but through the air by the help of holy angels, has been published in this city within the last few years, under the hand and from the pen of the present Roman bishop of St. Louis. A more foolish fable never was concocted by any marvel-monger. If we were to quote from accredited Romish authors the stories which have been published with all the gravity of indubitable verities, the transcript would be a defilement of our pages. We shall, therefore, let them remain where they are. After installing such fooleries as these to which we have already alluded in the sanctuary of faith, it will not be difficult to account for the boldness of the idolatrous worship paid to the Virgin. With a presumption unparalleled in any annals excepting those of Rome, Cardinal Bonaventure actually prepared, as a devotional book, the so-called " Psalter of the Blessed Virgin," which consists of the Psalms of David altered, so as to render them so many addresses and hymns of praise to the Virgin. The book may be said, in a word, to be a blasphemous travestie of the Psalms, requiring no qualification in the author other than a reckless audacity which shrinks from no excess of profanity. The hardihood of a man who can substitute the name of a creature for that of Jehovah, and call upon all men to offer to the Virgin the homage which is due to God alone, and mutilate the words of Divine inspiration for the purpose, is beyond all power of human censure. The pious heart recoils with horror from the blasphemy. Every sentiment of religion is shocked by the grossness of the outrage. We can do no more than leave the guilty perpetrators of this affront against the majesty of heaven in the hands of HIM who has said, "I am Jehovah, that is my name; my glory will I not give to another; neither my praise to graven images!" How insulting to the memory of the meek and lowly Mary is the disgusting homage which is paid to her, and the almost equally disgusting absurdities which have been fabricated with the avowed purpose of promoting Rome's superstitious veneration of the Virgin! Every saint on earth, as well as every saint in heaven, is willing to be nothing, that Christ may be all and in all. This absorption of every vainglorious feeling in supreme desire for the glory of the mighty Redeemer, is characteristic of all true piety, and surely the Virgin Mary is not an exception to this rule. The greatest dishonour, therefore, that can be shown to her, is that which they offer, who practically make her usurp the prerogatives of the Saviour. The homage which is paid to her proceeds on the supposition that she is the great agent of the redemption of those who are saved. This is an insult to her. She needed redemption, and was saved by the merits of Christ's atoning blood, just as any other daughter of Adam; and as one of the redeemed, she participates in the desire that ALL glory and dominion and power may be ascribed to the Lamb slain, because he ALONE is worthy. In this view of the subject, and it is the true one, the worship of Rome is a system of direct insult to the Virgin as well as to the Saviour. The boldest contradictions of the fiat of heaven, and the most blasphemous denial of Jehovah's prerogative to the honours of divine worship, is offered by those who call upon Mary as their "only hope." This the late Pope Gregory XVI. commanded all papists to do, in his last encyclical letter. Their ONLY hope! The Psalmist says, "My soul, wait thou upon God, from him cometh my salvation." The Church of Rome says, in her Psalter, "My soul, wait thou only upon Mary, from her cometh my salvation." The Psalmist says again, "My soul, wait thou only upon God." Nothing daunted, Rome responds, "My soul, wait thou only upon Mary!" And yet, in the face of all this, there are not wanting *charitable* Protestants, who would have us regard this sytem of damnable idolatry and blasphemy as entitled to respectful deference as a branch of the church of Christ. Worshippers of Mary are not *Christians*. They are Maryists. Their system is not Christianity; it is Mariolatry. We say this not with any feeling of hostility to the professors of this false creed. We pity them. But this devotion to the Virgin, about which the Pope and the late œcumenical Council are so urgent, is an insult to the name and church of the Lord Jesus Christ, and as such all good Christians deplore and resent it. Probably, comparatively few Protestants are aware of the blasphemous excesses to which the forms of worship in use among Romanists in our own country are carried. We need not advert to the Psalter of *St.* Bonaventure for examples in point. We can find them in the books of prayer in common use among Romanists around us. Take the following from "The Garden of the Soul," perhaps the book more extensively in use among papists in this country, than any other:

THE OFFICE OF THE BLESSED VIRGIN MARY.

At Matins.

V. Now let my lips sing and display,
R. The blessed Virgin's praise this day.
V. O Lady to my help intend;
R. Me strongly from my foes defend.
Glory be to the Father, &c.

The Hymn.

Hail Lady of the world,
  Of Heaven bright Queen!
Hail Virgin of virgins,
  Star early seen!
Hail full of all grace,
  Clear light divine!
Lady to succour us
  With speed incline.
God, from eternity,
  Before all other,
Of the world thee ordain'd
  To be the Mother.
By which he created
  The heavens, sea, land;
His fair spouse he chose,
  Free from sin's band.

V. God hath elected and pre-elected her.
R. He hath made her dwell in his tabernacle.

Let us pray.

O HOLY Mary, Mother of our Lord Jesus Christ, queen of heaven, and lady of the world, who neither forsakest nor despisest any, behold me mercifully with the eye of pity, and obtain for me, of thy beloved Son, pardon for all my sins: that I, who, with devout affection, do now celebrate thy holy conception, may, hereafter, enjoy the reward of eternal bliss; through the grace and mercy of our Lord Jesus Christ, whom thou, a virgin, didst bring forth: who, with the Father and the Holy Ghost, livest and reignest one God in Perfect Trinity, for ever and ever. Amen.

V. O Lord, hear my prayer:
R. And let my cry come unto thee.
V. Let us bless our Lord;
R. Thanks be to God.
V. And may the souls of the faithful departed, through the mercy of God, rest in peace.
R. Amen.

At Prime.

V. O Lady, to my help intend:
R. Me strongly from my foes defend.
V. Glory be to the Father, &c.

The Hymn.

HAIL Virgin most prudent!
House for God placed,
With the seven-fold pillar
And table graced.
Saved from contagion
Of the frail earth:
In the womb of thy parent,
Saint before birth.
Mother of the living,
Gate of Saint's merits,
The new star of Jacob,
Queen of pure spirits.
To Zebulon fearful:
Armies' Array;
Be thou of Christians
Refuge and stay.

V. He hath created her in his Holy Spirit.
R. And hath poured her out, over all his works.

Let us pray.

O holy Mary, Mother of our Lord, &c., *as before.*
V. O Lord, hear my prayer:
R. And let my cry come unto thee.
V. Let us bless our Lord;
R. Thanks be to God.
V. And may the soul of the faithful departed, through the mercy of God, rest in peace.
R. Amen.

OF THE VIRGIN MARY.

At Third.
V. O Lady, to my help intend:
R. Me strongly from my foes defend.
V. Glory be to the Father, &c.

The Hymn.
HAIL ark of the covenant!
  King Solomon's throne,
Bright rainbow of heaven,
  The bush of vision.
The fleece of Gideon,
  The flow'ring rod;
Sweet honey of Samson,
  Closet of God.
'Twas meet Son so noble,
  Should save from stain,
(Wherewith Eve's children
  Spotted remain,)
The maid whom for mother
  He had elected,
That she might be never
  With sin infected.
V. I dwell in the highest;
R. And my throne is the pillar of the clouds.

Let us pray.
O holy Mary, Mother of our Lord, &c., *as before.*
V. O Lord, hear my prayer:
R. And let my cry come unto thee.
V. Let us bless our Lord;
R. Thanks be to God.
V. And may the souls of the faithful departed, through the mercy of God, rest in peace.
R. Amen.

At Sixth.
V. O Lady, to my help intend:
R. Me strongly from my foes defend.
V. Glory be to the Father, &c.

The Hymn.
HAIL Mother and virgin!
  Of the Trinity
Temple; joy of Angels,
  Seal of purity.
Comfort of mourners,
  Garden of pleasure;
Palm-tree of patience,
  Chastity's measure.

430 THE IMMACULATE CONCEPTION, &c.

> Thou land sacerdotal,
> Art blessed wholly,
> From sin original
> Exempted solely.
> The city of the highest,
> Gate of the East;
> Virgin's gem, in thee
> All graces rest.

V. As the lily among thorns;
R. So my beloved among the daughters of Adam.

Let us pray.

O holy Mary, Mother of our Lord, &c., *as before.*
V. O Lord, hear my prayer:
R. And let my cry come unto thee.
V. Let us bless our Lord;
R. Thanks be to God.
V. And may the souls of the faithful departed, through the mercy of God, rest in peace.
R. Amen.

These extracts speak for themselves. If they are not the language of idolatry the most offensive, we know not where idolatrous worship can be found at this day. If Rome is free from this sin, then it cannot be laid to the charge of any devotee who has ever worshipped at the shrine of false gods.

THE END.

www.ingramcontent.com/pod-product-compliance
Lightning Source LLC
Chambersburg PA
CBHW022104290426
44112CB00008B/547